Killer Poker Shorthanded

Books by John Vorhaus

The Comic Toolbox: How to be Funny Even if You're Not

Creativity Rules! A Writer's Workbook

The Pro Poker Playbook: 223 Ways to Win More Money Playing Poker

Killer Poker: Strategy and Tactics for Winning Poker Play

Killer Poker Online: Crushing the Internet Game

The Killer Poker Hold'em Handbook

Poker Night: Winning at Home, at the Casino, and Beyond

The Strip Poker Kit

Killer Poker Online/2: Advanced Strategies for Crushing the Internet Game

Killer Poker No Limit!

Books by Tony Guerrera

Killer Poker by the Numbers

KILLER POKER SHORTHANDED

Shorthanded Hold'em Means Long Green for You!

John Vorhaus and Tony Guerrera

LYLE STUART
Kensington Publishing Corp.
www.kensingtonbooks.com

LYLE STUART BOOKS are published by

Kensington Publishing Corp.
850 Third Avenue
New York, NY 10022

All Kensington titles, imprints, and distributed lines are available at special quantity discounts for bulk purchases for sales promotions, premiums, fund-raising, educational, or institutional use. Special book excerpts or customized printings can also be created to fit specific needs. For details, write or phone the office of the Kensington special sales manager: Kensington Publishing Corp., 850 Third Avenue, New York, NY 10022, attn: Special Sales Department; phone 1-800-221-2647.

Lyle Stuart is a trademark of Kensington Publishing Corp.

First printing: October 2007

10 9 8 7 6 5 4 3 2 1

Printed in the United States of America

ISBN-13: 978-0-8184-0722-2
ISBN-10: 0-8184-0722-0

To action junkies everywhere:
We're one of you; you're one of us.

Contents

Foreword: A Difference Maker

by Phil Hellmuth, Jr.

To me, poker is all about winning the most prestigious poker tournaments and making millions of dollars (in that order!). And *Killer Poker Shorthanded* by John Vorhaus and Tony Guerrera will help you do both. To those of you who have read other *Killer Poker* books, you already know how they work: You strengthen your game through a combination of psychology, study, and pure power poker. If this is your first *Killer Poker* book, well, what can I say except, "Welcome!" Welcome to the wonderful world of shorthanded hold'em, where the cards you hold matter much less than what you can do with them. And there are so many crazy things to do!

Shorthanded play, and especially heads-up play, is hugely important in poker for at least four reasons: First, to win a poker tournament, you'll have to play shorthanded and, then, eventually heads-up for the title. If you're lucky, you'll win over $1 million for first or second place, but no matter how big or small a tournament you're in, there's a bigger cash difference between first and second than any other two spots. At the main event of the 2006 World Series of Poker, the difference between first and second place cash was a mind-blowing $6 million! Jamie Gold finished first, cashing $12 million, but don't feel too sorry for runner-up Paul Wasicka. He took home just over half of that for his troubles. So, yeah, shorthanded play, and especially heads-up action, can spell the difference between a big tournament win and a *huge* one.

The second reason that shorthanded play is important is that many times a game breaks down (as people quit), and you're forced to play shorthanded poker either to win your money back or to keep the game alive until help arrives. Often you'll find yourself facing the worst players in the game, and this should be a good opportunity for you to win some big money. However, you need to be careful: sometimes, the worst player in the fullhanded game is a good shorthanded player because the worst player knows how to play weak hands better than most. Often, this so-called worst player is a loser in the fullhanded game simply because he plays too aggressively and plays too many hands. Although playing too many hands and playing too aggressively are weaknesses in a full ring game, they're vital strengths shorthanded. So you can find yourself forced to quit a shorthanded game against bad players simply because you haven't honed your skills to the point where you're a favorite. Good news! *Killer Poker Shorthanded* will change all that.

The third reason shorthanded play is important is that you can gain invaluable insight into Texas hold'em (or whatever poker variant you play) by playing a huge variety of hands. Playing all the different hands that you would fold before the flop in a full ring game teaches you what it is like to play "fast." You will gain a clearer understanding of the tactics that the superfast players use. What was Huck Seed thinking when he moved all-in with J♦8♦ at the final table of the 1999 World Series of Poker? Or what was Daniel Negreanu thinking when he called a big bet before the flop with 8♣7♣ at the World Poker Tour's Doyle Brunson North America Poker Championship? Playing shorthanded and heads-up poker helps you see the rhyme, reason, and logic hidden in these plays.

The fourth reason that shorthanded play is important is that it's so read dependent. In general, if you're good at reading people, then you'll do well playing shorthanded and heads-up; if you're poor at reading people, then you'll be a weak shorthanded and heads-up player. If you're poor at reading other players, the good news is that you'll get some valuable practice reading your opponents by playing many hours shorthanded. If you can improve your reading abilities at all, then this'll win you more dollars in the long run in all forms of poker. Of course, my new book with Joe Navarro, *Read'em and Reap,* will help improve your reading skills as well (I know. I know. I'm always plugging something!).

Trust me—you'll want to be prepared for when someone like Howard "The Professor" Lederer comes at you raising every single hand on the button, as he is wont to do. How do you react to his raising every hand on the button? What do you do when someone like me comes at you playing super slow, almost never raising it up on the button—and then suddenly picks up the pace and raises it up almost every button? There are thousands of ways to play heads-up and shorthanded, and there are thousands of ways to adjust your play to the tactics that your opponent is using. Maybe, just maybe, you'll take the knowledge in this book and invent your own superstar way to play. Maybe, just maybe, I'll play you soon, heads-up, mano a mano, at the World Series of Poker. Bring your best game!

Acknowledgments

First, the usual suspects. Thanks to Greg Dinkin and Frank Scatoni, the stalwarts of Venture Literary, who have made it all happen since this series began. Thanks to Richard Ember at Kensington, as deft an editor as any poker scribes could want.

We acknowledge Nick Geber of Bluff Radio for his contribution of the Numpty and for teaching us, by negative example, how to play it correctly. Props also to Ben Brantley, who, for better or worse, earns the BenBucks sobriquet every time he plays. Thanks to Craig Vieregg for lending his insight into three-handed play and for contributing Slickerella to the linguistic stew that is poker slang.

Thanks to Phil Hellmuth, Jr., for contributing the foreword. Thanks likewise to all the other pros who shared their thoughts and insights with us, especially those who chipped in their "Words from the Wise" with no thought of recompense beyond helping others improve their game and, uh, free copies of this book. To borrow from Isaac Newton (and why not, since we've borrowed from everybody else), "If we have seen a little further it is by standing on the shoulders of giants."

Introduction:
The Short and the Long of It

What's the right number of players for a poker game? In California, no-limit hold'em (NLHE) games typically go nine-handed because California cardrooms are stand-alone affairs with plenty of room for plenty of tables. In Las Vegas, where space is at a premium because the poker room is often shoehorned in between a casino's sports book and keno lounge or in between the baccarat pit and the hooker bar, space is at a premium, tables are fewer in number, and the games go ten-handed. Most home games try to scrape together seven or eight players, enough to fit comfortably around the kitchen table or around one of those octagonal folding poker tables with the plastic cup holders, chip racks, and threadbare green felt that hasn't been replaced since pet rocks were popular. One memorable New Year's Eve, part of this book's writing team (the JV part) found himself at his in-laws', riding herd on a *twenty-three-handed* frenzy of hold'em with spirited action, no burn cards, and literally tens of dollars changing hands.

That was a bit much.

Thanks to our good friends at the World Poker Tour, many fans of poker have become used to seeing six-handed NLHE on TV. The six-way format makes a lot of sense for televised poker because with judicious postproduction editing, six players can easily be whittled down to a winner in the space of a single show. If you start that table nine- or ten-handed, it becomes much more difficult to bring a meaningful poker story to its conclusion in just two hours of TV time.

Still, popular as six-handed poker may be in TV circles (or twenty-three-handed poker may be at the in-laws'), full-handed no-limit Texas hold'em continues to be the game of choice for most cash game players, both online and in the real world. Likewise, fullhanded NLHE dominates the tournament scene. Does this mean that the average poker player doesn't need to bother honing his[1] shorthanded game? Of course not. We can think of many situations in which shorthanded tool-craft is the difference between surviving and thriving in poker. Consider...

You're playing in a Super Weekday tournament on Party Poker, and after some five hours of slogging through a field of about one thousand players, you're down inside the last two dozen. Here's the pay table for this event:

PLACE	PRIZE
17–20	$1,000
14–16	$1,300
11–13	$1,500
10	$1,600
9	$2,200
8	$3,000
7	$4,500
6	$6,000
5	$7,500
4	$9,000
3	$11,000
2	$19,000
1	$35,000

1. Fullhanded or shorthanded, and despite the growing popularity of poker among women, it remains true (and sadly so for the single half of

Having invested only $162 to play in this event, you may be content to settle for a thousand-dollar payday. Then again, having invested half a day's work and having come this far, you probably have your eye on a high-money finish. To snag the top dollars, though, you must battle through two short-handed situations: first when there are eleven to thirteen players left at two tables and, again at the final table, as the number of your competitors sinks toward none. While it's possible to get deep into a full-field tournament without shorthanded capability, it's *not* possible to win one outright unless the other nine players at your final table all go all-in on the same hand and everybody loses. So, yeah, (tournament poker) − (shorthanded skill) = (no victory).

Or how about this? You're at Las Vegas's newest casino, the oddly named Shih Tzu Palace, where the walls are all covered with velvet paintings of dogs playing poker, and you're feeling like a rottweiler in a very lucrative $400NL game.[2] You have two strong opponents and six real weakydeakies. Two of the deakies are off on a dinner break, and then without warning, two others go off to smoke. The game is now five-handed, and if you bail on it (which you may be inclined to do if you have no shorthanded skills), the game will probably break. To get back to your profitable fullhanded table, you'll need to weather a certain shorthanded storm. Now, you may find many reasons why you may not want to do this. You're up against known tough opponents; also, there's the rake to deal

---

this writing team, Tony) that, even at this late date, most poker players are male. So, and with profound apologies to the ladies in the reading audience, we will continue the *Killer Poker* tradition of representing players with masculine pronouns. We're not happy that the perfect he/she pronoun has yet to be invented, but we hope that whether you're ♀ or ♂ (or even Θ or ῶ), you'll cut us some slack on this issue.

2. Standard nomenclature for this book: $400NL means a no limit hold'em game with a fixed buy-in of $400.

with, and the rake will have a relatively higher impact in a shorthanded game. But it shouldn't be in your head that you're outclassed or outmanned in a shorthanded setting. If it is, then that's a hole in your skill set that needs filling. Otherwise, you'll never be able to play in a shorthanded game (even a profitable one against inept opponents) and will likely run for cover every time a few seats go vacant. For the sake of being a well-rounded cash game player and for the sake of being able to play through temporarily adverse situations, you need to have the shorthanded tool in your belt.

Then there's the good ol' sit-n-go (SNG), otherwise known as a single-table tournament (STT). These are insanely popular as stand-alone tournaments online and also serve ably as satellites, that is feeders into larger tournaments both online and in the real world. A typical SNG has nine or ten combatants and pays the top three. These matches quickly devolve to shorthanded, and then heads-up, confrontations, and the skilled SNG player must know how to play within the changing (shrinking) dynamic of the SNG setting. Of course, if you're a real action junkie (and we suspect that you are, or you wouldn't be reading this book—and by the way, so are we, or we wouldn't be writing it), you can find SNGs that start out with only six players or even heads-up. These tournaments are, of course, shorthanded from the get-go, and again, if your shorthanded expertise is missing or lacking, you yield substantial advantage to foes who are well practiced in the art.

Talking of six-player tables, so-called 6-max NLHE (or even 5-max) cash game tables have become all the rage online. Hands play faster, and the (relatively) low rake makes shorthanded play much more feasible online than in brick-and-mortar (b&m) cardrooms.[3] These shorthanded games can be

---

3. We have always wondered why realworld casinos are called "brick and mortar." Why not "lathe and plaster"? "Daub and wattle"? "Sears and Roebuck"? We clearly have too much time on our hands.

very, very profitable for a couple of reasons. First, you play more hands per hour at a shorthanded table. Thus, if you're skilled enough to earn 5 big bets per 100 hands (BB/100) at both fullhanded and shorthanded NLHE, you'll make more per hour at the shorthanded table simply because you'll plough through more hands. Second, since you're playing against fewer opponents, you have fewer opponents to "solve." If you're good at this sort of thing (and when you're done with this book, you will be), it won't take you long to figure out how to slice your few foes to pieces. Third, shorthanded NLHE attracts gamblers—impatient types who just don't like to sit around and wait for quality cards. Some of these gamblers may be tricky to play against, but at the end of the day they are gamblers, and properly conceived and executed battle plans will deftly separate these degenerates from their dosh.

Please don't imagine that we use the word *degenerate* in a prejorative sense. Some of our best friends are degenerates; hell, so are we. Both of us have gravitated to shorthanded play, especially online, because we are avowed action junkies who can fall in love with any two cards. We find shorthanded NLHE to be simply more fun to play than its fullhanded cousin. We know—as you know, too, no doubt—that at a fullhanded table the numbers dictate the action: bad cards are bad, good cards are good, and mostly the correct thing to do is fold, fold, fold. Not only that, but when you do see a flop, you often have so much company in the pot that clever play takes a backseat to dispassionate mathematical analysis. While we like dispassionate mathematical analysis as much as the next man, we're also fans of clever play and find that shorthanded poker gives our creativity *much* more room to move.

Plus we get to play more hands.

With all these great reasons to play shorthanded NLHE, why do some players yet hate it? It may be that they simply don't know how to play it. Most of us, after all, have been schooled in the typical tight-aggressive (TAG) approach that works so well in fullhanded games. Some of us have enjoyed great success in finding loose, weak, fullhanded games where we just sit around until premium cards come along. "If it ain't broke, don't break it," think these players, and they stick to their fullhanded habits. Others feel—or fear—that their imagined foes in a shorthanded setting will simply have them for lunch and, with hands spinning out at such alarming frequency, they believe that they have no place to hide and no way to protect themselves from the negative skill differential they perceive.

We think that's a shame.

We know from our experience how profitable and how much fun (and, in tournament poker, how vitally important) shorthanded play can be. So we did what we always do in such circumstances: we sat down and wrote a book. The book you're reading now. We hope and trust it'll help you overcome your fear (if any) of shorthanded play and give you the strategy and tactics you need to become a shorthanded beast.

If you've read a *Killer Poker* book before, you know that they're all about the interactive approach. In the past, this has mostly been a matter of participating with pen in hand: writing down discoveries and observations in your poker notebook, thereby deepening your understanding of both poker and yourself. This time, we're stretching that concept a bit to include exercises at the end of each chapter. Unlike paying taxes or spooning after sex, these are entirely voluntary. But we do recommend that you take a whack at them. As with hash brownies, the more you put into them, the more you'll get out.

Poker, it has been said, is the ultimate Darwinist card game, where the law of the jungle prevails. If that's true, then shorthanded poker is a tight little jungle surrounded by a steel cage.

It amplifies everything: your strengths and weaknesses; your skills and holes; and your courage and cowardice. Furthermore, mastering this challenge will force you to face yourself as the player you truly are and to rethink some things you've taken as given, probably, since you first looked at your first two hold'em hole cards. But once you've met that challenge, you'll find yourself better prepared to conquer any poker game you play, whether shorthanded, fullhanded, or twenty-three-handed at the in-laws' on New Year's.

So let's get into it, shall we? The long journey of shorthanded poker awaits.

Killer Poker Shorthanded

1

♣ ♠ ♦ ♥

SHORTHANDED THINKING

♧ ♤ ◇ ♡

*Whenever I see a nine-handed game in a casino, I
think, 'Wow, you could get three good poker games
out of this.'*

—MIKE CARO, AMERICA'S MAD GENIUS

How Short Is Short?

No-limit Texas hold'em has been called "a game of people
played with cards."[1] While we like that appellation, we also
find it true that, in fullhanded ring games at least, NLHE is
still pretty much a game of cards played with cards. That
is, your decisions are based more on assumptions about what
hands your foes hold than on assumptions about how they'll
play those hands. To take one well-known number, the odds
are about 4:1 against being dealt a hold'em hand containing
an ace or a pair. In a full ring game, then, if you don't have
a hand like that, you can figure yourself beaten in two places
going in—and figure that your best course of action in
most cases is to muck the Hammer (72) or the Numpty (62)

---

1. As strip poker has been called "a game of naked people played with
   cards."

1

or whatever other egregious piece of cheese you've been dealt.

In a shorthanded game, by contrast, the absolute number of premium holdings dealt each hand drops way down, simply as a function of fewer hands being dealt. Thus, in a fullhanded game, you begin with the assumption that, probably, somebody has a hand, but in a shorthanded game, you start with the assumption that, probably, nobody does. And the shorter the game gets, the more this assumption pertains. To reorient your thinking from fullhanded to shorthanded poker, then, begin with this question:

> *How can I win without cards?*

This is not a whiny rhetorical question, but rather the fundamental strategic query of shorthanded play. Before we begin to answer it, though, we must further refine our understanding of what we mean by shorthanded.

Traditionally, fullhanded tables consist of seven or more players, and shorthanded games consist of six or fewer players. Within the spectrum of shorthanded games, however, there's shorthanded and then there's *really* shorthanded. Just as a six-handed game plays differently from a ten-handed game, a heads-up confrontation plays very differently from its six-way cousin. Here is the full spectrum of shorthanded NLHE games:

- 6-handed

- 5- and 4-handed

- 3-handed

- 2-handed (heads-up)

Even though NLHE is a game that takes place across four betting rounds, our thinking about, and differentiation among, the different types of shorthanded games has mostly to do with the betting rounds where you find most of the action: preflop play and play on the flop.

Six-handed. Existing in a gray area between shorthanded and fullhanded play, six-handed games are neither precisely short nor exactly full. In six-way action, most flops are contested by at most three players—very rarely more—which sets six-handed poker apart from full ring games and their crowded, robustly contested "family" pots. So six-handed is not full-handed, that's for sure. Then again, at a six-handed table, the notion of early position still comes into play. If you call or raise from under the gun (UTG), which is to the left of the big blind (BB), you have half the players behind you yet to act, with only the two blinds sitting in front of you. This means that the majority of your foes will have position on you for the duration of the hand, and as we trust you know, putting in lots of money out of position (OOP) in NLHE can lead to real trouble. Six-handed games differ from shorter shorthanded games, then, in that early position plays remain vulnerable to significant action from a (relatively) large percentage of players in later, better position.

Five- and four-handed. We group five- and four-handed games together because in both cases while there's still a definable early position, if you enter a pot UTG, you'll never be out of position with respect to the majority of players yet to act. Though you still need to exercise positional caution, in five- and four-handed games, especially if the cutoff (CO) or button (B) or both are tricky, frisky players the notion of early position preflop play is pretty much gone. Furthermore, as a function of so few starting contestants, postflop play is almost exclusively heads-up or three-handed. Since it's unlikely that anyone yet contesting for the pot has much in the way of a hand, here's where the notion of winning without cards really starts to kick in. While six-handed games usually end up playing like shorthanded games after the flop, it's when you get to five- and four-handed games that the action can be said to be truly shorthanded from the start—and where, for consistent success, we have to start stepping outside the realm of tight-aggressive (TAG) hit-to-win poker.

Three-handed. Three-handed games are unique in that the only player who doesn't post a blind preflop is the button. Because of hold'em's positional advantage, three-handed games consist of a lot of blind stealing by the button. The blinds have to counter by finding a favorable mix of hands to defend with, but something very interesting happens here: because button raises are usually common in a three-handed game, they become almost meaningless. That is, no one believes that a button raise in any way equates with good cards. Even so, the blinds still can't freely play back at the button blind stealer because of the positional disadvantage they'll face in later betting rounds, whether the button has a hand or not. This is a specific instance of the more general phenomenon of knowing your foe is likely bluffing but being effectively powerless to stop him. The winning player in a three-handed game is thus usually the one who uses the power of the button most effectively.

Heads-up. We've already mentioned that cards don't mean as much in shorthanded NLHE as they do in fullhanded games; this idea reaches its logical conclusion in heads-up play, where the game is much less about holding cards and much more about establishing and exploiting profitable betting patterns. You (and your opponent if he's skilled) will be constantly changing gears, jockeying for position, and trying to get a foe leaning the wrong way. Some heads-up battles are won by whittling down an opponent through lots of small-pot poker. Others battles are won by laying big traps. This form of one-on-one combat is a unique subset of shorthanded play and probably deserves to have a whole book devoted just to it.[2]

Cash Games Versus Tournaments

Now let's look at the difference between shorthanded cash games and shorthanded play in tournaments. Because waiting for big cards isn't a viable shorthanded strategy, a looser, aggressive style of play becomes the norm. As anyone familiar with this style knows, loose and aggressive play leads, among other things, to increasing volatility. In a properly played shorthanded game, stacks may rise and fall like Roman empires, and in a cash game that's all right, assuming you're playing within your means, for you can always reload with available funds from your pocket, ATM, or wealthy maiden aunt.

In tournaments, of course, volatility is a potentially fatal problem. If your stack fluctuates all the way down to zero, you're done, with nothing to do from that point forward except repair to a cash game or the bar. Tournament play, then, requires that we strike a balance between chip accumulation and survival. In the shorthanded hothouse of a tournament's end stage, this balance can be hard to achieve. You must evaluate the chip expected value (EV) and subsequent payout EV of every move, and weigh these moves against the chip EV and

2. An idea we pitched to our publisher, who said something about blood from a stone.

payout EV of other possible moves on possible future hands. Moreover, since tournaments tend to get shorthanded at the exact moment when the pressure of rising blinds becomes extreme, we further have to weigh our choices as a function of relative stack size. Shorthanded tournament strategy, then, isn't just a matter of making the moves dictated by decreased hand values and temporary positional advantage. It's also a matter of gamesmanship, where considerations of a high money—or first place—finish come into play.

You may, for instance, be in a shorthanded tournament situation where every player has less than ten big blinds (10BB), or you may be in a shorthanded tournament situation where you have 5BB and your two opponents have 30BB each. The pure dictates of shorthanded play will be severely skewed (sometimes turned completely upside down) by the meta-considerations of tournament play.

Tournament play, then, differs from cash game play in that all our money moves exist in the context of greater strategic concerns. That said, the basis for sound shorthanded play lies in deducing chip EV for a particular hand and measuring that EV against what we know or can deduce or can manipulate about our foes.

A Crucial Truth

When we first started playing hold'em, most of us played in fullhanded, low-stakes games where the "any two will do" ethos prevailed. In those games, virtually every flop was contested by three or more players (often many more) (often everyone), regardless of whether or not there were preflop raises. The way to beat these games, we quickly discovered, was to play somewhat tighter than the mean, to try to hit our hands, and to bet the hell out of them for value when we did. Later we were introduced to the concept of pot odds, and then we learned to play drawing hands only when the pot was laying us the right price. Not too much sophisticated poker thought went into beating these games, but beating them was the first major step in our evolution as poker players.

As we advanced, we found ourselves in tougher fullhanded games, where our foes (curse them) didn't donate their money quite so willingly. Still, our standard, kosher, TAG, hit-to-win recipe continued to be a winning formula for even the relatively rougher fullhanded games. To improve our results, we started adding new weapons to our arsenal, such as bluffing in position and semi-bluffing some drawing hands. Even with these wrinkles though, the controlling idea for our fullhanded play remained hit-to-win. And you know what? Hit-to-win works. Why? Because with so many players contesting so many pots, somebody usually hits something, and therefore it usually takes at least a little something to take down the pot. Let's look at the numbers.

Suppose you hold two unpaired hole cards. The probability that you will flop one or more cards matching the rank of one of your hole cards is $1 - \left(\frac{44}{50}\right)\left(\frac{43}{49}\right)\left(\frac{42}{48}\right) \approx .32$.[3] You are a 2.125:1 underdog to hit at least a pair; it'll happen roughly one time in three. Now here's the thing: when you play in fullhanded games where many players see the flop, you are usually getting at least an immediate 3:1 on your preflop investment, so you are getting proper odds to draw to at least a pair.

Now let's shift to shorthanded play and see how the situation changes. In most shorthanded games, we'll have at most

---

3. If you want to learn how to set up such calculations easily, check out Tony Guerrera, *Killer Poker by the Numbers* (New York: Kensington, 2006). If you don't give a rat's ass about such calculations, check out JV's *Math? Bah!* (Nonexistington, 6002).

two opponents postflop, meaning we are usually only getting at best a 2:1 return on our preflop investment. If we're playing in a shorthanded game and only playing when we hit the flop, suddenly we're no longer getting the right price to play any hands at all. So we have to play *something*, and we have to base our play not on our cards but our foes. With this leap of logic, we step suddenly outside the whole hit-to-win mindset, and outside that mindset is where we absolutely need to be. Most successful fullhanded players who can't beat shorthanded games haven't figured this out. To aid in your transition, we offer the following crucial truth:

> *It's hard to hit a flop.*

Yes, it's so hard to hit a flop. Two times out of three, you will miss the flop—not so much as pair. Two times out of three, your foe will miss the flop—not so much as pair. Four times out of nine (more or less), you'll *both* miss the flop—not so much as pair. This means—and here comes the essential bedrock reality of shorthanded play—most flops will be contested over little or nothing at all. This is why our whole hit-to-win paradigm doesn't work shorthanded. Learning to play hold'em at fullhanded tables, we trained ourselves to "fit or fold," to wait patiently until we connected with the flop before we started getting involved. Good for us for learning how to play fullhanded games correctly, but that strategy simply doesn't work shorthanded. If we wait to connect with flops in shorthanded play, we will, not to put too fine a point on it, simply wait ourselves broke.

Just to make the picture abundantly clear, consider table 1.1, opposite. It assumes that the flop is unpaired and that you haven't at least paired. Here you see the probabilities that various numbers of foes likewise whiffed.

Table 1.1: Probability That None of Your Opponents Have a Hole Card Matching a Board Card on an Unpaired Flop If They Have Random Hands

NUMBER OF OPPONENTS	P(NONE MATCH A BOARD CARD)
1	0.65
2	0.41
3	0.26
4	0.16
5	0.09
6	0.05
7	0.03
8	0.01
9	0.01

As you can see in table 1.1, as the number of enemies increases, the likelihood of everyone having missed the flop drops like a rock. Against even three foes, the board helps no one only one time in four. Against five or more foes, it's a virtual certainty that someone has something. That's why hit-to-win (and fit or fold) works in a crowd—but not in a thin field.

Now let's assume that the probabilities in table 1.1 match the probabilities that your foes will fold if you bet into them. Of course, this assumption isn't entirely valid because your opponents may have draws or pocket pairs or may play back at you on stone-cold bluffs. Such caveats aside, the probabilities indicate that making a $\frac{2}{3}$ pot sized bet into one or two opponents when the flop has missed you is a potentially profitable play against certain players. Even if you have nothing, when they have nothing too, it's hard for them to call. For some of them it's impossible, for the simple reason that they don't know the real math of hitting the flop, as you now do. Knowing which of your foes you can run over is an important part of being a winning shorthanded player, and we'll show you later how to parse your enemies accurately. For now, though, just know this: that running over your foes is essential to shorthanded victory. Get used to it. Your level of aggressiveness is about to go way the fuck up.

Be a Codebreaker: Hacking 101

Live or online, shorthanded NLHE play features many more hands per hour than fullhanded play. Online, shorthanded games will boast a hand rate in the neighborhood of about 100 per hour. Thanks to the fast pace of play and the small number of foes, you get a whole lot of useful information in a very short space of time. This high level of so-called context density makes available to you a rich, meaningful data stream about your foes' betting patterns—a stream you never get in fullhanded games. In a full ring game, you might see a player use a certain betting progression only a handful of times, and there's a decent chance that you won't see a showdown any of those times, so you won't have a lot of hard information with which to make inferences. Shorthanded, those betting patterns repeat over and over again (because *everything* repeats over and over again), giving you plenty of reliable 411 to work with. Granted, some common betting patterns still won't lead to showdowns so that you'll still have to make some educated guesses, but in general, the shorthanded environment is much more information rich and information relevant than its fullhanded cousin.

And that's a good thing because with basic TAG play no longer a consistently viable path to profit, we need to find other ways of carving out our edge—and it turns out that analyzing betting patterns is a handy tool for this. We analyze our foes' betting patterns to discern who can be bluffed more profitably, more often. We use these trends to determine who we can profitably call with hands as weak as bottom pair. We let our enemies' tendencies show who will yield their blinds too often without a fight. These are small edges, but small edges are the bread and butter of shorthanded play. Fortunately, with all the hands we play, small edges add up quickly. Unfortunately, since the blinds come around so often in a shorthanded game, and also represent a higher overall percentage of pot size, not taking advantage of small edges can end up costing us a lot of money. So we need to push edges— which means we need to break codes.

As an example of how to break codes effectively, consider an online 6-max NLHE game. Say you have discovered that a minimum bet on the flop in this game usually means that the player making the bet has a draw or else a weak hand such as bottom board pair or middle board pair with no kicker. Armed with the information revealed by this betting pattern, what is your best course of action regardless of the cards you hold? Answer: overbetting the pot. Most opponents on draws won't call if you provide the disincentive of an overbet, and foes with weak made hands are similarly likely to fold because the whole point of their min bet was to reduce their financial exposure in the first place.

Shorthanded play, then, serves codebreaking two ways: First, by offering frequently repeating patterns in an environment of high context density, shorthanded play gives us plenty of hard information to work with. Second, by repeating common game scenarios so frequently, shorthanded play gives us abundant opportunity to put our counterstrategies to work.

To be a successful codebreaker (we prefer the happy term *hacker*), simply follow these three steps:

1. Identify a meaningful betting pattern.

2. Come up with a +EV strategy to exploit it.

3. Recognize that exceptions exist, and constantly update your hack.

Some opponents may be so slack-witted or stubborn that step 3 never comes into play (if it ain't broke, don't fix it), but the third step is usually important because once you launch a strategy to exploit a pattern, your opponents will usually begin to adjust. Say you've made some decent coin by overbetting your foes off their draws. How will they respond? Either by betting their draws bigger (to make them look less like draws) or betting their made hands smaller (to invite you to overbet yourself into a pickle). Each of these countermeasures requires yet another countermeasure from you, and so your hacking efforts are never a set-and-forget proposition. You're constantly breaking codes, constantly monitoring your foes' adjustments, and constantly responding to the changes you detect in their patterns. For instance, if you've been successfully bullying minimum bettors but suddenly find yourself in a situation where people are minimum betting their monsters and getting you overcommitted with understrength hands, you don't have a problem on your hands, but rather an opportunity. After all, by minimum betting huge hands, your foes are offering you highly favorable drawing odds, so you just thank them kindly for the gift and draw cheaply. If you're really fortunate, these tricky trappers will cough up big bets on later rounds, giving you maximum return on your implied odds. Even if they don't, their adjustment to your adjustment has made drawing hands more favorable than usual in a shorthanded game.

Bottom line: when you're a hacker, your opponents are *always* giving you something you can use.

Be a Codemaker: Cryptography 101

If your opponents aren't paying attention and adapting to your play, then your role at the table is exclusively that of a hacker. Crack everyone's code and comfortably play some +EV poker. Of course, sitting at a table where nobody's paying any attention is not very likely. More commonly, you'll be facing at least one other hacker, and in order to defeat your fellow hackers, you'll need to generate some meaningful and misleading code of your own. You'll need to present them with betting patterns that lead them astray and cause them to draw false conclusions.

Let's craft some code. Suppose you're still in that online 6-max game and you notice that, as just described, a fellow hacker always overbets the pot when someone makes a min bet. Holding pocket sixes, you find yourself heads-up against this criminal, when the flop comes T♥6♥8♦. Based on your hack, you can reliably predict that he'll take the bait of a min bet and overbet the pot. He'll have to, won't he? Either to protect something like top pair or good kicker or just to steal the pot from the weakass min bettor you appear to be. At that point, you can spring your trap with a big reraise or just call along and hope he'll oblige you by betting yet again on later streets. Now a couple of orbits pass, and you find yourself heads-up again against the same hacker—only this time you have the flush draw. Since you trapped last time with a min bet, he'll naturally be leery of making a big raise if you min bet here. He may just call along, giving you favorable odds for your flush draw or possibly even following a "won't get fooled again" line of reasoning, and fold right here. Either way, you've accomplished three worthy goals:

1. You've given yourself a great chance at winning two pots.

2. You've analyzed your foe's play.

3. You've misled him with yours.

This is called keeping your head in the game and also keeping one step ahead of the pack. In the name of exploiting small edges, it's exactly the sort of thinking and acting, codebreaking and codemaking, that you need to be involved with when you make shorthanded NLHE your game of choice. Remember that you only have a handful of foes to figure out, so figuring them out shouldn't be that tough a job. Really, it's the only job that matters. Shorthanded, you can't count on cards. You have to count on code.

Now, since each of your opponents has a different code, you'll probably have different misleads and countermeasures for each of them. What's really interesting is that you can use optimal play against one player to set up a profitable hack against someone else by wedding correct play to false code. To see how this works, let's say you're in a pot against a loose, passive player, a so-called Cally Wally, with the following attributes:

- On the flop he'll call a $\frac{2}{3}$ pot bet regardless of his hole cards.

- On the turn he'll call a $\frac{1}{2}$ pot bet with king high or better.

- On the river he'll call a $\frac{1}{3}$ pot bet with ace high or better.

Against shorthanded foes in general, your default game plan for many games will be to bet the flop heads-up with any two cards and, if you get resistance, to shut down on the turn and the river unless you have top pair. Against this Wally, though, your hack tells you that you can comfortably bet as little as bottom pair with a high kicker on the turn and as little as second pair on the river. This plan is a profitable way to play against the Wally—and it's secondarily profitable because even while you're beating him out of pot after pot, you're transmitting seductive false betting patterns to others at the table!

After a few hands in which you've shown down some sketchy, but winning, holdings, some of your foes will conclude that you're willing to bet your second and third pairs pretty hard. However, only the craftiest ones will recognize that you're making these bets exclusively against the Wally. The others will assume that you're generally wildly overoptimistic on the turn and river. If you exclusively bet into these others with just the high end of your spectrum—top pair or better—they'll pay off what they see as your promiscuous betting. Thanks to the Wally, and the primary target he presented, you now have fruitful secondary targets: your other opponents who'll no longer fold the hands they should on the turn and the river.

Playing different opponents differently is a great way to send out confusing signals to your foes, especially if you can do it in such a way that you're actually playing optimally against each individual opponent. The beauty of shorthanded play is, again, that you have fewer foes to solve, fewer foes to mislead, and many, many more situations where you're heads-up against a single foe whom you understand well, but who doesn't really understand you at all.

Just Say No to Ego

You're starting to get the sense, we hope, that shorthanded play is a much more mentally engaged and engaging version of poker than its fullhanded cousin. It's compelling. It commands all your information-gathering, information-processing, *and* information-blocking strategies. We here at KPHQ[4] like a fighter pilot metaphor: "Players in shorthanded hold'em are engaged in a perpetual dogfight, trying constantly to get inside each other's turning circle—and inside each other's head." Winning such dogfights feels good. Real good. So we feel it's only fair to warn you that feeling good, the buzz you enjoy from beating your foes, will become the tail that wags the dog of your shorthanded play. In short, ego—the emotional response to poker—is a greater problem in shorthanded hold'em than it is in full-field play.

All poker, of course, can be an ego-driven enterprise, as will any setting involving competition, money, glitz, glamour, and the chance to eviscerate and crush one's foes. Amplifying this ego impact is the close-quarter nature of shorthanded play, where personal—sometimes very personal—confrontations are the norm. It's easy to stay dispassionate in a fullhanded ring game when you're just sitting and waiting for hands. In shorthanded play, where every deal is a dogfight and where trash talk is often liberally applied (for edge or just for the hell of it), you'll find it's an extra struggle to keep one's ego in check. But wait, there's more.

In addition to all that competition, money, glitz, glamour, personal confrontation, evisceration, foe crushing, dogfights, and trash talk, shorthanded NLHE is a game where bluffing plays a pivotal role. In fullhanded play, bluffing is a luxury, a tool you may or may not choose to use. In shorthanded play, where it's hard to hold a hand, bluffing becomes de rigueur, and of course, the bluff packs an inordinate ego punch, whether it works or not. Our egos swell when we bluff successfully and shrink when our opponents bluff us successfully (es-

---

4. Killer Poker World Headquarters, a sanctum sanctorum not unlike the Bat Cave, but with far cooler technology.

pecially if they show their cards or trash talk it through). Shorthanded play is a bully's game, and no one likes to be bullied, so there's another opportunity for our emotions to become negatively engaged.

Ego pitfalls are everywhere. Suppose you're in a shorthanded game and just crushing it: raise, continuation bet (CB), everyone folds. *Next case!* Suddenly, a new player arrives, and he starts preempting all your bully behavior and bluff runs. At this point, it's natural to feel thwarted. Frustration blooms, and you find yourself thinking, "Who the hell does this dickweed think he is? This is *my* game, not his. I'm gonna show this bitch what's up!" Next thing you know, you're making decisions that are ego based, not hack based and then, well, you're doomed. Especially if you're shorthanded, where the pace of play amplifies small errors and turns tiny leaks into flash floods.

Shorthanded NLHE is a macho game, no question about it. The few seats at the table are often filled with hotheads, hotshots, and big, swinging dicks. To profit in this atmosphere, we *must* check our egos at the door. Let others take the glory road. Strive to be the emotionless assassin whose only interest is to kill as efficiently as possible. Treat all bets, bluffs, and confrontations as mere points of information: information you can feed back into your game to improve your performance and your results. It will help you detach from ego, and from emotional investments of all kinds, if you stop thinking of outcomes in terms of *good* and *bad*. In other words:

> *Avoid value judgments. Value judgments are bad.*

To borrow from the Buddhists, who are masters of this sort of thing, we ask you to contemplate the following Zen koan:

THE ABBOT'S GIFT

A Zen monk, early in his training, is preparing to leave the monastery and switch locations, for that is common in the Zen practice. Before he leaves he goes to the abbot of the monastery to say goodbye. He does so, but the abbot says he has a gift for him. Now, it is part of the Japanese way to accept gifts and be appreciative; to do otherwise is rude and, therefore, wrong. The abbot takes a pair of tongs and picks up a red-hot coal from the adjacent fire pit on which he has a teakettle.

The young monk starts to contemplate what he should do, and after a few moments, runs out of the hall distressed, for he cannot figure out how to act. He can take the coal and be burned, or he can refuse the gift of the abbot and be rude. Both, in his mind, are things he cannot do.

He meditates on the problem for the next week, and comes back to say goodbye. However, the same scene is played again, and the same frustration blooms when he tries to figure out what the abbot wants him to do.

He meditates further on the subject and feels he has discovered how to respond to the abbot's gift. He returns, for the third time, to say goodbye to the abbot, and as before the abbot picks up a red-hot coal and presents it as a gift to the young monk. The young monk simply replies, "Thank you."

The abbot breaks into a grin, nods his head, and returns the coal to the fire pit. "You may go now," he says.

Accept what is offered you, say the Buddhists.[5] A thing is not a good thing or a bad thing, it's just a thing that is. If

---

5. Also, don't make assumptions about what you'll be forced to take.

someone successfully bluffs you off a pot, even if he gloats and taunts, simply accept the outcome, make appropriate adjustments, and move on. In the swirling dogfight of shorthanded NLHE, the minute you let your ego get engaged, you're toast.

It will happen from time to time—and be a challenge to your ego—that you find yourself in a game that is unbeatable. Perhaps you are slightly better than your opponents are but not to the point of being able to overcome the rake. Maybe you're not even as much as slightly better. It could be that you're usually better, but on this occasion, your foes just have you dialed in. For whatever reason, if you determine that you're in an unbeatable game, don't try to come up with excuses. Instead, come up with a game plan that works. Here's the default game plan for meeting the challenge of difficult games:

Leave.

Of course, sometimes we're forced to play against tougher competition, as in a tournament where leaving is not an option. And sometimes we need to play against tougher competition in order to sharpen our skills. But we *don't* need to play against tougher competition just because our egos won't let go. That's a guaranteed way to blow your bankroll. Remember: just because they hand you a hot coal doesn't mean you have to hold it.

Exercises

1. Assuming that all players behind you are on the same calling distribution, what's an important difference between raising UTG in a six-handed game and raising UTG in a five-handed game?

2. Why does shorthanded NLHE require that you play outside the realm of hit-to-win poker?

3. Suppose you are in the cutoff seat with K♦T♣. Action has folded to you, and your three remaining opponents have the following distributions:

- Button: reraise with [AA,99]||[AK,AQ]; call with [88,55]||[AJ,AT]||[KQ,KJ]

- Small Blind: Reraise with [AA,KK]; if button calls, call with [QQ,22]||[AK,AJ]||[KQ]; if button folds, call with [QQ,77]||[AK,AJ]||[KQ]

- Big Blind: reraise with [AA,KK]; if button and/or small blind calls, call with [QQ,22]||[AK,AT]|| [KQ,KJ]||[JTs,76s]; if button and small blind fold, call with [QQ,22]||[AK,A7]||[KQ,K9]||[QJ,Q8]|| [JT,J9]||[T9s,76s]

What's the probability that you can steal the blinds?

4. Take the situation described in the previous question. Suppose that after you raise with your K♦T♣, only the big blind calls, and the flop is 9♥6♥2♠. The big blind checks to you. Estimate the profitability of a $\frac{2}{3}$ pot continuation bet assuming that, usually, the big blind will bet with top pair, but that he'll check-call with pairs worse than top pair or with a drawing hand for which, including implied odds, he's getting a decent price to draw.

5. After 150 hands, your opponent has raised preflop 35 times, and he has bet 20 flops after having raised preflop. Figure out whether your opponent is prone to continuation betting when he misses the flop.

6. Describe in your own words the meaning of the story of "The Abbot's Gift." How does this pertain to poker?

Answers

1. If all opponents behind you are on the same calling distribution, then participating in pots UTG in a six-handed game will put you out of position postflop more than 50 percent of the time (three players behind, two in front). Against the same players in a five-handed game, you'll be out of position only half the time. The shorter the game gets, the less negative impact bad position will have.

2. With unpaired hole cards, the odds against your hitting a flop are about 2:1. In fullhanded games, you usually have enough opponents contesting every hand to make it profitable to wait for odds-on situations. In shorthanded games, where the blinds come faster and cost relatively more, aggressive opponents will make you pay too high a price for patience. The first aggressor in shorthanded pots typically has an advantage, and so we must explore ways to play shorthanded NLHE besides just sitting and waiting to hit hands.

3. To make this calculation easier, we will assume that the probabilities of each player folding are independent of each other. In reality, they aren't, but as we saw in *Killer Poker by the Numbers*, using an independence approximation in such a problem will usually get answers sufficiently close to the true values.

   The button's playing distribution, organized in classes of hands with the same number of combinations, is the following:

6 combinations each: [AA]|||[QQ,JJ]|||[99,55]
= 48 total

3 combinations each: [KK]|||[TT] = 6 total
(because you hold one K and one T)

16 combinations each: [AQ,AJ] = 32 total

12 combinations each: [AK]|||[AT]|||[KQ,KJ]
= 48 total

This distribution consists of 134 combinations. Since there are 1,225 combinations of hole cards left, the probability that the button folds is $\frac{1,091}{1,225}$.

The only distributions of the small blind (SB) that matter for answering the question are his reraising distribution and his calling distribution when the button folds, for if the button calls, you already have failed to take the pot uncontested. The small blind's applicable distribution, organized in classes of hands with the same number of combinations, is the following:

6 combinations each: [AA]|||[QQ,JJ]|||[99,77]
= 36 total

3 combinations each: [KK]|||[TT] = 6 total

12 combinations each: [AK]|||[KQ] = 24 total

16 combinations each: [AQ,AJ] = 32 total

This distribution consists of 98 combinations, meaning that the probability that the small blind folds is $\frac{1,127}{1,225}$.

The big blind's applicable distribution, broken down with respect to available combinations, is the following:

6 combinations each: [AA]|||[QQ,JJ]|||[99,22]
= 66 total

3 combinations each: [KK]|||[TT] = 6 total

12 combinations each:
[AK]||[AT]||[KQ,KJ]||[K9]||[QT]||[JT] = 84 total

16 combinations each:
[AQ,AJ]||[A9,A7]||[QJ]||[Q9,Q8]||[J9] = 144 total

9 combinations each: [KT] = 9 total

3 combinations each: [T9s] = 3 total

4 combinations each: [98s,76s] = 12 total

This distribution consists of 324 combinations, meaning that the probability that the big blind folds is $\frac{901}{1,225}$.

To get the probability of all three players folding, just multiply together the probabilities of each player folding. The probability that you pick up the blinds, uncontested, is therefore $\left(\frac{1,091}{1,225}\right)\left(\frac{1,127}{1,225}\right)\left(\frac{901}{1,225}\right) \approx .60$. Think about it: against a button, small blind, and big blind with these fairly common raising and calling distributions, you will win without a fight about 60 percent of the time! No wonder preflop aggressiveness is so prized in shorthanded games. As always, the particular conditions of the game you are in will override any generalizations that we make, but you should keep this important number in mind—and use it to trigger your aggressiveness—every time you play shorthanded.

4. We have more precise knowledge of the big blind's distribution given that he checked to you on the flop. Using the assumptions given in the problem, the big blind's distribution, broken down with respect to available combinations, is the following:

   6 combinations each: [88,77]||[55,33] = 30 total

   16 combinations each: [AQ,AJ]||[A8,A7]||[QJ]||[Q8]
   = 96 total

12 combinations each:
[AK]|||[AT]|||[KQ,KJ]|||[QT]|||[JT] = 72 total

9 combinations each: [KT] = 9 total

4 combinations each: [87s] = 4 total

3 combinations each: [76s] = 3 total

This distribution contains a total of 214 hands. Out of these 214 hands, the following distribution consists of those hands that the big blind will call your continuation bet with. Again, the list is broken down with respect to the number of available combinations:

6 combinations each: [88,77]|||[55,33] = 30 total

4 combinations each: [87s] = 4 total

3 combinations each: [76s] = 3 total

1 combination each:

[A♥K♥,A♥T♥]|||[A♥8♥,A♥7♥]|||[K♥Q♥,K♥T♥]|||
[Q♥J♥,Q♥T♥]|||[Q♥8♥]|||[J♥T♥] = 13 total

The big blind will call you with 50 combinations, meaning that the probability that your continuation bet will get called is $\frac{50}{214}$. Assuming no further action after the flop, an estimate of the EV of a two-thirds pot continuation bet is the following:

$$\left(\tfrac{50}{214}\right)\left(-\tfrac{2}{3}P\right)+\left(\tfrac{164}{214}\right)\left(+P\right) \approx +0.61P$$

This result means that, for example, if the pot is $60 and you bet $40, your expected profit would be (.60)($60) = $36. Of course, we don't actually expect to make $36 every time we make this bet, because we aren't accounting for play on the turn and the river. However, this calculation again shows the merits of being the aggressor on the flop in shorthanded pots.

5. Ideally, we'd like to know the percentage of the time that our opponent makes continuation bets without a hand. This question is tough to answer analytically because we are missing some important information such as out of the 15 pots that this player didn't bet, how many of those were pots in which an opponent's action preempted his betting?

Though we cannot answer the question in purely quantitative terms, we can make a decent, logic-based guess. Since we know that with unpaired hole cards, one is about a 2:1 underdog to flop at least a pair, if an opponent is simply betting when he hits a flop, he should only be betting a third of the time. Even accounting for overpairs and semi-bluffs with big draws, the "true" betting frequency should get no higher than 45–50 percent. Anything over 50 percent should indicate that your opponent is making naked continuation bets at least some fraction of the time. In this case, our foe has made post-flop bets 57 percent of the time, so he is at least marginally capable of making continuation bets with nothing at all.

6. This space intentionally left blank.

2

♣♠♦♥

DATA MINING FOR FUN AND PROFIT

♧♤♢♡

Play Starts Before Play Starts

Poker is a game of incomplete information. This we know. This is not news. Absent a stunning run of cards, your results at the table will directly correlate with how well you piece together the fragmentary information available to you and, as we saw in the last chapter (and will see much more fully as we go along), how well you manipulate and misrepresent information about yourself and your holdings. The beauty of poker, especially online poker, is that you can observe a table, gathering copious critical information, before you ever sit down to play. This is a gift of the game's structure, but it's a gift that far too many players decline or reject. They're either too impatient to "do their homework" or too arrogant to consider it necessary. And you know what? In a full-handed ring game that might be okay. Since fullhanded hold'em is essentially a waiting game, those who choose to jump right into the pool can study their foes while they're at the table, waiting for playable tickets. We don't recommend this approach. We think that it's crucial to accept the gift of information, because we remember what our grandmothers once told us:

> *Always take cookies when cookies are passed.*

We like to suss out a game before we jump in—fullhanded or shorthanded, but especially shorthanded.

In a realworld casino, you often get time to study the tables simply because you often have to wait for a seat. Again, many players won't make the most of this time. They'll kibitz with friends or do Sudoku or watch the World Series of Darts on TV. But also in a realworld casino, you'll find damn few (none, in fact, that we know of) exclusively shorthanded games, so this whole waiting issue may be a moot point in the real world if you're a shorthanded specialist. Most of your b&m short-handed play will result from players leaving a fullhanded game you're already in. Therefore, much of the discussion in this chapter will focus on online shorthanded play. That said, we think that the notion of studying your foes and studying the game is valid—and vital—for all forms of poker, short-handed or fullhanded, online or realworld.

Most online poker rooms have many 6-max tables avail-able, meaning that you usually have the option of finding one with an open seat and immediately going to war.[1] If you are typically far better than the foes you face, then playing imme-diately will maximize your hourly return, and the advice in this section may not apply to you. However, if you are new to shorthanded poker or if you aren't a 10BB/100 player, then it's in your best interest to "stake out a table" before sitting down.

---

1. In fact, you *always* have this option, because if all the tables are full, you can go ahead and start a new table, meaning that you'll be in-volved from the first hand forward—against one or more completely unknown foes.

Now, when we tell you to stake out a table, we're not talking about watching a hand or two at a table or two and then jumping on in. We're talking about in-depth recon work. It's not enough to classify your future foes generally as "loose" or "tight," and their stacks as "large" or "small," and their play as "aggressive" or "passive." Folks, listen up:

> *If you're going to take the time to observe a table before you play, you might as well do it right.*

What follows are some of the specific things we look for before we dive into a shorthanded game. There's quite a lot to think about here, and frankly, it's impossible to think about it all without the synapse gaps starting to smoke. But you'll find that it gets easier as you go along—once, that is, you become serious about your commitment to studying the shorthanded playing environment.

As you consider the frequency of preflop raising, look to see who's driving the bus. Are all the players playing with roughly equivalent levels of preflop aggression, or is one person providing the fireworks while the others meekly call along? Also, look to see if otherwise tight players are throwing in a disproportionate number of their raises from the cut-off and button. Do they do this only if the pot is unopened, or regardless of whether or not other players have limped? This will give you a sense of their shorthanded philosophy: Some players so worship the God of Position that they almost have to raise in position—and almost cannot play at all out of it. Also, you want to see if loose in-position raisers are tight with their raises from the blinds, knowing that they will have to play the rest of the hand out of position. Someone who raises promiscuously in position, but almost never raises his own blind, is, of course, much more likely to have a big hand in the rare circumstances when he chooses not to "let 'em live."

From this brief discussion, we imagine, you can already see that there's much more to tight or loose than just tight or loose. Knowing where, when, and how your foes are tight or loose preflop is your first key to unlocking everything you need to know about how they play and about how to play against them. And remember, you're getting all this information free, without giving up a shred of data about how *you* actually play.

At this point, one of us (Tony) would be saying that the point of all this pregame study is to build a definitive template for each player's preflop raising distribution as a function of position, number of limpers, and raising amount. The other of us (JV) would be noting that you need to know who at your prospective table can raise with cheese anywhere, any way, anytime.

Next, you want to see how the players respond to aggression. On average, how many players call preflop raises? Do they call raises of standard size but fold to overbets? For that matter, is there such a thing as a standard size raise at the table you're observing? It's always good to know the "going rate" for preflop action. Also, check for the *limpede* phenomenon, where an early position flat-call seems to encourage everyone else to limp in as well. This will be important to your play of small pairs because you won't be getting the right odds to draw to your set unless you can reasonably count on generating a limpfest when you limp from UTG.

Then there's postflop play. What percentage of the time does a raiser make continuation bets on the flop? Does he only continuation bet if there are two or fewer foes? Only one? When he's last to act? Will he check if he missed? Will the button bet no matter what if no one else bets first? What's the size of postflop bets? Do people make min bets? Overbets? Does the size of their bets correlate to the size of their hands? Who will call postflop bets with little or no piece of the flop? Who's afraid of overcards on the turn and the river? Does anyone call flop bets with the intent of lead-bluffing at the turn? Does anyone check-raise or stop-and-go? Bet phantom outs? Slow-play monsters? Reraise bluffs? Bet the turn no matter what if no one bets the flop? Attack orphan flops? Defend orphan flops? Stand on their head and spit nickels?

Is your brain about to melt? Ours too.

The fact is that there are far more questions we could ask about betting patterns than we can reasonably expect to get answers to. Nor will these scenarios necessarily recur frequently enough (even shorthanded and even online) for meaningful patterns to emerge. Plus, at some point you're just going to get tired of watching and want to, you know, play. You also run the risk of getting shut out. There's nothing more frustrating than scouting a table for a while, working hard to get a sense of it, and then, just when you're ready to jump in, finding that the table has filled. To beat this vexation, simply grab your seat at the table and then sit out and watch till you're ready for battle. Being ready for battle, of course, is the whole point of the exercise. In *The Killer Poker Hold'em Handbook* (Lyle Stuart, 2004), JV writes about something called "the clear gestalt," which is the sense of full and complete understanding that an attentive player will eventually acquire in a poker game. Even after watching a table for a sufficient length of time, you may or may not have answers to specific questions—does *monkeyboy* raise out of position with middle suited connectors?—but the act of actively watching will get you dialed into the game just the same.

To help you attain the clear gestalt, consider using visual aids. A simple chart with appropriate check boxes will go a long way toward giving you a snapshot of the game you're about to enter. Let's say you're watching a certain 6-max table at pokerbeatsworking.com (our favorite phantom website) and within the space of thirty hands or so acquire the set of data shown in the table on pages 32–33.

You can tell at a glance who are the busiest, friskiest players (*Netherworld01* and *Janeysdaddy*), who are the tightest and meekest (*flurdelay*), and who are relatively tame (*Twinkee* and *bluff_or_die*). Armed with this information, you jump into the seat you've reserved, appropriately wary of the players to your left and ready to go to war with those on your right. Even if you don't know *everything* about these players, you know—literally—at a glance what sort of game you're getting into and what behavior to expect from the respective players. Therefore:

> *Even if you don't know* everything *about your foes, be sure you know* something.

On the next two pages, we include a blank version of this table for your photocopying pleasure. Just list the players across the top and observed actions down the left hand side. Don't restrict your choice of observed actions to ours; plan to track what you consider important. Then start checkmarking to your heart's content. When you've accumulated enough check marks for some patterns to emerge, you're ready to enter the fray.

Of course, if you really want to do this up right, you'll use your sniffer software (Poker Tracker or one of its competitors) to do deep profiling of your online opponents. If you run your sniffer in tandem with your active personal observation, then you'll have the best of both worlds: an analytical/statistical appraisal of your intended table, including stats for your heads-up display (HUD) when you play, plus a "gut" sense of those you're about to face.

If you really want to take care of business, always leave tables open on your computer and let your sniffer do your data

PLAYER NAMES	Twinkee	Bluff_or_die
OBSERVED ACTIONS		
Preflop raise	✓✓✓✓✓	✓✓✓
Preflop reraise	✓✓✓	
UTG limp	✓✓✓✓✓	✓✓✓✓✓✓
Defend SB	✓✓✓✓	✓✓✓
Defend BB	✓✓✓✓✓	✓✓✓✓
CO or B raise	✓✓✓✓✓✓✓	✓✓✓✓✓✓
CB	✓✓✓✓✓	✓✓✓✓✓
Postflop check after preflop raise	✓✓✓✓✓✓	✓✓✓
Attack ragged flops	✓✓✓✓	✓✓
Slowplay big pair	✓✓	

mining for you while you're at work, on dates, running marathons, having the cat spayed, or whatever. Some poker sites try to prevent players from this sort of set-and-forget data mining; however, third-party software is often available online to help you work around such measures. Remember, poker is a game where everyone has incomplete information. Your edge comes from making better decisions than your foes, and the key to that is having less incomplete information than they do.

Wave Functions and Poker

Shine light on electrons, you'll cause them to swerve.
The act of observing disturbs the observed.
—CECIL ADAMS

Netherworld01	Janeysdaddy	[reserved]	Flurdelay
✓✓✓✓✓✓✓✓	✓✓✓✓✓		✓✓✓✓
✓✓✓✓✓✓	✓✓✓		✓
✓✓✓✓✓✓✓✓✓	✓✓✓✓✓✓		✓✓✓
✓✓✓✓✓✓✓✓	✓✓✓✓		✓✓
✓✓✓✓✓✓✓✓	✓✓✓✓✓✓✓✓		✓
✓✓✓✓✓✓✓	✓✓✓		
✓✓✓✓✓✓✓✓ ✓✓✓	✓✓✓✓✓		✓✓✓✓
✓✓✓✓✓✓✓✓✓ ✓ ✓✓✓✓✓	✓✓✓✓✓✓✓✓ ✓✓✓		✓✓✓✓
	✓✓✓✓		✓✓✓✓✓
✓✓✓✓✓✓✓✓	✓✓✓		
	✓		✓✓✓

Poker, it has been said, is the perfect metaphor for life, and we here at KPHQ certainly sign onto that philosophy. Many is the time we've seen a lesson learned at the poker table—don't go on tilt; think things through; trust your gut—pay dividends in our lives and activities outside of poker. And certainly, we've seen many facets of "life out there" illuminate our experience of poker: everything from transactional analysis to Zen Buddhism to—quantum mechanics.

Quantum mechanics?

Oh, yeah.

In quantum mechanics, physical states are described by wave functions. A wave function, in essence, is a probability distribution that expresses a sample space of possible states for a physical system (technically, the square of the wave function is the probability distribution, but anyway—). Before a measurement is made, the wave function is the proper repre-

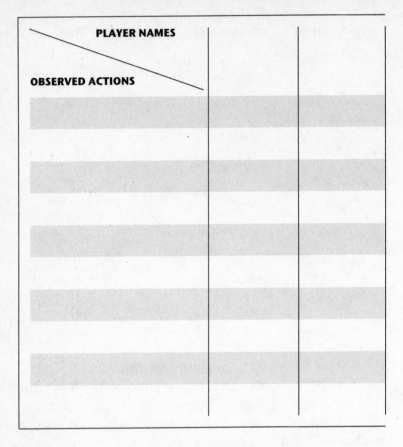

PLAYER NAMES		
OBSERVED ACTIONS		

sentation of the system. However, once a measurement is made, the wave function is said to collapse. What this means is that performing a measurement actually changes the state of a system. In other words, whenever we interact with a system, we impose a change on that system, and there's nothing we can do about it.

Examples of this are all around us. The mere presence of someone changing a flat tire on a freeway, for instance, can cause spectator slowing and a backup of miles. Laugh out loud in a movie theater, even if the movie's not funny, and others

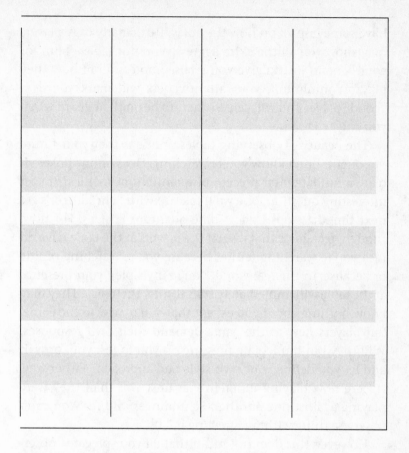

will laugh too. If you yell "Hi, Jack!" to your friend Jack Nicholson in an airport security line, uhm, guess what? You'll miss your flight.

Now let's bring this back to poker. Suppose you're in a casino—oh, let's call it Schrödinger's Casino, the one that's either always open or always closed, though you won't know which till you're inside—and you're waiting for a table. To pass the time properly, you stand and watch one of the tables you may end up playing at. The players at the table you're observing aren't blind. They see you watching, and this may have some impact on how they play. Particularly cagy players may show you a little extra aggressiveness or table a bluff for your benefit, just to give you a false impression of how they play. At minimum, your attentiveness will mark you as a "good" player and will cause others to be on their guard when you enter the game.

The beauty of observing tables online is that your future opponents don't know you're watching. Does online poker violate a fundamental precept of quantum mechanics? It's an interesting question, one we'll take up with Schrödinger's cat next time he stops by for some quantum Friskies. For now, though, recognize that even if the players at the table have no idea you're watching (either because you're watching online or because, in the real world, you're invisible), your presence at the table will immediately start to alter their play. They may know nothing about you except that you're new to the game, but players new to the game demand their own responses. Will they put immediate pressure on you to test you, or wait and let you define your own style and approach? Either way, they're now playing differently against you than they were playing against one another. Schrödinger said it: "You can't observe a thing without affecting it."

However, this does not mean that all your pregame observations are meaningless. Aggressive players will continue to trend aggressive. Passive players will continue to trend passive. While the pots you play won't play out identically to the pots you observed, there will be similarities, and the key to effective data mining is identifying these similarities and mapping out your play accordingly. The truth is that, collapsing waves notwithstanding, the data from hands you were not involved in will provide a firm foundation for the hands that follow your entrance in the game. Just keep in mind that your mere presence may make players play differently from how you observed them.

(JV here, with a note to add on this subject. It happens that from time to time when I play poker I'm outed or out myself, as "that Killer Poker guy." Players predictably respond in one of two ways: either they give me more respect than I deserve, or they take it into their heads to school Mr. Those Who Can't Do, Teach. My job is to know which way my foes are leaning and to keep pushing them in that direction till they tip over. Even if you're not that Killer Poker guy, you can readily use this tool. Simply observe how you are observed, identify the errors in others' appraisals—there's bound to be something—and encourage more mistakes of that type. Schrödinger was no fool. One thing he knew for sure was its better to be outside the box than in it.)

When You Enter a Shorthanded Game

First impressions are lasting ones. If you show up at the house of your girlfriend's father with a prison tattoo and a six pack of Mickey's Big Mouth, he's not likely to forget (or lift the restraining order). The question is, then, how do you want to start your shorthanded session? What do you want your first impression to be? In *Killer Poker No Limit*! (Lyle Stuart, 2007), JV outlines a game-entry strategy called "breathing in," wherein the player does nothing but watch and learn for the first thirty hands or so, creating a false impression of passivity and simultaneously soaking up all sorts of useful information about his foes. In shorthanded games, where play from the blinds is such a thick percentage of all hands, such obsessive circumspection is usually not a viable strategy. That said, tightness does have its place in shorthanded poker where, broadly speaking, your opening options are TAG or loose-aggressive (LAG). Each approach has its merit. Let's examine them in turn.

To start off TAG is to be a passive observer. If you did your homework and watched your table for a while before playing, there's really no advantage to putting in more time as a passive observer. We recognize, though, that *something* (impatience, arrogance, or alien mind control, say,) may have kept you from diligent watching, in which case a little in-game observing is called for. Of course, if you're tight and the rest of the table is loose, your more perceptive opponents will notice this and play differently against tight you than they do against each other. Tightness, as a class of poker behavior, is much harder to hide in a shorthanded game than a fullhanded one, so if you take the passive approach, just keep our talk about wave functions in the back of your mind.

One advantage of establishing a TAG stance is that it puts you in a position to steal some pots pretty soon. Most opponents will back down against aggression from a tight opponent. If you're facing such opponents (which you'll know from having observed them against other TAG players), starting off TAG will allow you to shift profitably into LAG mode for brief stretches of time. Just be aware that your TAG play could have the opposite effect, in that some players in shorthanded games delight in giving tight players a tough time. Instead of backing down, they'll call your preflop raises with the intent of bluffing on later rounds of betting. If you make a preflop raise and continuation bet, some players may call both with nothing but the intent to bet you off the hand on the turn. If you find yourself against such foes, just let them set this trap when you have a good piece of the flop so that you can get played with—which is to say paid off. The key is staying on your toes. Shorthanded play requires hand-by-hand adjustment to your image and your understanding of your foes' proclivities.

Starting off TAG is one way to go, but it's not the approach we prefer in most shorthanded NLHE games. Killer Poker is about aggression and establishing presence; thus, in most games, we propose generally coming out LAG, unless you're sitting at a table you've already observed to be maniacal. By starting off your shorthanded NLHE games LAG, you are an active participant, potentially the straw that stirs the drink. From this point forward, most of your data will be from pots you've been involved in, and will thus be more useful. It's the difference between knowing that "player A check-raises apparent continuation bets" and "player A check-raises *me* when I make apparent continuation bets." This is a subtle but important change in the quality of your information, in that it makes the data you mine more directly relevant.

When you start off LAG, plan to raise pretty much every unopened pot from the cutoff and the button, and continuation bet every flop that's checked to you when you're last to act. Plan also to continuation bet whenever you find yourself heads-up postflop, regardless of position. Your madness has its method: by this strong and sudden attack, you will discover which foes back down to your aggression and which play back. If the opponents who show resistance have position on you, you'll have to tighten up a bit. Beyond that, and this is really what the LAG strategy is all about, you start setting up your opponents to make the big mistake of overplaying a marginal hand in a big pot. By putting your foes back on their heels, by routinely putting them to tough decisions, you create for them the opportunity to make a wrong decision when it counts. At that point, of course, you'll need to have the goods, but you will, for it's this large pot you've been setting yourself up to win since you sat down.

Say, for instance, that you're constantly jousting with player *weakerthan*, who has revealed himself to be the sort to play aggressively postflop only when he hits top pair or better. You, meanwhile, are in there raising with everything from K9 offsuit to little pairs, and then continuation betting—and winning pots—postflop. Every now and then, though, when you continuation bet, *weakerthan* comes over the top. He's not doing this so frequently that you put him on rampant bluffs; rather, your reads tell you that he has the goods. Now comes the hand you've been looking for during this time: 6♥6♠ for you, A♣K♣ for him. The flop comes AT6 rainbow. You make your standard CB. Ah-ha! He springs his trap with TPTK!

And loses all his chips to your set.

Folks, this is what shorthanded NLHE is all about—diligent watching and careful planning in search of a big payoff. And it's why the LAG approach is so much more successful than its tighter counterpart is in shorthanded play. It gives your foes so many more chances to make big mistakes.

When a Fullhanded Game Goes Short

Let's look now at shorthanded games that have evolved from fullhanded games. This is often the case in b&m games (as opposed to online games that start short and stay short), so be sure to have a good catalog of realworld tells on the players you face. In fullhanded games that are becoming short-handed, a playing dynamic has already been established among all the players at the table, but that dynamic isn't necessarily relevant to the changing circumstance, since its patterns and strategies are based on fullhanded play. Many fullhanded players will have their battle plans in place but may not be prepared to change those plans in light of falling numbers. Therefore, the key to handling the game when it becomes shorthanded is to see which changes, if any, your opponents make. Are they raising more preflop? Are they calling more? Have they lowered their requirements for continuing with the hand past the flop? Do they, in short, know how to change to an appropriate shorthanded style?

In a game composed of fullhanded grinders, most will probably not make the proper adjustments to shorthanded play. You, on the other hand, are ideally situated to make a key, big adjustment from TAG to LAG. In the fullhanded game, with its premium on hitting hands, you probably have been playing fairly snug poker. Now that the game is short, you can radically change gears and start to take control of the table. This change will be most effective against players who don't know how to adjust to the shorthanded dynamic. Not everyone falls into this category, of course, so be on the lookout for other knowledgeable players making the same adjustment. Frankly, though, quite a few fullhanded players are lost at sea in a shorthanded game. In fact, the profit you can make from the rare times that your fullhanded games go short is reason enough to become a shorthanded specialist.

In general, you should try to seize control using the LAG strategy just discussed. Make sure to show most of your preflop aggression in hands where you'll have position for the duration. Do all your promiscuous preflop raising from the cutoff and button. If you raise from early position or the blinds, make sure you are doing so with premium hands. Remember:

bad cards + bad position = bad news

A fullhanded game that's trending toward shorthanded play is a choice morsel for the shorthanded specialist. You should do everything in your power to nurture and preserve the situation, and get the most out of it before the game breaks or fills back up. Especially in the real world, it may take some encouraging to keep other players engaged in shorthanded play. Here's where you really want to turn up the volume on your friendly, playful image. Try to come across as an action junkie who just wants to keep the game going.[2] Then try to disguise your increased aggressiveness, especially in position, by claiming that you're not playing fast, just running hot. While we're not huge fans of showing cards, this is one time when you might want to flip over a powerhouse or two if everyone folds to your preflop aggression. You're trying to milk the situation without killing the cow, and it's a delicate dance. Remember, most of your foes (again, this is in a realworld game) came to the cardroom with the intention of playing fullhanded poker. They know that the fullhanded game will be there. It's what they expect, and it's what they're comfortable with. A shorthanded game puts them outside their comfort zone. That's exactly where you want them: uncomfortable, but not so uncomfortable that they bail.

A good tack to take with this particular clueless parade is to trade small pots for big ones. The uninitiated, for example, won't know to attack your blind from position, which means that you'll see your share of flops in unraised pots. If you miss those flops, don't bother attacking the pot, even though you probably could. Be content to check the hand down, or check and fold, giving your foes the sense that they're winning their fair share. But when the situation is reversed, when they're in

---

2. "I'll play three-handed," JV proclaims in such situations. "I'll play heads-up. I'll play with myself if I have to." This gets some strange looks, but usually meets the goal of keeping things light.

the blind and you're in position, go ahead and raise to build a pot worth winning. Remembering the two-thirds rule (two thirds of the time a hand won't connect with the flop), you can go ahead and attack these larger pots with a certain amount of impunity, especially after you've passed this proposition back and forth a few times and gotten your foes well dialed in.

In a sense, it's completely unfair to your fullhanded foes in shorthanded games because they don't get to control the big pots, only the small ones. Let's say you're in the big blind in a game with $2 and $5 blinds. If someone calls from 'round back and the small blind folds, there's $12 (less rake) in the pot for the taking. Let 'em take it! When it's your button, you can go ahead and raise, either winning the pot outright or getting a loose call from a blind, creating a pot somewhere in the $30 range (depending on the size of your preflop raise and on who calls). Take that pot away on the flop and you're netting real profit, yet seeming to share the wealth. In the immortal words of Steely Dan:

> *Throw back the little ones*
> *And pan-fry the big ones*
> *Use tact, poise, and reason*
> *And gently squeeze them*

Thus do you yield the smaller pots but win the larger ones, all the while keeping the "fun" spirit of the game alive.

The Hand Distribution Model

Readers of Tony's *Killer Poker by the Numbers* will recall the hand distribution model (HDM) as an analytic way to read your opponents. As shorthanded NLHE is a game of deciphering betting patterns, putting your opponents on hands, and predicting their actions accordingly, a brief review of HDM is in order.[3]

Consider the hand outlined in table 2.1 (pp. 46–47).

We are faced with a $150 call on the turn for a $402 pot, and we will now use our data mining skills, in concert with the HDM, to try to put the worthy Player 5 (P5) on a range of hands. This is a more complex approach than just doing a rough calculation of the pot odds and diving in or diving out accordingly. By that strategy, we would first count the pot and see that there's $422 in it, but since we only have $150 left, we can only win $402. Next, we'd count our outs and arrive at 15, assuming our ace is good. So we are about 2:1 hitting our hand, and the pot is offering more than $2:$1, so we have to call, right? Wrong? Uhm—who knows? We're making an awful lot of on-the-fly calculations and some untested assumptions (is our ace *really* good?). The HDM method requires more work but yields more thoughtful and thorough results. As such, it brings the Killer Poker player to a certain crossroads: will you do the work to take your game to a higher level, or will you be content with gross approximations, rough guesses, and untested assumptions? Before you answer, we suggest that you really work through the HDM information presented in this section, and then decide for yourself if it's worth it. Know two things: First, this stuff gets easier—much easier—the more you do it, so you can consider you first attempts to be "sweat equity" that will pay you dividends downstream. Second, while the math can be cranially draining, it definitely engages your poker mind in the play of the game, and we don't know anyone who thinks that an engaged poker mind is a bad thing.

Okay, we start by presuming that you've been paying close

---

3. JV notes that this discussion barely scratches the surface of the HDM tool, and, at the risk of shilling for his partner's work, really recommends that the reader check out KPBTN. "It's a eye-opener, you betcha."

attention to the foes at your table, so you know from your observations of P5 that his preflop raise indicates a hand likely falling within the following distribution: [AA,88]||[AK,AT]|| [KQ,KJ]||[QJ].[4] Here we come to another crossroads, for if you haven't been paying close attention, then his hand distribution could be anything from pocket aces to "go fish," and we really can't help you at all. Note also that we speak of a "likely" distribution because no distribution that you ever assign to an opponent will be exact. A big part of understanding this process is being comfortable with a certain amount of uncertainty. The only times you can be certain about a read are when your opponents exhibit obvious physical tells or when they bet in an extremely predictable fashion given their prior betting patterns. (Or when they show their cards.) (Or when you're psychic.) In general, as the hand progresses, you'll add and subtract hands from your opponents' distributions to have the most accurate pictures of them possible.

So what information can we use to narrow our foe's hand distribution here? With your overcard, nut-flush draw, and gutshot straight draw, you bet into your opponent on the flop, and your opponent raised you. You have already observed that after raising preflop, he's been prone to making continuation bets when checked to on the flop; however, he usually folds when bet into. The times he's raised a bet on the flop he's either had at least top pair with a pretty good kicker or has been semi-bluffing with a big draw.

Knowing these things about your opponent, you start your analysis by thinking of the possible draws he could have. You have A♣T♣, so he can't have the nut-flush draw (you have it— don't neglect the information from your hole cards when de-

---

4. JV again: if this method of expressing hand distribution seems foreign to you, recognize that, for example, [AA,88] represents every pair from aces through eights, and that [AK,AT] represents the hands AK, AQ, AJ, and AT. I didn't get it at first, either, but trust me, it comes quickly.

Table 2.1: Sample Situation for an EV Calculation with Incomplete Information

Game: $200NL Hold'em
Structure: Small Blind: $2 Big Blind: $5
Comments: Home game with no rake. Action only recorded until P(layer)5's bet on the turn. What's your EV for the $150 call (you are P4)

	1(SB) XX	2(BB) XX	3 XX	*4* A♠T♣	5(B) XX
STACKS	$250	$150	$425	$270	$290
PREFLOP	b$2	b$5	>$5	$5	$20
	-	-	-	$20<	
STACKS				$250	$270
FLOP Q♣J♣2♥				>$40	$100
				$100<	
STACKS				$150	$170
TURN 4♠				>$0	$170
STACKS					
RIVER					
HOLE					

Comments: See text for analysis.

Legend: SB = Small Blind; BB = Big Blind; B = Button; X = Unknown Hole Card; b = Blind or Straddle; > = Beginning of Betting Round Action; < = End of Betting Round Action; - = Fold; d = Action in the Dark; c = Call; r = Raise; E = Exposed Card; M = Main Pot; S = Side Pot; AI = All-In; R = Rake

ducing your opponents' possible hole cards). Likewise, he can't have an outside straight draw with a draw to a king-high flush since he would need K♣T♣ for that, and you hold the T♣. Some players would semi-bluff here with K♣Tx, given

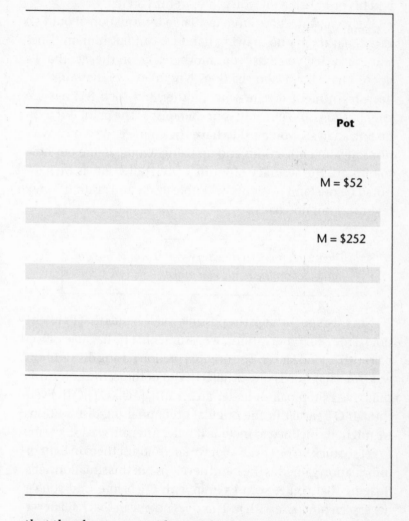

	Pot
	M = $52
	M = $252

that they have an outside straight draw with the king of clubs. In fact, some would semi-bluff here with any K-T, but from your observations of P5, you don't believe that he has offsuit K-T, for a hand that weak isn't consistent with his preflop and postflop raises. The only drawing hand you could be up against here is, therefore, K♣9♣, but given P5's preflop raise and his prior behavior, you can't put him on it.

We've now deduced from available information about P5's game that there's no drawing hand we can put him on. Does this mean that you'd bet your mother's life on the fact that P5 doesn't have a draw on the flop? Not unless you harbor some deep resentment toward your mother, but such feelings are your business and possibly your therapist's. The point is that to do any analysis, you need to have the courage of your convictions. If your convictions end up being wrong, figure out how to improve the accuracy of future convictions. But as we have noted before (and no doubt will note again and again till they take away our notepads):

> There's no point in making reads if you're not going to act on the reads you make.

Next, let's go through the possible made hands that P5 might hold. From our observations, we assume that he has at least top pair with a good kicker. The original preflop raising distribution was [AA,88]|||[AK,AT]|||[KQ,KJ]|||[QJ]. Out of these, the hole cards that give P5 top pair or better are [AA,JJ]|||[AQ,KQ]|||[QJ]. Even though QT wasn't in the original preflop raising distribution, we might be inclined to include it here. After all, we don't want to get so stuck on our reads that we fail to adjust them in light of information gained as the hand develops.[5] In this situation, let's imagine that you've seen P5 limp with QT before, and you've never seen him raise with it. This does not mean that he'll never raise with QT, but it's a reasonable assumption. The other hand

---

5.   There are two common errors made by players when they put their opponents on hands. First, they avoid putting opponents on better hands

not in the original preflop raising distribution that has you beaten at this point is 22. It seems very unlikely that P5 raised preflop with 22 because it's so far from his preflop raising distribution, so we can discount the possibility that P5 has a set of deuces.

Hey, check it out! We've narrowed P5's distribution all the way down to just seven hands: [AA,JJ]|||[AQ,KQ]|||[QJ].

The next step is figuring out the probability of winning against each of good ol' P5's possible holdings. Table 2.2 (p. 50) gives these probabilities, along with the number of possible combinations that exist for each of P5's possible holdings.

With the information in table 2.2, we can now do the EV calculation, the last step in our intensive shorthanded data mining exercise. Recall that winning the pot has a payout of +$402 and that losing the pot has a payout of -$150. Assuming that your $150 call is in the pot, you have potential payouts of +$552 for a win and $0 for a loss and your EV is the following:

AA   KK(with K♣)   KK(no K♣)   QQ   JJ

$$\left(\tfrac{3}{45}\right)\left(\tfrac{12}{44}\right)(\$552)+\left(\tfrac{3}{45}\right)\left(\tfrac{13}{44}\right)(\$552)+\left(\tfrac{3}{45}\right)\left(\tfrac{13}{44}\right)(\$552)+\left(\tfrac{3}{45}\right)\left(\tfrac{10}{44}\right)(\$552)+\left(\tfrac{3}{45}\right)\left(\tfrac{10}{44}\right)(\$552)+$$

$$\left(\tfrac{9}{45}\right)\left(\tfrac{12}{44}\right)(\$552)+\left(\tfrac{3}{45}\right)\left(\tfrac{14}{44}\right)(\$552)+\left(\tfrac{9}{45}\right)\left(\tfrac{14}{44}\right)(\$552)+\left(\tfrac{9}{45}\right)\left(\tfrac{12}{44}\right)(\$552)\approx\$155.56$$

AQ   KQ(with K♣)   KQ(no K♣)   QJ

---

because they've prematurely fallen in love with their own premium hole cards (e.g., they have A-A and do not flinch when the board is highly coordinated to high straights and flushes, or they recklessly bull ahead with their K-K against four opponents when an ace flops). Second, players unreasonably put their opponents on hands that beat them because they are playing scared. The key to being good at reading players is to be guided by your observations, not by emotions, hopes, or fears. Assign your distributions first, and then figure out how your hand compares.

TABLE 2.2: Number of Combinations for Each of P5's Possible Holdings and the Corresponding Values of P(Win)

HAND	COMBINATIONS	P(WIN)
AA	3	$\frac{12}{44}$
KK (with ♣)	3	$\frac{13}{44}$
KK (no ♣)	3	$\frac{13}{44}$
QQ	3	$\frac{10}{44}$
JJ	3	$\frac{10}{44}$
AQ	9	$\frac{12}{44}$
KQ (with K♣)	3	$\frac{14}{44}$
KQ (no K♣)	9	$\frac{14}{44}$
QJ	9	$\frac{12}{44}$

This equation says that given P5 has the defined set of hands, you will get $155.56 on average after investing $150. In other words, your expected profit from this call is $5.56.

Notice that in the equation, each term contains three numbers being multiplied by each other. The first two numbers, when multiplied together, give the probability of each event. For example, in the AA term, the probability that you win against AA is:

$$[P(\text{vs. AA}))(P(\text{win}|\text{vs. AA})] = \left(\tfrac{3}{45}\right)\left(\tfrac{12}{44}\right)^6$$

We see then, that we originally figured out the number of combinations for each of P5's possible holdings to get the

6. The "|" in the expression is read as "given that." Thus, the probability that you win against AA is the probability that you are up against AA times the probability that you win given that you are up against AA. Formally, this concept is known as conditional probability. Even more formally it's known as Sir Conditional Probability, but even for us that's a bit much.

probabilities of being against each one. Some people mistakenly say that since 9 hand categories exist, the chance of being up against each is $\frac{1}{9}$. Those who say this forget there is a total number of hand combinations that they are up against, and the true probability of being against a specific hand is therefore the number of combinations available for the specific hand divided by the total number of combinations. For example, there are more possible AQ combinations than QQ combinations, so it could not possibly be right to weigh them equally.

Well, there you have it: EV of +$5.56. A definite moneymaking call—given everything we think we know about P5 and given our ability to translate that knowledge into meaningful numbers. Is your head starting to sweat? That's quite normal. It's quite normal, in fact, to skim over pages containing calculations like this, like skimming over the names of characters in a Russian novel. So don't worry if you found that you "lost the plot" somewhere in through there. But do invest some energy in mastering the math, and maybe go back and read this section again. As we said, it gets easier with time and practice, and given that the shorthanded setting requires you to do more than play hit-to-win poker, this process, although exhausting, will be well worth it.

HDM Plus: Putting Players on Actions

When people talk about reading players, they typically refer to the type of analysis done in the previous section, where reading players is synonymous with figuring out what they have. In fullhanded poker, figuring out what they have, and comparing it to your own holding, is often enough. If you have your opponent beaten, you try to extract as much money as possible. If your opponent has you beaten, you see if you have odds to call, and if you don't, you typically fold. You *could* try to bluff, but in a fullhanded game where you generally have the luxury of patience, there's not a lot of motivation for tricky play when straightforward play will do.

But in shorthanded play, we need to take our ability to read players to the next level. We need to know not only what our foes have but also what they will *do* with what they have. And even with straightforward, nontricky players, there's not always a close correlation between what they have and what they'll do. We have two specific situations in mind: the first being when you put a player on a better hand but have a line of play that will make him fold, and the second when you put a player on a worse hand but his line of play will shut you out of the hand. Let's look at each in turn.

Consider the hand outlined in table 2.3 (pp. 54–55)

Originally, you called the reraise preflop with the intention of trying to flop a set. You didn't flop a set; however, the ace on the flop presents an intriguing line of play for the bold and opportunistic shorthanded specialist. With the ace on the flop, P6's hand distribution gives him 27 combinations of cards that equal at least a pair of aces and 24 card combinations that don't. Your $8 bet on the flop is the key to your play of this hand. Since P6's hand distribution precludes his being on a draw, you don't need to defend against that by betting a prohibitively large fraction of the pot. Your small bet here represents either weakness or a trap. P6 decides to put you to the test by raising you in position. A stop-and-go bluff from someone in your position isn't an uncommon play, so P6 is probing to see whether you're merely representing [AK,AJ]||[88]||[66] or whether you really have a hand. You call his raise and then bet $25 of your last $45 on the turn, again representing willingness to bet your bottom dollar. You know from data mining that P6 will fold unless he has AA or AK, and that's only 15 of the 51 combinations in his hand distribution. You win $42.50 with a probability of $\frac{36}{51}$, and loss $45 with a probability of $\frac{15}{51}$. This line of play has an EV of +$16.76 and shows that by putting your foe on a range of hands and by making keen note of his past actions, you can win a pot even when *every single hand* in your opponent's distribution has you beaten.

Now, consider the hand outlined in table 2.4 (pp. 56–57).

On the flop, P2 and P5 check to you, P6, and you make a standard semi-bluff on the button with a flush draw, acting on the assumption that you'll either take the pot or get a caller who'll check to you on the turn, therefore giving you a free card. P2 folds, but P5 puts in a large check-raise. P5 didn't raise preflop, so you're fairly certain that he doesn't have an ace. P5 has either a pair of kings or a pair of sixes, hands that don't necessarily warrant such a large check-raise. However, P5 may have changed things up by not raising preflop with a hand that he would've normally raised with preflop. Since you also didn't raise preflop, P5 might not put you on an ace or a king. P5 may assume (correctly) that you're semi-bluffing with a flush draw, and he has decided to shut you out on a pure bluff. His play works because you have, well, nothing and also, he has too short a stack to make bluffing him back a viable option. Thus, you have to fold. While there's nothing wrong with your calling in position preflop or taking a stab at the pot on the flop, P5 is able to take the pot because you didn't anticipate what action P5 would take. According to his hand distribution, P5 is a prohibitive favorite to miss the flop and should have folded. In this instance, putting your opponent on a worse hand—and even being right—isn't necessarily enough to win you the pot.

Table 2.3: Hand Illustrating a Situation Where You Put a Player on a Better Hand Distribution but Make Him Fold

Game: $100NL Hold'em

Structure: Small Blind: $0.50 Big Blind: $1

Comments: Online 6-max game. You are P4. P6's reraise preflop means [AA,TT]||[AK,AQ]. P6 is very aggressive on the flop, but he folds to most bets on the turn and the river unless he has top pair, good kicker, or better.

	1(SB) XX	2(BB) XX	3 XX	*4* 9♣9♠	5 XX
STACKS	$80	$160	$120	$75	$50
PREFLOP	b$0.50	b$1	>$1	$4	-
	-	-	-	$10<	
STACKS				$65	
FLOP A♣8♠6♥				>$8 $20<	
STACKS				$45	
TURN 4♠				>$25	
STACKS					
RIVER					
HOLE					

Comments: See text for analysis.

Legend: SB = Small Blind; BB = Big Blind; B = Button; X = Unknown Hole Card; b = Blind or Straddle; > = Beginning of Betting Round Action; < = End of Betting Round Action; - = Fold; d = Action in the Dark; c = Call; r = Raise; E = Exposed Card; M = Main Pot; S = Side Pot; AI = All-In; R = Rake

Misinterpreting opponents' actions when you put them on worse hand distributions, though, doesn't happen as often as misreading opponents' actions when you put

6(B) Q♥Q♦	Pot
$220	
$10	M = $22.50
$210	
$20	M = $62.50
$190	
-<	

them on better hands. Either way, reading opponents' actions is crucial to your success in shorthanded NLHE, where you and your opponents may be acting on the flop,

Table 2.4: Hand Illustrating a Situation Where You Put a Player on a Bad Hand Distribution, but He Makes You Fold

Game: $100NL Hold'em
Structure: Small Blind: $0.50 Big Blind: $1
Comments: Online 6-max game. You are P6. P5's typical raising
  distribution for opening in the CO is [AA,22]||[AK,A2]||[KQ,K8]|
  |[QJ,Q8]||[JT,J8]||[T9,T7].

	1(SB) XX	2(BB) XX	3 XX	4 xx	5 XX
STACKS	$80	$160	$60	$75	$50
PREFLOP	b$0.50 -	b$1 $1<	>-	-	$1
STACKS		$159			$49
FLOP A♥K♥6♠		>$0 -			$0 $15
STACKS					
TURN					
STACKS					
RIVER					
HOLE					

Comments: See text for analysis

Legend: SB = Small Blind; BB = Big Blind; B = Button; X = Unknown
  Hole Card; b = Blind or Straddle; > = Beginning of Betting Round
  Action; < = End of Betting Round Action; - = Fold; d = Action in the
  Dark; c = Call; r = Raise; E = Exposed Card; M = Main Pot; S = Side
  Pot; AI = All-In; R = Rake

the turn, and the river using sophisticated bluffs. If you know your opponent has QQ, the board is AK8, and you're representing that you have an ace or a king even though

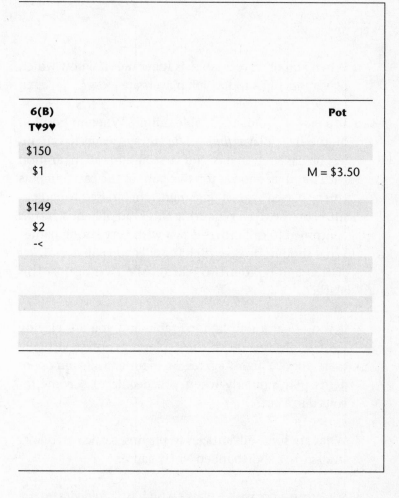

6(B)	Pot
T♥9♥	
$150	
$1	M = $3.50
$149	
$2	
-<	

you actually hold 56, it doesn't mean a damn thing if your opponent will still call you on the flop, the turn, and the river with QQ. Knowing how your opponents will respond to your bluffs is a vital part of playing winning shorthanded NLHE.

Exercises

1. When you observe a table, is it enough to know which players are tight and which players are loose?

2. You're at a five-handed table online. When in position on the river, player *fluffernutter* always seems to call unless he has a set; that is, you've seen him call in position with hands as good as top two pair. In the past four pots you've played against *fluffernutter*, he's raised you in position on the river, yet during this span of hands, he has continued to call others down with very strong hands. What should you do with hands like top pair, top kicker (TPTK) and bottom two pair on the river against this player?

3. If you are at a four-handed table and you are playing tight while the other three players contest virtually every pot in a highly aggressive manner, will your opponents play similarly when you decide to become involved in a pot?

4. What are some advantages to playing a calculated LAG strategy in a shorthanded NLHE game?

5. You are in a pot with a player who hasn't folded to many river bets even though top pair is the worst hand you've seen him show down. In this hand, you put him on top pair, but there's a diamond draw out. You've just identified an interesting opportunity to represent that you're

on the flush draw. If another diamond falls, you're going to bet or raise on the river to get your opponent to fold top pair. Is this a good plan?

Answers

1. No! No! No! Saying that players are tight and loose means nothing. Are you saying that they don't enter a lot of hands preflop? If that's the case, do they play differently postflop? What does a stop-and-go mean? What about a check-raise? Do they call a lot but rarely bet or raise? Using the terms tight and loose without doing some serious thinking beyond those labels will lead to careless—and ultimately bad—decisions in the game.

2. This is a tricky situation. From all the pots you've observed *fluffernutter* play against the other players at the table, it seems that TPTK and bottom two pair are no good. However, from his recent string of river raises against you, he seems to be playing differently against you. If he raises you in position on the river the next time you lead out, then you should reduce your calling distribution to include bottom two pair, and perhaps TPTK. You may also consider playing the river by check-calling out of position with a large range of hands (TPTK to middle two pair). You really need to figure out what his raising and betting requirements are against you specifically so that you can adjust accordingly.

3. Your seemingly loose opponents will probably tighten up against you. Games like this can be deceiving. You

sit and watch your aggressive opponents get tons of chips in with middle pair, and you think to yourself, "I just need to catch a hand." Sometimes, your loose opponents aren't thinking hard about their play. Other times, especially in shorthanded NLHE, your loose opponents are actually engaging in tactically sound aggressive play. You need to know the difference. It's tempting to get all your chips in with TPTK against seemingly reckless opponents, but against tactically sound aggressive opponents, your TPTK will be crushed in large pots if you've been observed playing tightly. You haven't shown yourself to be a guest at this party. Your foes will probably be more circumspect— and have better hands—when you finally do invite yourself in.

4. If you're LAG, you'll take down many pots uncontested simply because flops don't help players most of the time. Besides taking down a large quantity of small pots, your play will also force your opponents to play back at you more often, meaning that you'll be able to get more value from your made hands. If your opponents are tricky, then being too LAG will lead you to bleeding off a lot of chips, so you might need to back down at some tables. However, employing a LAG strategy, especially one where you take advantage when you have position, will generally take home the money in most shorthanded NLHE games you play.

5. It's good to recognize such bluffing opportunities; however, against the opponent described, this bluff is a horrible idea. As much as you'd like to move him off his top pair, evidence indicates that you can't. Scare-card bluffs like this should be in your arsenal, but use them judi-

ciously and only against foes who are capable of yielding to them. The bottom line is that there's no point in trying to run a bluff against this opponent on this hand. No matter how cleverly conceived it may be, all your diligent data mining indicates that it just won't work.

3

♣♠♦♥

DECEPTION TRENDS

♧♤♢♡

Weaving Tangled Webs

Assume that your opponents play systematically and you know exactly what their systems are. Unless your opponents have stumbled on an unbeatable Nash Equilibrium[1] strategy for deep-stacked cash game NLHE, there exist counterstrategies that will beat them. Everything we've talked about so far, from hacking and data mining to the HDM, has been aimed at the vital task of detecting and deducing your foes' systems and strategies. Other factors aid this task. Physical tells in b&m play, for instance, will give you reads on your opponents' hands and actions so that even when they're trying to play trickily, if their tricky play is betrayed by physical tells, you'll have them dialed in. In fullhanded play, this isn't necessarily enough.

---

1. The Nash Equilibrium was postulated by, and therefore named after, mathematician John Forbes Nash, who found such equilibriums in multiplayer games in which no player has anything to gain by unilaterally changing his strategy. So far as we know, it has nothing to do with Nash Bridges, Pluto Nash, or Canadian musical legend Nash the Slash.

Information on one player, even an airtight tell, is negated by masses of traffic yet to act. To take an extreme example, let's say that Gramps to your right is actually flashing you his cards so that you can see he's raising with pocket fives. You have two random cards and would happily go to war against Gramps, knowing that any high flop will give you license to steal. But Gramps is UTG, you're in early position, and the teeming multitudes wait behind so that your random hand has to compete successfully not just against the known hand but against all those unknown hands as well. That's why, sad to say, thoroughly hacking the betting pattern of just one player doesn't do you that much good in a fullhanded game. The edge you enjoy in shorthanded play is thus twofold: fewer foes to solve and fewer foes to screw up the individual solves you get.

But as we already know, you're not the only one trying to run a hack attack. Your foes, at least the keen ones, are hacking you, and if you play too systematically, your game will become an open book. Again, this is much less a detriment in fullhanded play, where patience and hand values reign supreme and where consistent lines of play may never even be discovered, thanks to the infrequency with which situations recur. Shorthanded, situations recur all the time. The game's high context density yields huge amounts of information about your play—information that, if you're not careful, will be highly vulnerable to hack and highly detrimental to your stack. You have to stay ahead of the curve! In this chapter we're going to talk about strategies for doing so—strategies, as it were, for weaving reliable tangled webs of deceit so that if your foes think they have you figured out they're wrong, and they can be majorly wrong in big pots, when the errors they make—errors you induce!—will manage to hurt them the most.

The first question you need to ask yourself is whether deception is necessary. Most of the time it will be, for there will be at least one or two opponents who are savvy enough to exploit undisguised consistency. It will happen from time to time, though, especially at lower limits, that you can play predictably and elicit predictably -EV responses from your foes. If you find yourself in such a situation, recall the words mentioned earlier:

> *If it ain't broke, don't break it.*

Some players have trouble with this. They get bored grinding out an easy win against unsophisticated foes who surrender their money without much of a fight. As such, these players run the risk of falling prey to what Mike Caro calls Fancy Play Syndrome or FPS. Remember, if deception isn't necessary, don't deceive. To do so is pure self-indulgence.

Most of the time, though, you'll have to build deception trends to use against your foes. And here we get into a certain stimulus-response situation, for as you introduce unpredictability into your own play, you inadvertently introduce it into your foes' play as well. This means that you not only have to keep your opponents guessing, but you have to keep guessing about *how* they're guessing. Are they making the adjustments you expect them to make, or are they outthinking you (or underthinking you) in ways you don't anticipate?

For example, suppose you've established that a check-raise from you means you have two pair or better. After establishing that betting pattern, you change things up and start tossing in some check-raise bluffs and some check-raises with marginal hands. You may be doing this simply to pick up more pots, or you may be doing it with the intention of later switching gears back to a check-raise with two pair or better. Regardless of your intentions, your increased frequency of check-raises may prompt an opponent to make an adjustment. If your foe starts calling your check-raises on the flop and your bets on the turn with a higher frequency, you can easily lose track of whether he's playing loose or playing to trap. If your check-raises are creating large pots and then if your opponent is bluffing you off those pots, you've got the deception trend running in exactly the wrong direction. In short, you want to baffle your opponents, but not so sufficiently that they start baffling you in return.

Actions and Situations, Situations and Actions

There are two convenient ways to think about deception trends: associating *actions with situations* and associating *situations with actions*. As an example of associating an action with a situation, suppose you bet $\frac{1}{2}$ pot in position with a flush draw. This knowledge prompts your foe to think that future $\frac{1}{2}$ pot bets in position also represent flush draws. You have built, in his mind, an association between an action and a situation. Later, when you bet $\frac{1}{2}$ pot in position with a set, your foe who associates that action with a drawing situation will ship you a lot of chips when he makes a large bet on the turn trying to shut out a suspected flush draw. This is why you have to monitor your foe's state of mind closely; you want to be sure that when he makes that big shut-out bet, it's for the reason you induced, not for some other reason—like having a better hand!

Now here's an example of associating a situation with an action. Suppose you later bet $\frac{2}{3}$ pot in position. Because your foe associates flush draws with $\frac{1}{2}$ pot bets, he won't put you on a flush draw here. When the flush card hits, it won't scare your foe because he "knows" that your $\frac{2}{3}$ pot bet is not associated with this situation. He'll feel certain in the knowledge that he has you solved—and will proceed to pay you off. You, of course, must be careful not to step into the same trap. Recognizing that savvy foes will mix up their play and that unsophisticated ones will simply act inconsistently, you need to weight all possible hands in your opponents' distributions carefully. Thus, if you see a $\frac{1}{2}$ pot bet used as a semi-bluff, you'll want to make an appropriate action-situation link, without completely discounting the possibility of the bet meaning something else at other times.

But it is a happy fact that most of our foes will not be aware of this distinction. Even at this late date, when gobs of good information about poker is available to even a casual student of the game, most will still not make the effort to get it and digest it. Most continue to play some variation of "when you get the goods, bet the goods" poker—a passive yet passable strategy in a fullhanded game, but death in a shorthanded joust.

Given that our unsuspecting foes will make lockstep associations of situations with actions and actions with situations, we must give some thought to how, specifically, to organize our deception trends. There are two broad options at our disposal: playing the same situation different ways and playing different situations the same way. Let's examine them in turn.

Play the Same Situation Different Ways

When opponents see you play a situation a certain way, many assume that you will always play the same situation that way. You can lead these foes into making mistakes by mixing up how you play these situations when they recur. Suppose, for example, that you flop bottom set against two opponents and you're first to act. You check-call the flop, check-raise the turn, and bet out on the river. You're called, meaning that your opponents get to see what hand you have. Provided they're paying attention, your foes will now associate that betting pattern with really solid hands. When they see you check-call and then check-raise, they'll put you on two pair or better, and think, "Oh, no you don't, you're not going to burn me with *that* trick again." Moreover, having seen you *drag* (slowplay) this hand, they may conclude that the slowplay is a staple of your game. Some may be acute in their analysis and conclude that you like to drag from early position, while others will tab you as "tricky" and assign that general value to all your play. This is an error, of course, on the order of labeling players as tight or loose and going no further than that. As such, it reminds us that there are all sorts of errors. There are errors of action but also errors of analysis. The whole point of generating deception trends is to exploit your foes' errors in analysis. You will find, in fact, that it's easier to exploit errors of this class because while poker players learn not to make action errors (e.g., don't make a bet on the river when the only hand that can call you can beat you), those errors of analysis are subtler and more difficult both to spot and to stop.

Once you know that your foes see you as a slowplaying mofo, it's time to make an adjustment, to play the same situation a different way. Next time you have a monster, go ahead and initiate aggression, especially in a situation where it looks like you're trying to steal. Since your opponents "know" that you slowplay, they won't read you for real strength. Note also that your check-call, check-raise pattern now becomes a useful platform for bluffing and—ah, but that's a case of playing different situations the same way. We're getting ahead of ourselves.

You pick up a flush draw on the button. Action is checked to you, giving you two options: check or semi-bluff. In this instance, you check and end up hitting a flush that you show down. Now your foes know you're a fan of the free card. Next time you pick up the flush draw, you can go ahead and semi-bluff, either winning the pot right there (because you're a fan of the free card with draws and therefore must have a real hand here) or giving yourself good implied odds for when you hit your flush (since you don't semi-bluff your flush draws and thus haven't hit it!). Can you think of other situations where you have two different but correct lines of play through a hand? Can you imagine what's going on inside your foes' minds when they see you use one approach and then default back to the other?

Most poker players think hand to hand. You, surfing your deception trends, are thinking many hands into the future. You're thinking beyond the battle, as it were, and into the war. Shorthanded play, especially shorthanded play online, brings these recurring situations around so quickly and so frequently that it's easy to gauge your opponents' thinking about your thinking. Once you've firmly established your line of play, you're ready to reverse it and confound your foes once again. And while this sort of "I know that *he* knows that *I* know" thinking is not always very sophisticated, it *is* very effective—especially against unsophisticated enemies. By playing the same situation different ways, you keep your foes in doubt.

Play Different Situations the Same Way

Playing the same situation different ways is important, but playing different situations identically will likely be your primary mode of deception in shorthanded NLHE. To do otherwise can, in certain circumstances, spell doom. Consider this: Since you'll be playing most flops heads-up or three-handed, against most opponents, you'll be bluffing a lot on the flop. You'll be raising preflop and continuation betting on the flop. *And you'll be doing this whether you have a hand or not.*

By using this same betting pattern regardless of your holding, you'll get your foes to fold sometimes when they should play back at you or to play back at you when they should fold. This one opaque pattern—playing a large range of hands identically—makes you very difficult to read, or to put on a hand. If you raise and continuation bet with AA and 7♣8♣ alike or push your TPTK and straight draws identically, how confidently can your opponents fight back? Note also that we're not just talking about playing different hands identically but, more to the point, with identical aggression. If you play a large quantity of hands hyperaggressively in a setting where your opponents don't have made hands most of the time, they're going to make mistakes unless they know your precise strategy. Thus we come to this:

> *Play weak hands strong and strong hands strong.*
> *Play all hands strong shorthanded.*

Whether you know it or not, you've probably been using this very form of deception as the rock and foundation of your shorthanded game. As you have already discovered (or will discover if you're yet new to shorthanded), this combination of aggression and opacity creates consistently large pots and profitable stacking opportunities in a shorthanded NLHE game.

A word of caution is in order. Suppose you take this notion of consistent aggression to such an extreme that whenever you're the cutoff or the button, you raise preflop with any two cards and with the intention of betting any flop that's checked to you. Against the clueless parade—foes who don't know shorthanded strategies or don't realize what you're doing—this "all roads lead to raise" deception will be highly effective. However, against players who catch on, you aren't really being deceptive at all. Instead, you're merely giving them a very well defined distribution to play against. Granted, the distribution is very wide ([All]); however, it's still a very well defined distribution.

You may think that a distribution such as [All] is no distribution whatsoever. But remember that the point of assigning hand distributions is to let one weight the probability of an opponent having a certain hand or hands. Thus, if your foe knows that your hand distribution is exactly [All], he can accurately rate your chances of having, say, a hand with a pair or an ace at 20 percent and give you a terrible time with reraises, since he knows that 80 percent of the time, according to your distribution, you're betting with little or nothing at all.

While we here at KPHQ are fans of uncompromising aggression—we know of no more successful approach to shorthanded play—you simply have to fold sometimes. The whole point of using deception is to make your opponents misread the distribution you're on. Therefore, even though playing multiple situations identically is important, it can be counterproductive if you do it in too predictable a fashion.

Phantom Outs

Because shorthanded NLHE is a game of naked bets and naked bluffs, let's take a look at one of our favorite bluffs—the bluff with phantom outs—and put it in the context of deception trends.

To motivate this discussion, consider a situation where you've found your way to the turn with a flush draw. You check in early position, and your solo foe bets $10 into a $30 pot. You are a $37:9 \approx 4.11:1$ underdog to make your flush, and you are getting 4:1 odds to call, so you call $10, assuming you have additional implied odds. For example, let's assume that you've played your hand in such a way that your opponent can confidently put you on a flush draw. Why can he do that? Perhaps you haven't been attentive enough to playing this same situation in different ways so that every time you've called a bet in this situation and then bet out on the turn when the flush card hit, you've been shown to have the flush. Now the flush card comes. You bet. Is he going to call? Of course not! You have no implied odds on the river. In order to make money on your drawing hands, you need to throw in some type of deception.

And not even on this hand.

Instead, you want to set up your extra profit in this hand by playing other hands the same way. Imagine another situation in which you're looking at a suited board on the turn but you happen to have no cards of that suit. No problem. You call on the turn, a move perfectly consistent with your pattern for playing drawing hands. Then when the flush card comes on the river, you go ahead and bet it as if you've made the flush. At this point, one of two things will happen: either your foe will fold, yielding you the pot, or else he'll call, snap off your bluff, and expose you as a big lying liar. Is that a bad thing? Not necessarily, for the next time you actually have the draw, you'll get paid off on both the real odds *and* the implied odds. By using these nonexistent outs—called *phantom outs* because they don't actually help your hand but can be represented as if they did—you net pots you're not entitled to or set up profitable drawing situations downstream or both.

This is yet another example of putting each hand in the context of the contest as a whole. Viewed through this filter, there are no bad outcomes, because no matter what happens on any individual hand, *some* exploitable impression will be created in your foes' minds. In fact, it's often worthwhile taking a tiny stab at a small pot just for the sake of getting caught and putting doubt in your foes' minds. It's okay to swap small -EV now for big +EV later.

Changing Gears

If your primary mode of deception is playing different situations nearly identically, your opponents will eventually catch on. Once they do, they can potentially formulate the correct strategy to counter you. Even if you're playing a highly complicated strategy, once your foes know it, you're done, unless for some bizarre reason your opponents are shrewd enough to puzzle out your complex strategy but yet not shrewd enough to counter it.

Even relatively unsophisticated foes will make adjustments, adjustments they may not be aware of, except on a gut level. If you raise *all* the time, for instance, even the tightest foe will know to loosen up. If you never bet anything but monsters, even the nonrocket scientists in the house will ultimately stop paying you off. Your deception trend, then, always carries your foes' response trends in its wake. To prevent them from gravitating toward proper countermeasures, you need to keep tweaking and modifying the strategy you're using. This can be a daunting matter if you don't know exactly where you're at. Are you supposed to be playing "same-situations-differently" now or "different-situations-same"? In other words, we know we have to change gears, sure, but which gears, when, and how?

Pictures help, so let's look at one now.

Imagine that you can represent the set of all possible strategies on a line, where each point on the line represents a specific strategy, such as *raise with cheese, bet phantom outs, order a pizza*, and so on. Just as you have a line of strategy, your foe has a line of counterstrategy. In a wild flight of imagination, let's call these lines ℓ_1 and ℓ_2, respectively, shown here in figure 3.1.

Your line, good ol' ℓ_1, represents the set of all strategies available to you. Your foe's line, ℓ_2, represents the set of all counterstrategies available to him, winners and losers alike.

Figure 3.1: You and Your Opponent, Represented Artistically as Lines

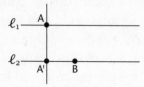

As B gets closer to A', you must shift to a new strategy:

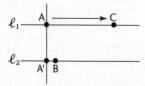

The point *A* represents the strategy you are currently using. The point *A'*, directly under *A*, represents a winning counter-strategy against *A*. As your opponent rides along ℓ_2, he tries out various strategies, eventually discovering and implementing *A'*, the one that works.[2] Now you have to change to a new strategy, C. If you don't, clearly you will lose.

Occasionally, you will encounter opponents who are stuck on a losing strategy and can't, or won't, adjust. If you're +EV against them, with no conceivable way of extracting more +EV from them, then there's no need to change gears. But such situations rarely pertain, and rarely last, for such players quickly find a new equilibrium, the Cash Equilibrium, as in— they haven't any.

Normally what happens is that your opponents will start to

2. If there is, in fact, no strategy B that works, you have stumbled upon the aforementioned Nash Equilibrium; stop reading this book and write your own. Also note that there may be multiple strategies, A', that are winning counters to A.

get a sense of your strategy, look for confirming evidence, and then make a change. This dynamic is described in *Killer Poker No Limit* (page 251) with the phrase, "Third time's the adjustment." That book recommends, and this one reiterates, that you get out ahead of your foe's adjustment, actually anticipating how he'll change gears, and switch strategies to counter his moves before he even makes them. In other words, while he's busy gearing down from B to A', you've already jumped to C, and have him completely turned around.

Gradual Versus Sudden Adjustments

It's said that if you put a frog in a pot of boiling water, it'll jump right out and not be harmed, but if you put it in cold water and gradually turn up the heat, the frog won't notice and will placidly remain where it is until it, you know, croaks. While noting that no frogs were harmed in the writing of this book, we'd like you to keep this story in mind when you contemplate the difference between gradual and sudden strategic shifts.

Let's say that while your preflop raises are appropriately abundant, your preflop reraises are so rare that your foes figure them to mean [AA,QQ] and will only tangle with you postflop (if they call your preflop reraise at all) when they have two pair or better. To maximize this moneymaking opportunity, widen your reraising distribution slowly and slightly so that the increased frequency of your reraises goes largely unnoticed. If you work this trick right, you can now continuation bet the flop after every reraise and steal some extra pots. Your foes don't make a strategic adjustment because they're not even aware that one needs to be made.

Now look at what happens when instead you alter your reraising distribution abruptly and radically. If you're suddenly in there banging away with a lot of preflop reraises, your foes will quickly change their appraisal of your reraising distribution from [AA,QQ] to [AA,TT]||[AK,AJ] or maybe all the way to [WTF?]. This will naturally trigger your opponents to make abrupt, radical, strategic shifts of their own. Some will wilt in the face of your shock and awe campaign, cut back on their preflop raises (for fear of your counterattack), and give you complete control of the game. Others will devalue your reraise and start mixing it up with you with a wider range of hands postflop.

What you risk when you loosen up your opponents' postflop play is the chance to lose big pots when your foes flop monsters. What you gain, though, critically, is that your opponents are now playing your game. When their adjustments are a *response* to your *stimulus* and not plots of their own invention, they may find themselves unprepared to play the game they're now playing. Especially when you loosen up tight (and timid) foes, you move them out of their comfort zone and into unfamiliar territory. At best, from your point of view, they'll end up playing larger pots with lesser hands. In sum:

> *When you change gears gradually, you increase your EV incrementally. When you change gears radically, you destabilize the table.*

Every time you change gears, then, ask yourself not just how you intend to pace the change, but what strategic end you serve. Are you trying to squeeze out some extra stealth profits, or are you waving a red flag in front of a bull? The choice is yours, but it's a choice you should arrive at consciously, with a definite goal in mind.

Deception trends, then, are about more than just staying

inside that enemy fighter pilot's turning circle. They actually shape the fight. When you're using your power of deception not only to cloak your real strength or real intention but also to make your foes make mistakes, either by misreading you or simply by being unable to keep up with you, you're using this power appropriately.

But the fact is that most players don't use deception appropriately. That is, they think they're being tricky and they think they're mixing up their play, but all their devious deviations are really just variations on a theme: the theme of who they really are. In the next chapter we're going to look into this issue in more depth and discuss how to peel back the layers of other players' deception.

Exercises

1. Why is it easier to take advantage of information about individual opponents in a shorthanded game?

2. What are the primary modes of deception available to you?

3. What is one aspect of adding deception to your play that possibly makes your decisions in a hand more difficult?

4. You are pummeling your opponents, but your strategy is very straightforward. You raise preflop if you have the option of being the first player in or if you have a premium hand. You continuation bet whenever you are heads-up and miss the flop, and if you get resistance, you shut down. You only bet the turn if you actually have a hand. Should you change your tactics at some point?

5. What are phantom outs, and in what types of situations are they useful?

6. When should you change gears?

Answers

1. Because of the high context density of shorthanded poker, the information you have is generally more reliable. Also, in shorthanded poker, you don't have to worry about the actions of several players remaining to act behind you. In other words, in shorthanded poker, you have fewer opponents to interfere with the strategies you've formulated for heads-up situations against individual opponents.

2. The primary modes of deception available to you are the following:

   • Play the same situation different ways.

   • Play different situations the same way.

3. Adding deception to your own play implicitly adds unpredictability to your opponents' play. As they become aware of your deception, they start to make adjustments, but you don't necessarily know what those adjustments are. Thus, it's not enough simply to be deceptive. You need to clock your foes' adjustments and nail down how they're responding to your deception.

4. You don't need to change your game until it's clear your opponents are making adjustments that will end up beating you. If your opponents aren't adjusting—even if

they know what you're doing—then there's no need to change gears. The key to changing gears is timing. You don't want to change gears too late, but you don't want to change gears prematurely. Ideally, you want to change gears just as your opponents begin to stumble upon a winning counterstrategy.

5. Phantom outs are cards that, from an opponent's perspective, look as if they've helped your hand. Scary boards, such as those containing flush and high straight draws, are the best candidates for phantom out play. If a scare card falls, you can try to bluff your opponent, representing that the phantom out hit your hand.

6. You should change gears once you think your opponents are making adjustments that will beat your current game plan. You may wish to change gears even before your opponents start changing strategies. However, if you have a winning strategy and your opponents aren't making any adjustments, then changing gears is a bad idea unless you are changing to a strategy that has a higher EV than the one you're presently using.

4

♣♠♦♥

SORTING THE SHORTIES

♧♤♢♡

In General, Don't Generalize

We've already seen how such broad categorizations as tight and loose don't really do a poker player much good, especially in shorthanded play where each of our (good) foes has a fluid, dynamic style of play. In some circles this need to label things is known as the "squished pigeons" paradigm: if you try to put everything into a neat and cozy little pigeonhole, all you end up with is a bunch of squished pigeons.

Still, it's human nature to taxonomize.[1] Especially in these days of information overload, we look to classes, types and kinds, orders, phyla, and kingdoms to help us make sense of the data-dense world around us. Since poker is about data management, why wouldn't we use the same tool, and why wouldn't it be effective? Well, for one thing because most players use it as a blunt instrument. Consider the word *loose*. When you describe a player thus, what does it really tell you

---

1. TG: And it's JV's nature to neologize. The things he calls words—sheesh!

about him? That he plays a lot of hands? That he calls a lot pre-flop but folds a lot postflop? Will he chase to the river? Draw without proper odds? Call river bets with ace high? How, exactly, is this guy loose?

As you can see, without proper qualification, a label like loose is useless.

Worse, it's misleading: In most players' minds, the word "loose" has become synonymous with "bad." We theorize that this is an artifact of the postmodern poker philosophy that preaches TAG poker, as if tight-aggressive were a divinely inspired playing style and everything else was, you know, running with scissors or smoking in bed. Forgetting for the moment that the core idea of any good poker philosophy should be "it depends" and granting, even, that TAG play is generally a winning approach to fullhanded NLHE, where does that leave us shorthanded specialists? If we're loose in a short-handed game, are we bad by definition or merely flexibly responding to circumstances as we find them?

Interestingly, this pejorative use of the word "loose" is a big reason why so many players don't play shorthanded NLHE well or even like to play it at all. In a shorthanded setting, where the traditional reliance on starting hand values no longer serves, these players become self-conscious, afraid to look like bad players in the eyes of their peers. As veteran full-handed players, they have become so used to the comforting ideal of snug play that they've lost the willingness to be adventurous—even when, as in shorthanded poker, adventurousness is not a luxury but a necessity.

If you're making the transition from fullhanded to short-handed play or even just trying to take your game to a higher level according to your own vision, then at some point you'll have to consider what's worse: being caught making a gutsy, but +EV, move that your friends don't understand or getting blinded to oblivion and having your friends sympathize with you about how unlucky you were not to have caught any cards. We know where we stand on this: To play Killer Poker, you can't give a rat's ass about how others judge you. You've got to be ready to make the best possible decisions based on the best available information and your own view of correct play. And if the small minds don't like it, why they can just go smoke in bed.

Disconnecting from Loose/Tight Tags

Such is the nature of subjective reality: You've just started data mining a 6-max NLHE game on pokerbeatsworking.com, and on the first hand you watch, you see player *opheliabeans* call a preflop raise out of position, bet the flop, turn, and river, and lose to late position raiser *MarkTheNarc*'s pocket fives. *Wow*, you think, *that's some stinky bad play*. You don't know who's worse, *opheliabeans* who bet into a preflop raise three times with cheese or *MarkTheNarc* who ignored the warning salvos of three shots across the bow. But you assign them both the tag loose and find yourself just itching to get into the game. You figure they're both a lock to dish you their chips.

Oh yeah?

Before you go blithely attacking these simplistically labeled loose players, pause to consider that each of them may be acting on information *you don't have*. Maybe *MarkTheNarc* knows *opheliabeans* to be an inveterate bluffer, from whom three shots across the bow are not abnormal or to be feared. Perhaps, in turn, *opheliabeans* knows that *MarkTheNarc* is perfectly capable of calling all the way to the river without a pair, and surrendering there. Unfortunately for opheliabeans, this time he had a pair, but that's not the norm, and meanwhile *MarkTheNarc* knows his play to be +EV. Each, then, was playing the hand correctly according to his own understanding.

The only one making a mistake, really, would be someone standing on the sideline making untested assumptions about the "god-awful looseness" of the players in the game.

In a similar vein, consider watching a player who never shows down a hand unless he's a clear winner. Does that mean he's tight? Does that mean he's good? Is he making great reads and staying out of trouble, or is he just yielding too much to the pressure of bluffs and folding like an origami crane? It's one thing to assign a provisional label to a player—for the specific purpose of then refining and expanding your understanding of his play—but it's another thing, a dangerous thing, to go around making snap judgments. These judgments are usually refracted through the certain prism of "Why I can beat this guy." Such thinking is a function of arrogance, and while we acknowledge that arrogance is what confidence wishes it was, blind arrogance isn't thoughtful play. It's just bully behavior, and it leads to careless mistakes born of laziness—death in any poker game, but especially deadly in short-handed games where your opponents should be constantly changing gears and adapting to your play. Not to put too fine a point on it, the good players at your table will pick you apart.

Your Digital Allies

Have we put the fear in you yet? Have we made it clear that shorthanded NLHE requires an intellectual rigor—a commitment to superb play—that must not flag for even a single hand or two? Well, wait, campers, 'cause you ain't seen nothing yet. We're about to delve into the world of sniffers, and if you think it requires effort to play just organic shorthanded poker, wait till you see what these babies take.

Sniffers, by way of reminder, are computer programs that track online poker players' statistics, and associated HUDs that overlay these statistics on your computer when you're playing online. Though sniffers do a great job of collating information, the onus is on you to interpret all this data, and, as with the HDM, it can be a bit of a job. However, as with the HDM, using sniffers will get your head in the game at a much higher level. Not to be too blunt, but if you're playing poker online, the best player you can be is the one who uses sniffers. Obviously if you don't play online, then this section won't apply to you—but read it anyhow for it approaches shorthanded play from the perspective of the game's deeply underlying math, and when you know the math of your opponents' play, much of their strategy is likewise laid bare.

Preflop Sniffer Stats

As we use sniffers to move beyond the gross generalizations of loose and tight, the first important statistic to consider is the percentage of hands that a player Voluntarily Puts money In the Pot (VPIP). This number helps to tell us what mixture of hole cards your foe considers "go" cards.

For example, suppose a player has a VPIP of 25 percent. Since we know off the top of our heads that there are 1,326 possible hole card combinations,[2] we're looking for the 330 or so hole card combinations that comprise roughly 25 percent of 1,326. Presumably, we're looking for the top 330 hands, but the question is, how deep does that list go?

We start by noting that there are 6 combinations for each pocket pair, and 16 combinations for each set of unpaired cards.[3] It's probably a good assumption that our opponent is

---

2. You knew that, right? Yeah, we knew it too. We learned it in sixth grade, right after we learned that the capital of Kiribati is South Tarawa.

3. You knew that, too, right? Us too. The chief export of Kiribati is copra.

playing any pocket pair, so [AA,22] gives us 78 combinations, leaving us with about 252 combinations to find. Next we look for 16 unpaired hands to add to our distribution, since 16 • 16 = 256, and that's roughly the number of additional combinations we need to reach that 25 percent VPIP. Now it's Christmas for our foe as we start awarding him playable hands. We give him [AK,AT] for 4 hands or 64 combinations, and then [KQ,KT] for 3 hands or 48 combinations. We'll add [QJ,QT] into the mix, for 2 more hands, 32 combinations, and [JT] for 1 hand, 16 combinations.

Having endowed him with 10 hands from among the obvious quality hands, we now need 6 more possibilities from the likes of A9, A8, K9, J9, T9, 98, 76, and 65. Coming up with an exact distribution isn't going to be possible, but look what we've accomplished: by using the sniffer's hard data—that 25 percent VPIP—and wedding it to some not-too-taxing thought about what that number represents, we've determined that this player is at least straightforward enough and tight enough (now that that word means something) not to be banging around in pots with the Numpty or up-down hands like K3 or Q5. We know for sure that even in a shorthanded game,[4] when he voluntarily puts his money in the pot, he has at least a fair-to-good hand. That's a useful thing to know, and it's a thing we can know with confidence, since it's backed both by software and logic. Note also that even if you're not using sniffers—in fact, even if you're not playing online—it's worthwhile just to think about what the top 25 percent of hold'em holdings look like. If you're up against a player who seems to be calling *some* but not *too much*, well, we'd argue that those values are woefully imprecise, but at least you can

---

4. Worth noting: Make sure you have your sniffer draw a distinction between your foe's shorthanded and fullhanded play. Otherwise, you'll get numbers that are irrelevant at best and dangerously misleading at worst.

knock pure crud out of his distribution of playable hands pre-flop.

While this look at VPIP gives you a good handle on what your foe considers a playable hand, it only goes partway. It doesn't give you positional information, for example, so you don't know if this particular 25 percenter is someone who's tight up front and loose 'round back or if he's someone who plays uniformly irrespective of position. You also don't know for sure what proportion of those hands were played in ultrashort situations, such as three-handed, where any decent shorthanded specialist is going to be entering puts from the button just on general principle. At full 6-max tables, most players will have a different VPIP for each position, so the opponent just mentioned is probably playing late position hands like all connectors, medium aces, and the odd Q9, but not playing UTG with hands like QT. Sniffers will usually provide position-dependent VPIPs, so if you want that information while you're playing, you can have your sniffer open. Even without that, you can sort of adjust the VPIP for position on the fly. Considering that players will be looser in later position, if a player's VPIP is x, then his VPIP in early position will be $x - y$, and his VPIP in late position will be $x + z$, where y and z are the hands that you, probably, wouldn't play in early position but would play in late position.

The VPIP is a lumped statistic that doesn't separately consider raised pots and unraised ones. This can create a false picture of a player, for you wouldn't want to assume that someone with a 30 percent VPIP plays in 30 percent of unraised pots *and* 30 percent of raised ones. Naturally, players voluntarily put money into fewer raised pots and more unraised ones, and again, this is an instance where you have to wed your intuitive sense to the sniffer's analytical one. Just know that if you have two foes with VPIPs of 60 percent and 10 percent, respectively, the 60 percenter is the one you're gonna have to deal with most. The 10 percenter is only in pots (raised or unraised, ceramic, clay, or copper bottom) with super-premium hands and can be dealt with accordingly.

Okay, with the VPIP stat, we've moved a step up from generic tight and loose tags, but we still don't have much information about the mix of playing strategies our foes employ preflop. Limps, raises, reraises, and cold-calls are all lumped together in VPIP. We therefore need another stat to abet the VPIP. One that'll help is the percentage of times an opponent calls a preflop raise. Especially in a shorthanded setting, where we'll be generating a lot of preflop heat, we'd like to know exactly how much preflop heat an opponent can stand. Unfortunately, most sniffers put this information in terms of *number of raises called per total number of hands* "played". We would prefer to see the fraction expressed as *number of raises called per total number of raises* "faced." But it's not a perfect world, and we don't recall seeing the words "life is fair" printed on the contract.[5] Nevertheless, there is a workaround, and that's to estimate the percentage of raises that your opponent faces preflop. This'll be essentially the total percentage of raises at the table, less the raises originating from the foe in question.

For example, suppose your opponent's VPIP is $\frac{31}{108}$, and the percentage of times he's called a preflop raise is listed as $\frac{5}{108}$ — five hands out of a total 108 seen. If you estimate that players other than your specific opponent in question raise 50 percent of the hands at your table preflop, then the percentage of hands where your opponent has faced a preflop raise is also 50 percent—54 hands. This means that the relevant percentage of hands that he calls a preflop raise with is actually $\frac{5}{54}$. $\frac{5}{54}$ is about .093, meaning that he's calling with about 123 combinations of cards. Skimming the cream from our card distribu-

---

5. Actually, they are there, but down at the bottom it says, "void where prohibited."

tion, as before, we conclude that he'll call raises with hands such as [AA,55]||[AK,AT], a distribution consisting of 124 combinations. Now we not only know *how* tight he is (he'll call about one raise in ten), but we also know, to a fair degree of guesstimation, what hands he holds when he calls. We're starting to get him figured out.

Now let's consider when this guy has himself opened for a raise. The percentage of hands that a player raises is his Preflop Raising Percentage (PFR), and the higher this number is, especially when culled from hundreds of hands, the more generally aggressive you can expect him to be. Now all you have to do is differentiate his "real" (out-of-position) raises from his blind steals. Sniffers aid you in this with a specific stat, [ASB], which tabulates Attempts to Steal Blinds [ASB]—raises in unopened pots from the cutoff seat, the button, or the small blind. Since stealing blinds is so big a part of hand-in-hand-out shorthanded play, it's really useful to know, to a degree of statistical certainty, how well your foes use this tool. To do this, compare a player's ASB to his PFR arising from situations other than potential blind stealing scenarios. If his ASB is much higher than his adjusted PFR then yeah, he likes to steal blinds and knows he must in order to prosper here.

You can see, we're sure, how such information will arm you for battle. If you note an inveterate blind stealer (as revealed by his ASB), you can go ahead and play back at him from the blinds, knowing that he usually won't have much of a hand when he raises in late position.[6] If that same player were to

---

6. How you play back, of course, is another story entirely. Do you reraise him preflop? Do you call him preflop and lead out on the flop no matter what falls (the good old stop-and-go)? Do you call him preflop and look to check-raise bluff a continuation bet on the flop? Most likely, you'll be using a mixture of these and other plays, but it's important to have a well-calculated plan for how you expect to play back instead of just "I'm going to play back at this blind-stealing dillweed."

raise in early position, though, you could judge him to be betting true values. And yes, we know that this all seems fairly intuitive: even unschooled players know to be tighter earlier and looser late. But suppose your sniffer search reveals a foe who's loose early and tight late? Wouldn't you like to invite him to (be) lunch? The point of using sniffers is so that you don't have to assume or guess. Knowing how to use them properly is as vital to your "homework" of shorthanded play as thoroughly scoping out a table before you sit in.

One last preflop stat for your sniffer to consider is the percentage of times your opponent folds to blind steal attempts. If it's a high number, you can attack with a wide range of hands (recognizing, of course, that your foe may eventually adjust). If you see that your foe rarely folds to preflop raises, you'll want to dial back on your own aggression—or, heck, continue it and play the rest of the hand in position against this staunch defender. It would be nice if sniffers sorted this data by the size of a preflop raise so that you could know who will defend against 2.5BB but surrender to 3BB. Alas, the current generation of sniffers can't do that, so just be aware that while sniffers are helpful, they don't give a completely nuanced picture. Nevertheless, the statistics discussed (VPIP, percentage of raises called, PFR, ASB, and folding percentage against steals) provide a pretty good picture of an opponent's preflop tendencies.

Postflop Sniffer Stats

We'll start our discussion of sniffers and postflop play with this key observation:

> *What you really want to know in shorthanded NLHE is how often a foe folds to a bet on the flop.*

Remember that in shorthanded NLHE, you'll usually have at most two opponents postflop, especially if you enter most pots with a preflop raise. Because you have few opponents, the math of the game dictates that they most likely won't hit the flop. When your opponents don't hit the flop, you'd like to be able to take a lot of pots by betting on the flop with or without a hand. The key to knowing when such a line of play will work is knowing the percentage of times your opponents fold to bets on the flop. If you are heads-up in a pot against an opponent who has only folded to 2 out of 20 bets on the flop, chances are that you are facing an unbluffable opponent. If you're facing someone who has folded 15 out of 20 times, go ahead and bet, for that pot is yours for the taking. Typically, opponents who fold to more than two thirds of bets on the flop are looking to hit flops and will likely only hang around with straight draws, flush draws, or made hands at least as good as top pair. These are the foes who will let you continuation bet them into oblivion.

Meanwhile, players who are folding to less than half of the bets they face on the flop are usually calling with hands such as ace high, overcards, and gutshot straight draws. On paired boards—so-called orphan flops, like 883 rainbow—they might even be calling with king high or queen high. They may also be calling with nothing, looking to take pots away on the turn. For more than one reason, then, players who call a lot on the flop are to be treated warily, as they're generally not bluffable, or if they are, they may require more than one bullet to kill. Against this type of player, just go ahead and play straightforward positional value poker. Even though shorthanded NLHE is a game where players usually don't have made hands, extremely loose callers actually give you odds to hit hands in the long run, especially if they're willing to give you free cards on the turn and river.

Another important postflop number to crunch is your opponent's Aggression Factor (AF), the relationship between his aggressive and passive actions. AF is the ratio of bets or raises made to calls made; the higher the ratio, the higher a player's AF. Your foes will typically have different aggression factors for each round of betting, and your sniffer and HUD should separate them out for you.

The aggression factor can help you in a few ways. It will tell you which foes will or won't be likely to give you free cards, as well as telling you whether their range of betting/ raising hands is narrow or broad. And it will guide your actions and keep you from stepping on certain avoidable landmines. For example, TPTK against a passive, trappy opponent who almost never bets or raises could be a lot of trouble.

We expect our opponents to hit the flop about one third of the time, so an AF bigger than 0.50 should indicate a player who is being aggressive with more than just his made hands. However, there will be times your opponents are semi-bluffing draws. Furthermore, against very tight players for whom pocket pairs constitute a large percentage of playable hands, AFs between 1.00 and 2.00 may be indicative of preflop selection rather than postflop aggressiveness, since those players will have a higher percentage of made hands on the flop. In a typically aggressive shorthanded game, tight players will either be betting big hands or be exiting out of the pot altogether, so their AFs are likely to be skewed high toward 4.00 or 5.00 (possibly more in some cases). To get a truer sense of a player's aggressiveness, look for a correlation between AF and bluffing frequency and remember to temper your reading of these statistical tea leaves with judgments based on what you are actively observing with your own eyes. Always be aware that a foe's current state of play may be a wild departure from his statistical norm. He could be trying out a new strategy, letting his cat play, or pounding the Mickey's Big Mouths. You just never know.

Use sniffers, then, as a training tool for improving your poker thinking; use them to remind you how familiar foes typically play; use them to reinforce (or contradict) the conclusions you draw from foes' betting patterns and deception trends; use them, in all events, to keep your head where it belongs: in the game. Just don't use sniffers as a crutch or as an excuse to put your game on autopilot. Especially in short-handed play, where nefarious rascals will try anything, you can't be sure whether any given foe is playing situational poker or pure card poker. Does his reraise from the big blind mean he has pocket aces, or has he just gotten tired of you pushing him around? Does his early position bet on the flop mean he's running a stop-and-go, or did he hit the board hard? Does a call on the flop mean a draw, or a take-away plan for later streets? Sniffers go a long way toward defining your foes, but you always have to go the last mile yourself.

Exercises

1. Are loose players bad and tight players good? Are good players tight and bad players loose? Is it sufficient to tab your opponents as loose or tight?

2. A player sees 70 percent of all flops. You have 7♣7♠, and the flop is 3♣5♦Q♥. You bet, and the player just described calls. Should you value bet the turn?

3. You are playing online, and after 200 hands, an opponent has a PFR of 15 percent. Come up with a raising dis-

tribution assuming that this opponent is raising with the top 15 percent of hands.

4. How valid is the assumption in question 3 that your opponent is always raising with the top 15 percent of hands?

5. For the first two hours at a table, the player to your right either folds or just completes from the small blind whenever action folds to him preflop, but the past six times he's been in this situation, he has raised to 3BB. What does this mean, and how should you adjust?

Answers

1. The words loose and tight don't tell us whether a player is good or bad. Some good players may be tight, and others may be loose. Many different playing styles can win, especially in shorthanded NLHE. The best players adjust their strategies and adapt to whatever their opponents are giving them. Likewise, some bad players may be loose, and others may be tight. Losing players (God love them) come in all forms.

2. We haven't given you enough information to answer this question. The opponent described sees 70 percent of all flops; however, when he sees the flop, what distribution of hands will he stay in with when faced with a bet? It's very tempting to extrapolate his loose preflop play to his play postflop, but until you have some evidence linking the two, you can't draw any conclusions.

3. Fifteen percent of hands represent 198.9 combinations. The phrase "top 15 percent" of hands is a bit vague because some players may not assign hands like low pocket pairs to the top 15 percent of hands, given how tough they can be to play properly postflop. For argument's sake, let's just start off with the following distribution: [AA,77]|||[AK,AT]|||[KQ]. This distribution makes up 128 combinations, leaving about 70 more to account for. If we toss KJ and QJ in the mix, the total goes up to 160, and if we also include [66,55], we are now at 172 combinations, leaving about 26 to account for, which we'll find in hands like QJ and QT. This player's raising distribution therefore probably consists of something like [AA,55]|||[AK,AT]|||[KQ,KT]|||[QJ,QT]. Maybe QT and KT are sacrificed in favor of hands like A9 and A8; it's hard to say precisely, but the numbers are at least a point of departure for your own thoughtful analysis.

4. Every raise from this opponent will not represent a raise with the top 15 percent of hands. From early position, perhaps this opponent raises with a much tighter distribution. When he's the cutoff or the button and everyone has folded, he might be raising with a much wider distribution. Though your sniffer tells you how *many* times a foe raises, it's up to you to discern *which* hands he's raising with, always adjusting for factors such as position, tilt, and whether he's letting his cat play.

5. The first one or two times he raises you are justified in thinking that the small blind has a huge hand. However, his six consecutive raises from the small blind indicate that he has changed gears. If you are in a five- or six-handed game, you probably don't have to worry too much about this shift. If you are in a shorter game,

then you have to start making adjustments. Either call or reraise more often when you have two big cards, depending on which action will lead to more favorable postflop play. You have position on the small blind, which means that you can defend somewhat more liberally than if the button were trying to steal.

5

ARCHETYPES

Introduction

You've learned to tie your shorthanded foes to trends and patterns, rather than static generalizations about their play. Now
let's begin the long (but fun) process of carving out strategies
to use against these foes. In this long (but fun) chapter, we'll
look at some commonly encountered shorthanded NLHE
playing archetypes. The authors have devised these archetypes based on betting trends, sniffer data, and our own obsessive observations. By presenting them to you in this
form—without the laborious work leading up to their cre-
ation—we hope to give you the ability to "know 'em when you
see 'em" and to choose from among the palette of strategies
and counterstrategies on offer here.

In fairness, we have to say that this information isn't the
definitive guide to every shorthanded foe you'll face. Your actual enemies will deviate from these profiles, and you may
find foes who play in a way not remotely close to anything you
see here. In that case, we strongly urge you to build profiles of
your own—and to share them with us if you like. In all events,

allow your thinking to be flexible, dynamic, and strategic. Use your enemies' weaknesses against them while building your own strengths (your observational and adaptational skills), as you grow into a shorthanded juggernaut.

Tighty Tighterson
Modus Operandi

Most shorthanded NLHE tables, especially low buy-in games, feature at least one Tighty Tighterson.[1] Preflop, Tighties fold most of their hands. When a Tighty enters a pot, he has a strong holding or, if many have limped before him, a drawing hand like suited connectors. In the face of a preflop raise, though, these drawing hands will go in the muck, for Tighties favor cheap draws and will avoid big pots even with favorable pot odds. A large reason for this is that Tighties have highly conservative estimates of their implied odds. While it's good to err on the conservative side with implied odds (many players wildly overestimate—or overesteem—them), the conservatism of a Tighty is usually too extreme.

Based on his general playing philosophy (hit-to-win), a Tighty's starting requirements look something like [AA,22]|| [AK,AT]|||[KQ,KT]|||[QJ,QT]|||[JT]|||[T9s,65s]|||[J9s,64s]. Here's where

---

1. You may find something comic, and perhaps pejorative, in the Tighty Tighterson sobriquet, or the other handles we use in this chapter. No criticism is implied, for people are entitled to play as they see fit. Furthermore, adopting an archetype described here could be a viable counterstrategy against a particular foe. Yet each of these archetypes is exploitable in some sense, and it is by exploiting the exploitable that we make money. Besides, whimsical handles give us a psychological edge over our foes. "To name a thing is to own a thing," says JV at frequent intervals—while Tony calls him Nelly Neologizer behind his back.

hand distributions can be misleading, for how can a player be said to be tight if his distribution includes hands like 64 suited? The answer is that in a five- or six-handed game, a Tighty may fold up to half of the hands in this distribution from early position and will only play the bottom end of the spectrum—the suited connectors and one-gappers—in late position with at least two limpers already in.

Preflop raising distributions for typical Tighties will range from [AA] to [AA,99]||[AK,AJ]. It's also possible that you will encounter a player with a similar profile but with a larger raising distribution. If so, most of our advice about handling Tighty Tightersons should still apply; just be aware of potential points of departure.

Postflop, a Tighty's play is fairly straightforward. If he doesn't have a good hand, he's out. If he has a good hand (at least top pair with a good kicker), he's in unless he thinks that he's beaten. When a Tighty has a bad hand, he will check-fold. He'll call with a draw if he thinks he's getting the right price; however, as he tends to estimate implied odds pessimistically, he'll usually fold his draw to the pressure of a pot-sized bet or perhaps even a $\frac{2}{3}$ pot-sized one.

Tighties who raise preflop with unpaired hole cards like AK usually will not continuation bet when they miss the flop. When they have draws, they usually will not semi-bluff, though some will semi-bluff in position if they think they can get a free card. And that's about as sophisticated as a Tighty Tighterson gets. We mention this not to cast aspersions on his approach but to give you an idea of what level of expertise to expect.

Consistent with that level of deception, some tighties will slowplay their big hands. Some enjoy check-raising. Others passively call with their big hands on the flop and the turn, only suddenly to turn aggressive on the river. Still others will come right out betting with their made hands; since they won't be betting anything else, you'll know exactly where you stand in the hand when they do.

The bottom line is that Tighties employ very little troublesome deception. Once you know whether a Tighty Tighterson you face prefers to lead out or slowplay, you shouldn't lose many chips in hands where you're behind.

When He's Not a Blind and You Have Position on Him

To be in position over a Tighty is a consummation devoutly to be wished. With few exceptions, he reliably raises preflop with his premium hands, meaning that his limps usually won't be slowplayed monsters, but rather hands he doesn't like to play in raised pots. An exception to this might be something like AK UTG, a hand with which he not only will limp but also call raises. As a rule, though, you can assume (and your sniffers will confirm) that a Tighty will usually fold to a raise after limping. If the players remaining to act don't call many raises, a pot-sized raise preflop is a great way to pick up the blinds and an extra limp without having to see a flop. This hole in Tighty Tighterson's play is a real gift to you, but you have to be careful not to abuse it, lest the players behind you start to fight back. Then again, it's worth considering the secondary benefit of this line of play, as this is a case where correct play against one foe can induce incorrect play in others. If having a maniacal image at your table will loosen up your other opponents in a profitable way, then go ahead and raise Tighties mercilessly when they limp.

What if Tighty Tighterson makes an adjustment and starts calling your preflop raises with a higher frequency? No problem. He may be calling you more often, but he's still calling in hopes of hitting the flop, and when he does, he'll stick to his familiar plan of betting out, check-raising you on the flop, or check-calling on the flop with the intention of showing aggression later. Usually, Tighties like to try to trap their aggressive opponents. Should that deter you from betting? No! That's just what Tighty Tighterson wants: passive postflop play from you and free cards for him. But the math of poker remains the math of poker. Most of the time he'll miss the flop, and most of the time he'll fold. Therefore, whenever you're heads-up against a Tighty Tighterson and the flop has less than two face cards, go ahead and make that continuation bet, no matter what cards you hold. You may even be able to continuation bet flops with two face cards, but this will depend on your opponent, on your current image, and on the image you wish to project. Again speaking in terms of secondary benefits, this line of play may involve some -EV moves in small pots, but it sets you up to capture a big one down the road.

So to win against a Tighty Tighterson, lean heavily on the fact that the flop usually won't help him. Isolate him preflop and pummel him with continuation bets on the flop. Since this type of player will usually give up immediately on the flop, consider a call from him to earmark a real hand and shut down your betting. Since he's done you the favor of defining his hand for you, you should return the favor by not paying him off.

If others at the table interfere with your plans to isolate Tighty Tighterson, then you must slow down preflop. When you're in the cutoff or on the button, raise less and limp more. While your preferred strategy against Tighty Tighterson is to punish his limps with raises, you have to remember that you interact with all your opponents at a poker table, not just the ones you've chosen to abuse.

Playing in Position When You Hit

Since you'll miss the flop a majority of the time, our discussion to this point has focused on continuation betting when you miss. But what happens when you hit? Say you've got top pair with a good kicker. Tighty Tighterson will probably check to you, since that's what he does. Should you slowplay? Nup. Since you've been continuation betting so much, you might as well bet out on the flop and hope that this time Tighty Tighterson has a hand. If he folds, oh well, next case. But when he calls—that's when the fun starts.

Following his check-call on the flop, go ahead and bet on the turn, remembering to bet enough to deny him the right price for a draw. A call from him here will show real strength, and if he checks to you on the river you should probably check behind, unless you think you can value bet (i.e., make a bet such that more than 50 percent of Tighty Tighterson's calls will come from hands worse than yours). Meanwhile, if Tighty Tighterson bets out on the turn or the river, or if he check-raises you, and you just have top pair, you can easily get away from your hand. Remember, this is a player who (1) has shown no penchant for bluffing, (2) probably has a big hand, and (3) will give you ample opportunity to steal back your chips on subsequent deals.

There's a special line of play you can use against this player if he bets into your solid hand on the turn, especially if his betting distribution is on the broad side for a Tighty. Go ahead and raise him in position on the turn, sizing your raise so that you'll pay less by raising on the turn than you'd expect to pay by calling on the turn and the river. If your opponent calls the raise on the turn and then leads out on the river, you'll need at least a good two pair to win; otherwise, if your top pair is good, you'll get a free showdown.

Also, note that if a straight draw or a flush draw hits and a

Tighty bets into you, he has most likely hit the draw. Unless it's the turn and you're getting odds to draw to a better hand, you need to give up. Remember, this is a player who doesn't know about phantom outs. He won't typically go looking for bluffing opportunities, and he usually won't bet into someone who might have hit a draw. The controlling idea here, again, is to avoid giving action to this player in unfavorable circumstances when he offers you so many ample opportunities to beat him.

Instead of checking to you on the flop, now suppose that a Tighty leads out on the flop and you have top pair. Your two options are to call and to face a bet of unknown size on the turn or to raise on the flop and seize control of the hand. We'd like to see you raising the flop, because it'll tell you where you stand on the turn. If Tighty Tighterson calls and then checks the turn, you can bet into him. If he calls on the turn and checks the river, check behind. If he bets into you on the turn or the river after you've shown aggression or if he check-raises you, consider your top pair no good, and let your hand go.

When you have two pair or better, you will typically bet on all three rounds if a Tighty checks to you. If he bets into you, raise him on the flop and the turn, but just call instead of raising on the river unless you have at least top two pair, for at that point, there aren't many hands he can have that you can beat, so you can't raise for value. Also, remember not to lose the plot when a possible draw hits. If a Tighty is still throwing chips into a pot after a potential straight or flush has hit, you need to be very careful even when you have a set.

Since Tighty Tighterson is very straightforward, your main job is to measure your hand against his distribution when he calls you or starts showing aggression. If your hand warrants value betting against the distribution, then value bet. And if Tighty Tighterson has you beaten and you know it (and you *do* know it), don't waste chips trying to move him off his hand. It may be possible to fire three bullets (of increasing caliber) and get him to fold, but since he's being patient and waiting for hands, he's probably not going away against an aggressive foe like you. Likewise, don't throw chips away making crying calls with losing hands. When Tighty Tightersons show aggression, your own discipline is your best friend and saving grace. While hands like bottom two pair are assumed by most to be monsters in a shorthanded game, one of the biggest mistakes people make in shorthanded NLHE is not laying down hands simply because the game is shorthanded. What matters is how your hand stands against *this* opponent in *this* pot—not its typical strength in a shorthanded game.

Perhaps if a game gets three-handed, a Tighty will broaden his distribution, but even so, until you have evidence to the contrary, don't go overboard calling a Tighty down to the river with top pair. Show some aggression earlier in the hand so you can control the betting action, and get some information. Then, trust the information you get. In other words:

> *If you're beat, retreat.*

Moving on . . .

Playing in Position Against a Raise

When you have position on a Tighty who has raised preflop, there's good news and bad news. The good news is that his raise represents a well-defined distribution. The bad news is that it's a big hand. Different Tighties have different raising distributions, but the one you face will likely be on a specific distribution, for most players of this ilk play a very systematic game. As described earlier, expect a raising distribution in the range of [AA] to [AA,99]||[AK,AJ]. If this particular player is on a very tight raising distribution, then the only hand you should consider reraising with is AA, despite your positional advantage. If he's on a looser raising distribution, you may consider reraising him periodically with any two cards to represent big hole cards with which you can continuation bet on the flop.

You may also consider flat-calling some of his preflop raises with the intention of bluffing on a later betting round. Such lines of play are effective if the Tighty you face doesn't usually continuation bet or trap. Should that be the case, you have an invitation to steal many pots. Even if he traps occasionally, those occasional traps shouldn't deter you from pursuing adventurous positional play because he probably won't be trapping often enough for you to be worried about his checks. Putting a different spin on it, assume your opponent checks to you every hand; if he traps every time he has a hand, he won't have a hand about two thirds of the time of checks. You're home free.

However, what you're really looking for when a Tighty Tighterson raises preflop is to hit a monster against a foe who's likely to have a big hand that will be tough to lay down. Calling raises with small and medium pocket pairs to flop a set is huge against Tighties who can't get away from that AA or KK they've been waiting for.

To recap, we've established that when in position against a Tighty, you'd really like to be able to isolate him and take advantage of him postflop. The only big pots you'll win are the rare ones where you both hit very good hands, so your primary source of profit is taking all those pots where neither of you has hit the flop. If you're in a game where other foes thwart you and give you isolation frustration, you might not be able to abuse Tighty as much as you'd like. Let the table dynamic dictate your line of play. To avoid overinvesting in tough situations, just raise less and limp more when you're in late position. This will give you the opportunity to steal pots on flops that are checked to you and simultaneously give you proper pot odds to hit flops.

When He's Not a Blind and He Has Position on You

Now let's give Tighty Tighterson position over you and see how that affects play. Right away we can see one benefit: with him behind you, you're effectively playing one position later, since the infrequency with which he'll call or reraise your preflop raises means that he'll be a nonfactor in most hands. When you're to the right of the cutoff, you can treat yourself as in the cutoff; when you're in the cutoff, you can treat yourself as on the button. Good times! Not only do you get to play more hands in virtual late position, but you also have only infrequent, and easily solved, problems when Tighty gets involved. When that happens (bearing in mind that you raised in front of him) his calling distribution will likely look like [QQ,TT]|||[AK,AQ]. Some Tighties will flat-call with KK, and others may even do so with AA so as not to reveal the strength of their hand (but it's usually the case that they'll reraise with [AA,KK]). Conversely, lower value hands like [99,88] and [AJ] will be in the calling distributions of some Tighties.

If you miss the flop, one option is to throw a continuation bet out on the flop, just to see what happens. He might have missed as well, and obligingly fold. There are pitfalls, though. If you've been really aggressive with continuation bets, your opponent may be willing to call with a pocket pair lower than the high board card (not likely, but it's a possibility to be aware of). So maybe you want to check to him on the flop to find out if he does, in fact, have something from the pocket-pair side of his distribution. He won't bet if he didn't pair and also won't bet if the board has a card higher than the rank of his pocket pair. He'll only bet if he flops top pair or an overpair. If he bets and you're beaten, you fold. If he checks and the turn card comes lower than the highest ranked card on the flop, go ahead and pitch in a $\frac{1}{2}$ pot bet on the turn. This play, the Delayed Continuation Bet (DCB) works great here, for apart from a two-outer to an underpair, there's probably no card lower than the top board card that will make Tighty Tighterson call your bet.

If you hit the flop, say top pair or better, you should bet, for there's not much point in checking to an opponent who's not likely to bet. You might as well hope that he has hit the flop hard, but not as hard as you have so that you'll get money in on all betting rounds. You may want to slowplay top set with no draws on board, in the hopes that your tight opponent will turn something that he'll pay you off with, but the sad fact is that against a Tighty it's going to be tough to make any real money with top set.

Tricky situations arise when a Tighty gives you resistance when you have top pair or an overpair. For example, you have T♣T♦ and the flop is 9♣6♥3♠. You raise preflop, and Tighty Tighterson calls. You bet half the pot on the flop, and he calls again. What could he possibly be calling with? A9 isn't in his preflop calling distribution, meaning that he probably has [AA,88]. The only hand in that distribution you beat is 88. Not a good situation for you. If he called with a hand like [QQ,JJ] and an overcard falls, then a bet on the turn may scare him off. But as a rule, you shouldn't be looking to get a lot of chips in the pot out of position against a Tighty who has shown some bottle. A similar situation is having AT on a ten-high flop. TPTK is a strong hand shorthanded, but you have to know your foes and know when to slow down. Again, think about his hand distribution, weight the possibility of his having pocket paint, and be prepared to muck your TPTK if need be.

The trickiest situation is when you raise preflop with something like QQ, and Tighty Tighterson calls. So far, so good, but now let's say that on a flop of 9♣8♥3♦, either you make a typical flop-fraction bet and Tighty raises, or he calls you on the flop and then raises on the turn. These two betting patterns are problematic for you and your pocket queens, for you won't know quite what you're up against. Does he have a set? Is he behind but thinking he's ahead with TT or JJ? Did he smooth-call preflop with KK or AA? While you can discount all his unpaired holdings (for he'd fold those on the flop), the remaining hands in his distribution put you in something of a pickle.

Because of the size of the pot at this point in the betting, the pot odds usually favor your playing the hand to the river *if* you can do so cheaply. The way to do this is to employ *blocking bets*, undersized bets that discourage larger ones. If you are raised on the flop, lead out with a $\frac{1}{3}$ pot bet on the turn and the river. If you are just called on the flop, employ the same bets. If a Tighty raises you on either the turn or the river, you have to assume that your queens are beaten. If for some reason, a raise on the turn does not convince you that you are beaten, you can employ a stop-and-go by calling the raise on the turn and betting $\frac{1}{3}$ pot on the river.

This would be a better situation if you were in position, for you'd only have to bet the turn instead of the turn and the river. However, since the circumstance we're describing doesn't occur too often against a Tighty, having one to your left isn't a disaster. Just know when blocking bets and stop-and-gos are in order, and don't hesitate to lay down top pair or overpairs if the betting suggests that you're beaten. Again, shorthanded NLHE is all about knowing your foes.

A further word on blocking bets, if we may. These bets are

one of your key lines of defense in many of the marginal situations you'll encounter in shorthanded NLHE. To keep them working for you, it's important that you use them with some of your very big hands as well as your marginal ones. If you don't, they'll lose their deterrent force as your more observant opponents start raising them and forcing you to fold winners. You probably don't have to worry about this against a Tighty, but there are other foes out there, and they're probably paying attention.

Play in the Blinds

Raising against Tighties in blind-on-blind action is both profitable and straightforward. If you are in the small blind with a Tighty in the big blind and action folds to you, raise the big blind and take the pot immediately. If you're in the big blind with Tighty in the small blind and he limps in, raise the small blind and take the pot immediately. If you're limp-reraised and you don't have a premium starting hand, fold immediately, unless you have a small-to-medium pocket pair and proper odds to draw to a set. In other words, playing a Tighty in the blinds is pretty much like playing him elsewhere. He's weak in the face of aggression, so be aggressive.

Of course, if you're too aggressive too long, you're liable to irk this would-be patient player. Eventually he'll morph into someone else. He might even become a Cally Wally.

Cally Wally
Modus Operandi

Like Tighty Tighterson, Cally Wallies are common fixtures at shorthanded NLHE tables. Some Cally Wallies simply have a psychological disposition toward loose play without aggression, no matter what game they're in. Others play a conventional TAG game fullhanded, but become Cally Wallies in shorthanded games because they know that they need to play more hands, but don't quite know how. In both instances, these are players who play more hands (sometimes a *lot* more hands) but rarely in a way that will give you much trouble.

Whatever its basis, it's the "any two will do" mentality that brings Wally into the pot. Preflop, he'll be in a large percentage of unraised pots. "Hell, it's only a big blind," he'll think to himself—or possibly say out loud, for Wallies are frequently Talkies, maximizing the social aspect of the game as they happily limp in.[2] Truly dreadful hands might find their way into the muck, but generally, almost anything is good enough for a Wally in an unraised pot.

Raised pots are a different story. Only the most extreme Wally won't differentiate between a raised and an unraised pot. That said, while his overall calling frequency will go down, you'll still see him calling into more raised pots—especially minimally raised ones (2–3BB)—than he should.

When it comes to initiating aggressive action, this player's raising distribution will track fairly closely to Tighty Tighterson's, so if a Wally raises, you can be sure he has a real hand. This may seen counterintuitive, but we have some Wallies in our Poker Tracker databases with VPIPs of 60 percent and PFRs of 1 percent over hundreds of hands! It doesn't matter that a player has shown the ability to call with the Hammer or the Numpty; if this is his second raise in hundreds

---

2. While Cally Wallies may say such things, not all players who say them are Cally Wallies. Good players will try to manipulate their foes with such banter, portraying themselves as someone they're not. Scoundrels! Guess that's why they say a poker table is a gold mine of misinformation.

of hands, know that he's in there with aces, kings, or queens for sure. Remember:

> *A loose caller is not necessarily a loose bettor.*

Postflop, a Cally Wally will continue his calling spree with a wide range of holdings. He'll sometimes call down to the river with ace high. With most of his draws, he'll call regardless of whether he's getting the right price, for concepts like pot odds, implied odds, and reverse implied odds are either foreign to his understanding or irrelevant to his approach. He's playing hit-to-win, and damn the cost!

The big issue with Wallies is figuring out how they play when they hit the flop. Some will bet out with top pair and a bad kicker; others will just call with it. Some will slowplay their big hands; others will play them aggressively. Wallies who like to slowplay are problematic because their infrequent calls with good hands resemble their frequent calls with bad ones, so it's hard to know exactly where they're at. In a live game, you may get some physical tells to help you out, but if you're playing online, you only have betting patterns and hand distributions to work with.

Wallies will often change their postflop calling requirements as a function of the number of players in the pot. Interestingly, these changes flow in opposite directions. Some Wallies turn timid in traffic, figuring that their ragged preflop holding is now no good. Others, however, look at large fields as a justification to chase slim draws. This betrays a fundamental misunderstanding of implied odds in NLHE. Whereas in a limit game, you derive your implied odds from many callers at fixed limits; in no limit, your implied odds come from getting a worse hand than yours on the hook and stacking him off.

Wallies employ little deception. Likewise, because their hand distributions are so wide, including many hands that are just plumb no good, your basic game plan against them should involve very little bluffing and driving, and lots of straightforward value betting. And remember that if a Wally shifts into aggressor mode, he definitely has a hand.

Though Wallies are among the easiest foes to face, you'll still have some tough decisions against them. For instance, to derive maximum profit, you need to think very carefully about when to value bet the river, for if you value bet too frequently, you'll be losing EV on your river play due to the times Cally Wally has a hand; however, if you're too conservative with your value bets, then you won't be making as much money as you could. You'll also want to give some thought to the price a Wally will pay on a value bet. What you're looking for—and this varies from player to player—is his "what the hell" line, the amount of money he considers insignificant in light of having come so far in the hand. When you can get a Wally thinking (or saying—and they will say this), "I know I'm beat but what the hell," then you'll know you've got him sussed.

When He's Not a Blind and You Have Position on Him

With Tighty Tightersons our primary game plan was to pummel them with brute force and bully them out of pots. Bullying a Wally is not that easy; you can't bully someone who is unwilling to fold. At first, this may seem frustrating in a shorthanded NLHE game. After all, a major theme of this book has been that no one hits the flop in shorthanded games. If you can't bully people and force them to fold when no one hits the flop, how are you supposed to win?

One thing you could try is to increase the size of your pre-flop raise and push Wally outside the comfort zone of his calls. Trouble is, this may have the effect of tightening him up, and since his calliness is his fatal flaw, you definitely don't want to move him off it. Plus, overbetting with other players yet to act may result in your playing lots of inflated pots against the Cally Wally *and* against other foes who now have sufficient odds to play a profitable sit-and-wait game. Overbetting, then—not the way to go.

Should you then stop raising preflop? Of course not! Raising preflop is the strength of your game shorthanded, and you're not going to relinquish it just because Wally can't get off the pot. Particularly if raising will likely buy you the button and drop the blinds, go ahead and raise with something along the lines of the following wide distribution: [AA,22]|||[AK,A2]||| [KQ,K2]|||[QJ,Q9]|||[JT]|||[J9s,64s]|||[T9s,65s].

Some of these hands are worse than random, so you may wonder why we advocate raising with them. The answer lies in an interesting little math anomaly of a limp-caller like Wally. Say you are playing in a shorthanded NLHE game with $1–$2 blinds. If Wally limps, a sensible preflop raise would be to $8 (3BB+1BB for every additional caller). Assuming that the blinds fold and Wally is your only foe postflop, you're getting 11:8 on your money. If you were simply to deal all the board cards with no further betting, your hand would need to be better than 42 percent against Cally Wally's distribution. Bringing betting back into the picture, you also get to play your position in all subsequent betting rounds. This is a huge +EV situation, espe-cially considering that your worse-than-random hand may very well be matched by one of Wally's own.[3]

---

3. We acknowledge that this discussion neglects the impact of opponents remaining to act. Sure, your raise is meant to make them all fold, but of course they won't fold all the time. So save your true junk raises for ta-bles where the players behind you are tight enough to be likely to fold.

When the Wally you've raised checks to you on the flop, you should bet anytime you hit a flop, anytime you have ace high or even king high with a good kicker, and anytime you have fourteen or more outs. All of these are value-betting opportunities, and value betting is the key to beating a Wally, so much so that we'll box the thought for your attention and inspection:

> To beat a Cally Wally, value bet him to death.

In addition, in cases where you have a big draw, or even a small draw like overcards, betting the flop will most likely get you a free card on the turn. Granted, you'll probably be getting a free card anyway, unless you're up against a special Cally Wally who will bet the turn with middle pair after his opponent has shown weakness on the flop. Therefore, when you have a draw against a Wally, you should generally check behind and take a free ride to the river against someone who doesn't fold a lot.

If you rate yourself as better than fifty-fifty to win the hand with two cards to come, go ahead and bet. Not to beat the dead horse of this, but *value bet, value bet, value bet*. This is why you want to clear out the rest of the field preflop so that you can have the Wally—and his chips—all to yourself. Apart from isolating Wally in position, your preflop raise deals you another edge, in that if you miss the flop, you'll most likely get to see the turn for free, giving you four cards instead of three in your quest to hit a hand or pick up a draw.

Well, as you can imagine, life with Wally isn't nearly as idyllic as we've just described. Your more observant foes at the table know what you're up to; heck, they want to do the same thing themselves. Since they know you're raising with a wide distribution, they may either start calling your raises more liberally or start reraising you more often. When you face such resistance, you need to tighten up your raising distribution, especially if your lingering foes in the fight will have position on you postflop.

If you're on the button with Wally to your right and the blinds are giving you lots of trouble, you can't let them take away your positional advantage. Since you'd still like to be in lots of pots in late position, just adjust by limping with some of your weaker holdings and keep raising with all your premium hands and your nonpremium hands containing two wheelhouse cards.

What happens when a Wally wakes up and turns aggressive? First, remember that there are different kinds of looseness and that, critically, loose calling does not translate into loose betting. If the Wally you face is betraying real strength with his lead bets and raises (and you should assume he is), then you should have no problem knowing what to do: just be cautious in all circumstances. Playing against an aggressive Cally Wally is much like playing against an aggressive Tighty Tighterson. You know he has a good hand, so you simply need to evaluate where your hand stands relative to his distribution and go forward from there.

Preflop, you should muck most hands except for pocket pairs, AK and possibly AQ, the vaunted Big Slickina, a.k.a. Slickerella. Choose between calling or reraising as a function of your particular Wally and the players remaining to act behind you. With smaller pairs, since Cally Wallies will typically give you great implied odds, you can usually call preflop raises with any pocket pair, looking to flop a set, even if you anticipate being heads-up. In many shorthanded NLHE games, people go crazy with overpairs, so your implied odds tend to be better. Of course, if your specific game conditions are such that you don't think your implied odds are great—for example, you are likely to face a preflop reraise from hyperaggressive and tricky players sitting behind you—you should fold instead of calling to flop a set.

Postflop, if you think your hand is good enough relative to the pot odds you're getting, you can elect to call down an uncharacteristically aggressive Wally. But don't discount the possibility of taking back the initiative. Remember, anytime your hand is better than 50 percent against Cally Wally's distribution, you should raise, regardless of whether he aggressed. Also, remember that raising in position on the flop or turn is a good way of saving some money in uncertain circumstances. Against a bettor who is going to bet $\frac{1}{2}$ pot or more on the river, raising in position earlier in the hand will result in you putting less money in the pot, provided that your aggression in position will put the brakes on a river bet—as it often will against a wide variety of foes, not just a Wally.

Of course, if you have a hand like top pair or something else that doesn't look very good when faced with a reraise against a normally passive opponent, then you probably need to abandon ship. You will also have to consider bailing with hands like top pair if a Wally pulls a stop-and-go, but no problem—you have still saved money relative to calling down from the flop to the river.

In summary, when you have position on a Cally Wally, your primary strategy is to isolate him heads-up with a wide range of hands preflop because of the huge implied odds you have in postflop play. Your default strategy on all betting decisions on all rounds will be to value bet. As long as you're always firing bets when your hand is at least 50 percent against a Wally's distribution, you're doing all you need to (and all you can) in order to derive a healthy profit. Meanwhile, beware of unexpected aggression from this player, and look to save money in uncertain circumstances by raising in position to slow that Cally Wally down.

When He's Not a Blind and
He Has Position on You

Unfortunately, if a Cally Wally is to your left, you won't be able to raise to seize a positional advantage for the rest of the hand. Also, with Wally calling behind you, others will likely jump in, so your raises will result in many three- and four-way flops. As a result, you'll need to limp with hands like JT and other hands you'd normally consider raising with as CO-1 or CO.[4] Similarly, you can no longer raise with drawing hands like suited connectors. You can limp with them if you're in the cutoff and earlier foes have already limped; otherwise, muck.

Having a Cally Wally to your left forces you to adopt more of a sit-and-wait game. The good news is that, since you'll be limping a lot more, you'll be getting at least 2.5:1 on your money most of the time preflop. You'll be winning fewer pots, but the percentage of money you'll be putting into each pot will be lower. This is a rare instance in shorthanded NLHE where hit-to-win isn't just a viable strategy but probably the best one you've got.

Let's say you do raise preflop and end up facing Cally Wally heads-up out of position. Since your hand is high cards, medium pocket pairs, or high pocket pairs and his is [WTF?], you are pretty sure to be a favorite against a Cally Wally's distribution. If you have at least second pair, you should bet out on the flop, and you should consider betting again on the turn if called on the flop. An argument can be made for betting the flop against extremely loose Wallies if you have bottom pair with an ace or king kicker, but such betting may not be good value when you are out of position. When you have top pair or better, lead out on all three betting rounds if your opponent doesn't aggress. If a Cally Wally raises you, then simply evalu-

4. That is, cutoff minus one or cutoff.

ate where you are relative to his raising distribution, and if you don't have a monster, choose the right course of action from among fold, stop-and-go, or check-call to showdown.

It's tough to be profitable out of position, but despite the edge you lose when you lose position, diligent pattern reading and intelligent value betting should still make it +EV to whack away at a Wally, even from in front. It's best to be to the left of virtually all players in a hold'em game, but you obviously can't be to the left of everyone.[5] So when you have to choose between yielding position to Wally or to tougher foes, go ahead and put Wally on your left. If his pockets are deep, you'll get your share no matter what.

Play in the Blinds

If a Cally Wally likes to call when he's not a blind, imagine how much more he likes to call when he's already put money in a pot. Blind money is really dead money, but a lot of players, especially Cally Wallies, don't think that way. When you're on the button, play Blind Wally the way you otherwise would in position. The only difference is that when he's in the blind, his calling distribution is even wider, if such a thing is possible.

When you're in the small blind with Wally in the big, you have to tighten up your raising distribution a tad. Bearing in mind that it's hard to get value by betting with nothing upstream into someone who won't fold, restrict your small blind raises to good aces, pocket pairs, and the odd KQ. Otherwise, take your favorable 3:1 odds and limp. When you're in the big blind and Wally limps from the small blind after everyone has folded, you should raise with a somewhat tighter distribution than normal behind this limper. While you still have position,

---

5.   At least not in this universe.

there's no dead blind money from other players in the pot, meaning that your raise is a 1:1 proposition. Therefore, it's only a good play if your probability of winning the hand is at 50 percent or more. Push your combined edges of position and cards, of course, but avoid becoming too aggressive and straying from calculated value betting. Sheer aggression alone works against Tighty Tightersons, but it doesn't work against Cally Wallies.

Finally, if Cally Wally turns aggressive from the blinds, give him the benefit of the doubt and assume he has a good hand. It's not in his nature to be tricky from the blinds. It's not in his nature to be tricky at all.

Serial Dater
Modus Operandi

Serial Daters constitute another class of players who know that it's correct to play more hands in shorthanded NLHE without knowing, er, how. Serial Daters get involved in lots of pots. They will limp in most unraised pots and call a fair share of preflop raises. Their preflop play usually resembles that of a Cally Wally. As a class, though, Serial Daters are more aggressive preflop. When facing such a player, the key thing is to link his preflop actions to his corresponding hand distributions.

Serial Daters have problems with commitment; they don't like being in pots for the long term. They fool around preflop only to fold most hands postflop. When they are in a hand past the flop, they have a good hand or a very good draw. The degree to which Serial Daters are aggressive postflop will vary. Some Serial Daters are willing to semi-bluff, but others only aggress with made hands. Likewise, some Serial Daters come out firing, but others prefer to slowplay. The main theme is that if a Serial Dater is putting in chips postflop, he's not trying to bully and he's usually not speculating with garbage.

Serial Dater is a blend of Cally Wally and Tighty Tighter-son, being a slightly more aggressive version of the former pre-flop and a slightly looser version of the latter postflop. Thus we have a profile where not only can the tags tight and loose not be assumed to travel between betting rounds, but they ac-tually, and by design, conflict.

When He's Not a Blind and You Have Position on Him

Let's first assume that a Serial Dater limps preflop. His MO is to fold postflop unless he hits a flop. Therefore, your line of play is to raise preflop in an attempt to isolate him heads-up. If he checks to you on the flop, you will make a $\frac{1}{2}$ pot or $\frac{2}{3}$ pot con-tinuation bet to which he'll fold about two thirds of the time.

What happens if, after you raise preflop, a Serial Dater bets into you? Since Serial Daters are fairly stringent with their postflop playing requirements, the most likely scenario is that he has top pair or better. If your hand holds up against his dis-tribution, you should usually raise the flop and then bet the turn if he checks to you, with the intention of checking down on the river (if you have a huge hand on the river, you obvi-ously will bet again). If a Serial Dater check-raises you on any round of betting, you should be done with the hand unless you have at least two pair, preferably including the highest board card. If you have a draw and he bets into you on the flop, semi-bluffing can be a highly effective line of play that either gets you the pot immediately or gets you a free card on the turn.

If your opponents see what you're doing and start calling your preflop raises with a higher frequency, you need to tighten up your raising requirements. In circumstances when you do raise, maintain your loose image by tossing in a fair number of continuation bets against one or two opponents. But don't look to splash around more than necessary. As with other players on the weak side of the archetype spectrum, your goal is to get heads-up against Serial Daters, but you can't be so single-minded in pursuit of this goal that you leave yourself open to attack from stronger players.

When a Serial Dater raises preflop, you need to know his raising distribution. This is where your awareness of betting patterns is key, for different Serial Daters vary widely on this. If he's a loose raiser who doesn't make a large number of continuation bets, then you can call his raises with the intention of controlling postflop action, or even reraise, both to thin the field behind you and to get more money into the pot against a player whose predilection is to fold when he misses the flop. However, if the Serial Dater raising here is a tight raiser, then you should probably throw away all but your best hands. Holding just a small pair, for instance, you'd need more traffic behind to justify drawing to a set. You'll know from observation whether you're likely to get those callers, but since you know for sure that the Serial Dater is on a strong hand, there's nothing wrong with folding many indifferent holdings, including small pairs, here. You won't get proper implied odds with a small pocket pair if he's capable of laying down an overpair in the face of lots of postflop heat, and while it may be tempting to attempt a fancy bluff on a player willing to lay down an overpair, the thin return you might get on such maneuvers probably isn't worth the risk.

When He's Not a Blind and He Has Position on You

When a Serial Dater has position on you, expect him to call a high percentage of your preflop raises. In the ideal circumstance, the players behind a Serial Dater are tight and likely to fold to your preflop raise, leaving you heads-up to complete your raise-call perfecta. Though you're out of position, you're not in bad shape, because your lead bet on the flop will win a majority of pots. In this sense, playing out of position against a Serial Dater is easier than against, say, a Wally, for most pots will end on the flop, meaning that you're only out of position for one betting round instead of three. Your continuation bet won't have quite as high an EV coming from early position, but it will still be profitable against most Serial Daters. If you get resistance, then treat the Serial Dater like you would a Tighty Tighterson out of position, and if you don't have the goods, then get the hell out of Dodge.

Play in the Blinds

If you are on the button or in a heads-up blind situation against a Serial Dater, you want to raise almost any hand preflop with the intention of continuation betting all flops. Granted, your Serial Dater may eventually make an adjustment if he figures out what is going on. However, in all likelihood, you will not only be deriving big +EV against your Serial Dater, you will also be giving yourself a loose, aggressive table image that will work in your favor in pots against other players at your table. Here is another example of a correct play against one foe simultaneously sending usefully false image signals to others—so much so that we might call this move Double Happiness.[6]

If your Serial Dater does begin to catch on to your antics in

---

6. Tony here: Double Happiness is a Chinese ideogram that represents a bride and groom and really has no application here. Note to self: keep JV on shorter leash.

the blinds, an option is to change up your play by sometimes limping and then betting the flop after limping, for your limp will represent an even wider range of hands than usual for you, any one of which could have hit the flop. Subjective reality is your ally in this: a foe who is predisposed to fold will easily persuade himself that the visible junk on the board matches the hidden junk in your hand. You can also choose to refrain from always continuation-betting. Just remember that the norm against a Serial Dater is to get dead money in the pot preflop, then to get it surrendered to you on the flop.

BenBucks
Modus Operandi

BenBucks is a player with lots of money at his disposal, and he's not afraid to use it to put you to difficult decisions. He's very aggressive, and many of his raises are the result of the weakness he perceives in others, rather than any particular hand strength of his own. When faced with calling decisions, he may be—let's call it creative and optimistic—in counting his outs, which makes him very difficult to bluff, especially considering that he also has no qualms about bluff reraising. Being aggressive, creative, and unafraid, he's a very tough opponent to play in a shorthanded NLHE game. If you're not prepared, he'll clean your clock.

Preflop, BenBucks enters pots with a large mix of hands. He enters almost any pot when he's on the button, and he's a vicious blind defender in suspected blind-steal scenarios. BenBucks raises a fair amount of hands preflop, but his raises have less to do with his hole cards than with reads, situations, table trends, image, momentum, and other considerations from the "art" side of the poker ledger. Given this, he's capable of raising with any two cards at any time—but don't assume that he's raising with any two cards all the time. When facing a preflop raise, his calling requirements are also highly situational in nature. He could decide you're stealing or decide from the outset that *he's* going to steal. He's got moves within moves and, in the pantheon of players we've discussed so far, he's one who can give you fits.

Postflop, BenBucks's aggressiveness increases as his number of foes goes down. He'll show some restraint in shorthanded poker's rare four- to six-handed pots, but in the two- and three-handed pots common in shorthanded NLHE, he comes out swinging most of the time. When he has a drawing hand or when he's on a bluff, he'll be highly aggressive with it and make his bets and raises large with respect to the pot—not overbets, but usually pot sized. BenBucks plays his mediocre and good hands similarly to how he plays his draws, further clouding our picture of him. However, when BenBucks has a monster, he generally switches into calling mode. He sometimes goes into calling mode with mediocre hands to switch things up, but don't let his ploys fool you. When he hesitates and starts calling, then you can be pretty sure that he has at least two pair.

With all his aggression and apparently loose calling, BenBucks loosens up everyone around him. He knows he has this effect, and plays to it. Through image and chat— BenBucks loves to chat—he pries his opponents open, widening their calling distributions considerably. Having done that, he keeps up the heat by being much more aggressive postflop than most opponents you'll face in shorthanded NLHE games.

The theme, then, of BenBucks's game is tricky aggression. This can be a double-edged sword, sometimes making him too tricky for his own good. For instance, he's susceptible to calling off large stacks of chips when he's way behind as a result of mentally devaluing his opponents' hand distributions. All in all, though, this is a player long on chicanery and short on weakness. It's going to take all our guile to put this worthy adversary in his place.

When He's Not a Blind and You Have Position on Him

Your goal when in position in hold'em is to raise when your hole cards and your positional play put you at an advantage against your foes. Against some opponents, like Serial Daters, the cards don't much matter when you have position, but against others, you can't win simply by abusing your position. BenBucks is one such foe whom you can't beat with position alone.

Because BenBucks is tricky, your goal is to avoid getting involved in many heads-up pots in which you don't have a huge edge. There are two ways for you to deal yourself an edge: The first is to limp behind him with a wide range of hands, encouraging others to join the parade and giving you good odds to hit a big hand. Since you know BenBucks is going to be tricky postflop, this will give you a lot of positional flexibility with big hands and big draws alike.

The second way to seize advantage is to raise your very strong unpaired cards like [AK,AJ] when you have position. In these circumstances, it's okay to get heads-up against BenBucks, because you'll likely go to the flop with the better hand. If you miss the flop and BenBucks checks to you, you should continuation bet a high percentage of the time, only occasionally checking behind to take a free card on the turn. Your continuation bet here is, in some senses, a value bet, since your ace high may be better than a good chunk of hands he'll call with. But know this: if he checks on the turn and you check behind, BenBucks will generally bet the river, figuring that, hey, if no one else wants the pot, he'll take it. Since this means that you frequently won't get to a showdown for the price of a bet on the flop, then the continuation bet on the flop goes from being a partial value bet to being almost completely a one-shot bluff. You could try to fight fire with fire and shoot multiple bullets into the pot, but if BenBucks has a read on you (or even if he doesn't), he may check-raise bluff the turn or the river. The possibility of him playing back at you shouldn't necessarily scare you or deter you, but you should know what you're stepping into—and consider whether you want to step into it at all. Per classic poker wisdom:

> *Don't challenge strong players, challenge weak ones. That's what they're there for.*

BenBucks may be somewhat loose and reckless, but he's a keen hacker, so while you want to raise primarily for value preflop, you should throw in some image raises, just to keep BenBucks off stride. Hands like 98 suited are good for the occasional raise, for if BenBucks tabs you as a standard TAG player, this hand won't be in the distribution he puts you on. Furthermore, with a BenBucks in the game, doing his darndest to loosen it up, such a raise might actually get three or four callers, simultaneously tempering BenBucks's postflop friskiness and giving you a good multiway pot for your drawing hand.

Postflop play against BenBucks can get very interesting. In the ideal, you'll battle him heads-up with something like top pair with a good kicker or better, for if he's driving the hand from the start (which he'll do a lot), you can call him down on every street with a hand much better than the usual cheese he plays. Trouble is, he'll often know where you're at when you do this, and he'll shift to value-betting mode instead of bluffing mode, heavily betting into your top pair when he's on a set or two pair. Simply calling BenBucks down can thus be a dicey way to go with top pair. Let's think of other ways to play him.

In the judo nature of using an enemy's strength against him, consider raising most of his flop bets, checking the turn, and inducing bluffs on the river. Your raise on the flop will thin the field behind you (if it exists), while your check on the turn will telegraph (false) weakness. BenBucks knows you may be playing him; even so, he may simply not be able to resist taking a shot at the pot on the end. This will put you in good shape with hands like top pair, though it must be noted that you are giving him a free card on the turn, which could come back to haunt you. Also, if BenBucks decides to lead out on the turn, you have a tough decision. He may be sensing your strength and trying to maximize his value on a made hand— or he may just be representing that line of play. Such is the difficulty of playing against a fearless, creative type like this. And if he is creative on the turn, figure him to be creative again on the river, either leading at the pot with something or nothing or preparing to check-raise with something or nothing. You can try to slow him down by raising his lead bet on the turn, which may net you a check on the river. That raise in position is a great ploy against most players, but it works with only mixed results against BenBucks.

The real key to playing against BenBucks in position is to know that each pot is a potential high-variance skirmish. If you're scared of variance, you need to find another foe—or another game altogether. If you aren't scared of variance, just play simple hand-distribution match-up poker, staying out of BenBucks's way unless you can go to war in large pots with TPTK or better. Sure, you won't win every hand with TPTK, but as long as the mean hand you're giving action with is higher than the mean hand he's giving action with, you should derive a decent profit when you're in position against BenBucks.

When He's Not a Blind and He Has Position on You

You typically don't want to be in this situation. You should be actively looking to change seats or change games, rather than yield position to a player who can do much with this edge. In the times that you have to play BenBucks out of position, your priority is to try to get him involved in pots with many players. Of course, if you are playing heads-up or three-handed, that'll be impossible (so just leave), but if you are in a five- or six-handed game, then you want to get other money in the pot where the larger volume gives you better pot odds and the higher traffic slows BenBucks down.

To avoid being heads-up out of position against BenBucks, you severely need to limit the hands you raise with preflop, for a raise by you and a call by BenBucks will eliminate players behind. It's better to limp and let BenBucks limp behind you, which he'll often do because while BenBucks is somewhat aggressive preflop, he's nowhere near maniacal. An action player (and then some!), he's looking for any excuse to join any pot, and the prospect of a limpfest will tilt him toward calling with a variety of mediocre hands. He figures that his edge comes from being able to outplay everyone after the flop (you; the other players; Johnny Chan; God), and so he welcomes a full field, even though he shouldn't, since it takes away so much of his bluff equity.

If you do end up heads-up against BenBucks postflop as a result of having raised preflop, and you miss the flop, employ a mixed strategy of continuation betting about half the hands and checking the rest. You can't simply check-fold when you miss, or you'll embolden BenBucks to steamroll you. A battle with BenBucks is a battle for control. If you yield control, you're toast.

If you flop top pair or better, you have to be prepared to go to war. If he raises you on the flop and there's a draw on the board, you should often make a slightly oversized reraise. Another option is to call the raise on the flop and immediately make a pot-sized bet on the turn. Or, you can check-raise on the turn. There will be times when he'll have you beaten, but quite a few times when he won't. Remember that BenBucks is prone to overestimating his outs. For instance, if he has JT suited, you have QQ, and the board shows 962 with two of his suit, he may count his overcard outs as good when they're not. This'll skew his math and put him in many -EV situations. The biggest thing to keep in mind, again, is that you want the mean of your playing distribution to be higher than the mean of his. Sometimes he'll beat you, and sometimes you'll beat him; you'll make your profit on the margin of your mean—if you last that long, and if you can stand the variance! Shorthanded NLHE against BenBucks is a roller coaster ride. Either keep a very level head, or simply decline to ride.

Play in the Blinds

Visiting again the concept of subjective reality—what you see depends on where you stand—know that a tricky player like BenBucks sees tricky play in everyone. He's apt to read raises in blind play situations as steals, so the best route to go is the straightforward route. When you're in the small blind, you might not even be able to limp because BenBucks will typically raise your limps mercilessly. Fold your garbage small blinds to him, and when he limps in the small blind, you should often check behind in the big blind. Don't let relentless aggression on his part anger you, arouse you, or put you off your game. You aren't sitting around waiting for aces in the big blind, but you don't want to let ire prompt you to get overexposed with hands like A2. Try to keep pots small preflop, and make most of your money from large implied odds postflop. Blind-versus-blind play is one of BenBucks's (many) strengths, for he has long experience of playing raised pots with blind-quality hands and of drawing many inexperienced and unsuspecting foes into this web. Again, straightforward poker and a level head are your best defense against this trap.

BenBucks is a formidable foe—but one worth watching and modeling. At the end of the day, we reckon, it's easier to *be* BenBucks than to beat him.

Location Station
Modus Operandi

Preflop, a Location Station's play tracks close to a Tighty Tighterson. However, there is one huge difference. When a Location Station has the cutoff seat or the button, he will raise with a huge range of hands if the pot is unraised, usually regardless of how many limpers are in.

After he has raised preflop, he will usually continuation bet all flops that are checked to him by one opponent and sometimes two opponents. If someone bets into him, he will usually raise in position with hands at least as good as top pair or as a semi-bluff. Some Location Stations will raise your bet in position no matter what if you are heads-up, but most have a "be first in or be out" policy. Not a bad policy to have, by the way.

On the turn, the Location Station will bet many hands that he will probably check behind on the river. He usually won't semi-bluff the turn. His semi-bluffs on the flop are usually done to take the pot down on the flop or to take a free card on the turn. When he is out of position on the turn, he usually employs blocking bets.

On the river, when he's in position, he will typically be a skilled value bettor, for a strength of his game is playing hands in position against foes who have limp-called into pots larger than they originally intended to play. He'll check behind when he doesn't anticipate getting called by a worse hand, and he'll bet if he senses the slightest +EV to be gained. As on the turn, he'll use blocking bets out of position on the river to tamp down others' aggression. He'd rather risk a $\frac{1}{3}$ pot bet with a marginal hand by betting out of position than check and be faced with a very tough $\frac{1}{2}$ pot or full pot bet.

A Location Station is something of a hybrid between Tighty Tighterson and BenBucks, and he may be among the toughest opponents you face in a shorthanded no-limit game. He's going to force you to pay the highest price possible in most pots. Meanwhile, he won't give much up when he's behind. Furthermore, because of his frequent aggression, he can often get his opponents to overplay hands in bad spots. Online, watch his VPIP percentage numbers, which do not take position into account, and compare them to your actual observations. A Location Station can easily have a VPIP of around 40 percent in some games, but you'll see that he will rarely put money in out of position. He relentlessly deals himself the advantage of acting late or last. For this reason, be wary of a Location Station getting involved out of position; he probably has a hand.

When He's Not a Blind and
You Have Position on Him

The first situation to consider against a Location Station is when you are in a four- to six-handed shorthanded game, and the Location Station has limped. He typically doesn't slow-play any hands because of the loose raising image he's established with most players at the table who don't know what's actually going on. Thus, when he limps, he doesn't have a great hand. If you raise preflop, he'll most likely fold all hands except for pocket pairs trying to hit a set. Even then, he'll probably lay down his smaller pocket pairs unless he has at least one other caller to give him appropriate implied odds. It's also valid to include suited connectors in his calling distribution if the pot is three-way or more. Thus, if you have position on a Location Station who limps preflop, you can usually pick up the pot by raising preflop, provided the table dynamic is such that the players behind you will fold to a raise. In other words, a good way to beat a Location Station is to become one yourself whenever you have position over such a foe.

When a Location Station calls your preflop raise and then checks to you on the flop, go ahead and make a continuation bet. If he bets into you, raise with top pair or better. Also, raise with almost any hand if the Location Station you are facing employs stop-and-gos with pocket pairs. Since most Location Stations understand the math of the flop helping no one, employing a tricky stop-and-go is not out of the question for the Location Station you are facing. You can also blow him off his blocking bet with a big reraise in position on the flop. In general, though, you should typically follow the top pair or better rule when facing aggression from a Location Station in response to aggression from you.

If the Location Station leads out on the turn, he was either trapping on the flop by calling, or he's making a blocking bet with top pair or a draw. Your best line of play, provided you have top pair with a good kicker, is to raise again on the turn. Either you will take the pot there, or the Location Station will call and check the river. If he does bet again on the river (or reraise you on the turn), your top pair is probably no longer good. Looking at this line of play, if you have two pair or better, you should simply aggress on all betting rounds, except that if a Location Station bets into you on the river, you should call instead of raising with hands worse than something like top two pair.

When a Location Station raises preflop from positions other than the button or cutoff, figure that he has a good starting hand. This type of player underscores the danger of recklessly applying general tags like loose and tight to your foes. Location Stations have a huge preflop raising percentage, but that high percentage comes from ruthlessly abusing position when they have it. If you are playing online shorthanded NLHE, such a player can have a PFR in the 20–30 percent range. However, despite that big PFR, Location Stations have solid hands when they are neither the button nor the cutoff. Playing the Location Station when he raises out of position is pretty much like playing a Tighty Tighterson except that his continuation-betting percentage with unpaired hole cards like AK will be much higher. Despite the higher continuation-betting percentage, your primary game plan when a Location Station raises out of position is to have a hand, hit your hand, or skip the hand.

You'll also have position against a Location Station when he's the cutoff, and you are the button, but in this case, you can expect him to be raising with a wide range of hands. Since you have position on him, reraising him with [AA,66]||[AK,AT] is a good way to go. This may earn you a check from him on the flop, when your weapon of choice will be the $\frac{2}{3}$ pot bet. Given his wide raising distribution, you might reraise preflop with a much wider distribution to try to slow him down. Another option is to flat-call his raises more frequently; however, since he'll be tossing a lot of continuation bets your way, tend to keep reraising until he gets wise to your tricks. If he starts pulling stop-and-gos by calling your reraises and leading out on the flop, then you need to either raise him some fraction of the time on the flop as a bluff or start reraising him less preflop.

When He's Not a Blind and He Has Position on You

Since a Location Station is going to raise a large percentage of pots in position, a good strategy is to beat him to the punch by raising preflop before he has a chance to. Location Stations *hate* this. They just don't like to get involved in pots in which they aren't the primary aggressor, so most of the time they'll fold to your raise preflop.

Cases where a limp may be warranted are the times that you have a big hand and want to limp-reraise. The obvious problem of limp-reraising is that it's an obvious play. You may have to disguise it by limp-reraising with hands other than your best ones. Otherwise, you won't get much more money out of the Location Station, as there's a good chance that he'll just fold his hand to your limp-reraise. We've said that loose callers aren't necessarily loose bettors, and the converse is also true:

> Loose raisers aren't necessarily loose callers.

Therefore, the way to employ the limp-reraise is to expand your distribution to hands like [AA,88]|||[AK,AQ]. You don't necessarily want to limp-reraise every time you get these hands. To keep a proper limp-reraise percentage to slow him down, you may actually widen this distribution a bit more, but use a mixed strategy as to when to raise outright with [AA,88]||[AK,AQ] and when to attempt a limp-reraise.

Regardless of the particular distribution and mixed strategy you use, understand its goal. Against other players, you'd be limp-reraising to capture their initial preflop raises. Against the Location Station, you're limp-reraising to slow him down and move him off his very effective line of play: unmolested aggression in position.

Postflop, if you find yourself heads-up against a Location Station when he has position, you have a few options—one of which *isn't* to check-fold every time you miss and bet out or check-raise every time you hit. Because of the (in)frequency with which you hit flops and because a Location Station is going to shut down as soon as you show any aggression, he's not going to pay you off when you actually do hit a flop. The key to beating a Location Station is to introduce a percentage of bluffs where you lead into him or check-raise him on the flop. You may also wish to include a third class of bluffs in which you check-call the flop and lead-bluff the turn. You don't want to overdo these moves because you want the Location Station to continue to think that you have a hand when you bet. Mix in a small percentage of bluffs, and play your bluffs the same way as your made hands, thus tipping the scales of EV in your favor.

That said, you really shouldn't be getting involved in too many pots out of position against this player. You can try to slow him down, but the other way to beat him is to let him loosen up the rest of the table while you sit back. Though if you play ultratight, your attentive opponents won't give you lots of shots at their chips. So first see if your opponents will allow you to lay out. If they will, that's great. If they won't, then you need to give yourself a looser image, and one reliable way of doing that is to become a Location Station yourself.

Play in the Blinds

When you are a blind and action is folded to a Location Station in the cutoff or on the button, the Location Station will try to steal the blinds an overwhelming percentage of the time. Because of this, you'll be very tempted to start defending your blinds more often than you should. When you are the big blind and a Location Station raises to 3BB or less, you are justified in defending your blind when you have two high cards; however, you aren't getting the right price to call a large percentage of his raises from the small blind. Also, since you're out of position, you shouldn't be reraising too often. If you do, you'll find yourself playing a lot of big pots out of position, and that's not how to win at shorthanded NLHE, no matter how much of a blind stealer your opponent is. The unfortunate reality is that you'll have to surrender to many of the Location Station's steals in four- to six-handed games. In a three-handed game, you'll have to defend somewhat liberally as the big blind, but again, don't make the mistake of reraising too much. Against a Location Station or just in general, for success in shorthanded play:

> *Play small pots out of position and large pots in position.*

When you are both in the blinds, you can probably take a fair number of pots by raising from the big blind when Location Station limps from the small blind. If he raises from the small blind when it's folded to him, clock him to see if he habitually raises in this situation or not. It's very tempting to extrapolate his positional play to his play in the small blind; however, not all Location Stations will actually do so, since they know they'll be out of position and since they prize position so highly. Assume, then, that he has a legitimate holding the first two times and play accordingly. If he does it three consecutive times, it's time to start reraising him occasionally to play some bigger pots in position (recall that "third time's the adjustment"). Because of the implied odds associated with his continuation bet, combined with the money already in the pot and your positional advantage, you are able to call with more hands.

Dr. Overbite
Modus Operandi

All the players discussed so far tend to make their bets in proportion to the size at the pot. Dr. Overbite, though, is an overbettor who doesn't really care about pot size. Well, he does care, but his bets are usually overbets anyhow. Preflop, he'll open for 8BB or 10BB or—in the classic Grandstand Overbet—everything he's got. When he reraises, he tends to slam in at a minimum of five times the amount of the previous raise. Postflop, his bets are generally two to three times the pot.

Some Overbites are loose and get involved in lots of pots. Other Overbites are tight players who simply do not want their opponents to draw out on them. Still others are not normally Overbites but may become so when they have good hands, and they believe that they can trick their opponents into thinking that they are bluffing. Some just have no clue.

In a fullhanded setting, you can afford to sit and wait against Overbites, for there the only question is usually just which player is going to take down the inevitable large pot and send Dr. Overbite home. Unfortunately, in shorthanded NLHE, especially three- or four-handed games, you can't always afford to sit and wait as you would in a fullhanded game. You need to know what kind of Overbite you're facing, and once you know that, the proper game plan will materialize.

When He's Not a Blind and You Have Position on Him

With this player, we need to reevaluate how we think of pre-flop play. Against most opponents, you aren't getting proper odds to call and hit a flop unless they make a mistake and give you big implied odds. Overbites are different, though. Suppose you're in a game with $1–$2 blinds and your Overbite opens to $10. You have AJ. Assuming the most likely scenario that everyone folds behind you, you are getting $13:$10 on your money. When you call, the pot will be $23. Most likely, the Overbite will put in a bet that's at least the size of the pot on the flop, meaning that you are really getting $36:$10 on your call, and we haven't even considered further betting action. Granted, you have to consider reverse implied odds; however, against a player who likes to make very large bets, you're getting good odds to hit a flop—if you have the stomach for it. Your stack size will be more volatile, so it's imperative that you don't let your stack fluctuations affect your psychological state.

Because the pots get large with Overbites and you'll be faced with pricey decisions, you need to be in the pot only with hands that give you a good shot at hitting a big flop. You want to have top pair with a very good kicker to continue past the flop. Even though the Overbite is probably raising with a large range of hands—many of which you could possibly beat—you can nevertheless afford to wait for a premium hand because of the sizes of his raises relative to the blinds. Be patient. You'll get your shot.

When you have high pocket pairs, you probably want to reraise the Overbite immediately preflop and put him to a decision for his stack right there. If he demonstrates that he'll back down in the face of aggression, you may wish to reraise occasionally with [AK,AQ] and possibly a few other hands. Just remember that since his bets are so large compared with the price of an orbit, you are in no rush to get involved.

When He's Not a Blind and He Has Position on You

Depending on how often he raises preflop, you may consider a limp-reraise with your strongest hands, especially if the Overbite you face is not observant and won't notice that you've screwed down your starting requirements against him. Against most players, the limp-reraise won't get you a whole lot, but since Dr. Overbite's raise is much bigger than average, limp-reraising is actually a viable way to squeeze out some extra value.

With your weaker raising hands, you are better off just taking the initiative and raising preflop. This is especially true if the Overbite will usually back down in the face of aggression. However, if the Overbite likes to reraise, then you need to tighten your raising distribution. Also, if the Overbite likes to reraise, you should immediately raise with hands like AA instead of looking to limp-reraise.

Postflop, when you hit a hand, you want to bet into an Overbite, luring him into coming back over the top. Before responding to that move, stop to consider what the Overbite's over-the-top distribution is and decide whether you want to go all-in. Many players are tempted just to call the raise.

However, if tricky cards—cards that can complete draws—might fall in favor of an Overbite, the worst thing you can do is slowplay a big pot. Each pot against an Overbite is big, so any mistake you make in a pot against an Overbite is potentially catastrophic. Therefore, against aggressive Overbites, you want to get the money in whenever you are sure you are ahead in the hand.

Play in the Blinds

Because his raises will be large with respect to the blinds and because he'll have position on you, it's usually not a good idea to defend many blinds against an Overbite. You can afford to sit and wait, so do so. It may be frustrating letting a fair number of your blinds go, but the Overbite is betting so much with respect to the blinds that it doesn't matter. Given the distribution of quality hands, if you're heads-up or three-handed against an Overbite, your stack will get blinded down about 5BB, and then you'll get in a big pot. You'll be blinded down another 5BB, and you'll be in another big pot. Of course, you won't win every big pot, but you should stand to win more big pots in the long run.

If you and an Overbite are both blinds and you are the big blind, you should raise a fair number of hands preflop behind an Overbite's limp to get a bigger pot when you have the positional advantage. By inflating the pot, you're forcing the Overbite to invest a larger quantity of chips. Being somewhat aggressive in these scenarios also gives off the image that you aren't simply waiting around for the nuts. It's going to be hard for you to get paid off, even by an Overbite, if you come across as a nit.

Because of the inflated pot sizes, your hands against an Overbite can be the make-or-break hands of your session.

Similarly, a heads-up match against an Overbite is a high variance affair. Practice patience, keep your cool, and avoid pissing contests. Eventually, Dr. Overbite will hang himself with his lengthy and jubilantly tossed rope.

Closing Words Regarding the Player Archetypes

The profiles presented in this chapter reflect the playing styles we commonly encounter when we play shorthanded NLHE. Recalling the squished pigeon paradigm, don't expect to find players who fit these archetypes precisely, and don't attempt to bend reality to fit your preconceptions. You'll certainly encounter players who mix attributes of various archetypes and also players with tendencies not discussed. It's a good idea to assign archetype values to the players you face—to name a thing is to own a thing, yeah?—and to adapt the strategies outlined here to fit the foes you face.

The key thing to remember is that neither you nor your opponents will hit the flop. Given that by-now well-given given, just go to work and figure out your specific edges against specific foes. Some players and tables are so aggressive that your biggest advantage will be patient waiting. Others will let you hammer away at them and completely control the action. Against yet other opponents, you'll need to tease out the betting patterns that lead to successful bluffs. And finally, some foes will require maximum creativity and fortitude or—never a terrible move—a strategic retreat.

Exercises

1. What are the defining characteristics of a Tighty Tighterson and basic strategy against him?

2. What are the defining characteristics of a Cally Wally and basic strategy against him?

3. What are the defining characteristics of a Serial Dater and basic strategy against him?

4. What are the defining characteristics of a BenBucks and basic strategy against him?

5. What are the defining characteristics of a Location Station and basic strategy against him?

6. What are the defining characteristics of a Dr. Overbite and basic strategy against him?

7. You are the cutoff in a five-handed $200NL game with $1–$2 blinds. A Tighty Tighterson (stack size about $180) limps UTG. The button is a Cally Wally (stack size about $140), the small blind is a Location Station (stack size about $300), and the big blind is a Tighty Tighterson (stack size about $250). You have QT suited. What's your decision preflop?

8. You are the big blind in a four-handed $600NL game with $3–$6 blinds. A Location Station raises to $20 UTG. The button and the small blind fold. You have K♥T♥. What's your play?

9. Suppose you call in the situation described in question 8. The flop is Q♥7♥2♦. What do you do?

10. You're in a shorthanded $50NL ($.25–$.50 blinds) game that has just gone two-handed, leaving you heads-up against a Dr. Overbite who has now raised four consecutive hands from the button to $4. You are in the big blind and the Overbite raises to $4 again. You hold A♥T♦. Before the hand started, you both had $80. What's your line of play?

11. Same situation as in question 10, but now you and the Overbite have $20. What's your line of play?

12. You are in a six-handed $100NL game with $1–$2 blinds. You limp UTG with K♣J♠. UTG+1 folds. The cutoff, a BenBucks, calls. The button folds. The small blind, a Cally Wally, completes, and the big blind, a Tighty Tighterson, checks. The flop is K♦T♣5♦. The blinds check to you, and you bet $5. BenBucks raises to $20, and the blinds fold. BenBucks has about $70 left, and you have about $50 left. What's your play?

13. If you had to define yourself in terms of these archetypes, what label would you assign?

Answers

1. A Tighty Tighterson only enters hands with strong holdings. Some Tighty Tightersons will raise with hands like AQ unsuited, but others will just call with them. With really strong hands like AA, some Tighty Tightersons will raise while others will attempt to slow-play. After raising preflop with unpaired hole cards, they usually don't continuation bet when they miss the flop.

Postflop, Tighty Tightersons employ very little trickery. When they bet or raise, they have something. When they check, they don't. When faced with a bet, a Tighty Tighterson typically needs top pair or better to proceed.

When facing a Tighty Tighterson, you want to throw bets in early to push him out of hands. When you get resistance, you need to back down unless you have a holding that matches up favorably against his distribution.

2. A Cally Wally plays lots of hands, and he typically does so passively. He may play somewhat tighter in raised pots, but he will be in a large percentage of those too. Even though he's in a lot of hands, a preflop raise means that he has something good. Cally Wallies are generally passive in nature.

Postflop, Cally Wallies will call with a wide range of holdings, especially when the bets they face aren't prohibitively big. When they have draws, they seldom consider whether they are receiving proper pot odds to justify drawing; they simply call and hope to hit their draws. Though Cally Wallies call a lot, aggression on their part means that they've hit the board at least relatively hard. However, some Cally Wallies slowplay their big hands by playing them passively like they play their other holdings.

To win money from a Cally Wally, do two things: First, beware his raises, for they signal real strength. Second, value bet his ass to death.

3. Preflop, a Serial Dater is similar to a Cally Wally in that he will be involved in a ton of pots, veering possibly to a more aggressive stance preflop.

Postflop, a Serial Dater resembles a Tighty Tighterson.

To stay involved in the face of aggression, he needs a solid hand or a draw for which he's getting great odds. In terms of their own aggression, Serial Daters will vary. Some Serial Daters will bet made hands and will sometimes even semi-bluff. Other Serial Daters may bet hands like top pair but slowplay monsters like sets and flopped straights.

To beat them, just press them, for they will back down easily when faced with aggression.

4. A BenBucks is generally defined by his aggressiveness and lack of fear. Preflop, he tends to enter lots of hands, either pressing hard with a bully's stance or limping along, calling raises, and looking for postflop opportunities. His preflop raising requirements have more to do with situational analysis than cards. Really, he is capable of anything from raising with 23 offsuit to smooth-calling a raise with AA.

Postflop, a BenBucks is typically highly aggressive. When he senses weakness, he bets and raises, regardless of his holdings. He's sometimes exceedingly optimistic about counting his outs, so pushing him out of pots can be difficult. He loves to semi-bluff his draws, but when he has a big hand he looks to lay back and let his foes throw chips at him. He occasionally makes unwarranted calls, but he's far from being a bad player. To the contrary, a BenBucks is usually a tough foe to play against.

The key consideration against a BenBucks is that cards do not matter nearly as much as situations and perceptions of what his opponents will do. He focuses on outplaying his opponents rather than simply waiting for hands to win. To beat him, you must match him thought for thought, bet for bet, and ploy for ploy. He will test you, so be prepared to be tested.

5. When not the cutoff or the button, a Location Station plays very much like a Tighty Tighterson. When he's either the cutoff or the button, a Location Station plays very aggressively with a wide range of hands, provided that no one has entered the pot yet. Some Location Stations will be highly aggressive with a wide range of hands even when limpers are already in. Typically, a Location Station wants to get heads-up postflop where he's likely to take the pot down with a continuation bet. In the face of aggression, he'll fold all but the best hands when he's the cutoff or the button.

The reason that Location Stations are so aggressive preflop is that they like to be the primary aggressor postflop. Postflop, Location Stations are very aggressive against passive opponents. When their opponents take initiative in a hand, Location Stations often back down. With tough hands like top pair, Location Stations like to use ploys such as raising on the turn to get a free showdown on the river. When out of position, they tend to use blocking bets. Location Stations use ploys like these so they don't have to make decisions about difficult calls.

To beat a Location Station, steal his initiative by stealing his position through frequent preflop raises. Also recognize his blocking bets for what they are...an (unsuccessful, one hopes) attempt to slow you down.

6. Dr. Overbite is characterized by his practice of making bets that are inordinately large with respect to the pot size. Preflop, his standard opening raise will be to eight or ten big blinds. Overbites vary in how many hands they play. They are typically mildly loose, but it's best not to make assumptions; rather, let your observations speak for themselves.

Postflop, Overbites will typically bet amounts

around two to three times the size of the pot. Some Overbites are habitual bluffers, while others use their overbetting as a ploy to deceive their opponents into thinking they're bluffing when they're not.

Patience is the key to winning against Dr. Overbite. Give him time and he'll give you money, it's really as simple as that.

7. The Tighty Tighterson who just limped will most likely fold to your preflop raise, unless his limp UTG is a slow-play. The players in the blinds are also likely to fold to your raise if the Cally Wally on the button folds. Your major problem is that the Cally Wally to your left will most likely call your raise, putting you heads-up out of position against an opponent against whom a postflop continuation bet will have no benefit. If Wally's call should bring in the blinds, you will end up in a multi-way pot without benefiting from last action and holding the very modest QT. This situation is not really desirable either. The best play here is to limp to keep the pot small and to give yourself better implied odds for the times you make a big hand. In NLHE generally, you want to play small pots in marginal or uncertain situations and save the building of big pots for when you have a clear edge.

8. This is a tough problem, especially without more nuanced information about your opponent. Let's first examine pot odds. There's currently $20 + $3 + $6 = $29 in the pot, and you have to call $14, meaning you are getting $29:$14, or about 2:1, on your money. These are very marginal odds considering you have to play the rest of the hand out of position. Still, you're not without options and not without lines of play.

You know that the Location Station will most likely continuation bet when he misses the flop, meaning that one way of playing the hand is to check-raise when you hit the flop. If you get reraised or called, you'll face some tricky decisions on later rounds, but the most likely outcome is the Location Station folding to your check-raise. In fact, you may wish to throw in a small percentage of check-raise bluffs here as well.

Another line of play is to call the preflop raise and then bet at the flop no matter what it is. If the Location Station won't play back unless he has a hand, this is a great line of play. If the Location Station will raise such a bet as a bluff or call with the intention of bluffing on a later round, then use the stop-and-go only when you hit the flop. You can also consider check-calling the flop with the intention of bluffing later in the hand.

While you may consider reraising the Location Station preflop, this will result in your playing an inflated pot out of position. Though it will signal to him that he can't run over you with sheer aggression, it may open the door to his winning lots of easy large pots. It's better to keep pots small when you're out of position.

There's nothing wrong with folding here, as it will keep you out of trouble when out of position—always a good thing. While KT would probably be good against the Location Station's hand if you could get to the river with no further betting action, considering that you need to survive three rounds of out-of-position play, the value of your KT goes way down.

Depending on the texture of the particular game you are in, your overall strategy will be heavily weighted toward calling or folding. When you call preflop, you should primarily use check-raises and stop-and-goes to control the action from the flop forward.

9. You flopped a nine outer, probably a twelve outer, or possibly even a fifteen outer (if your ten turns out to be good, though that ten can be tricky, because you don't want to get caught on second pair against an aggressive opponent when you are out of position). Bet out or check-raise on the flop, considering both of these actions to be semi-bluffs, for you'd rather win the pot on the flop than get stuck playing your draw out of position on the turn and the river. With all your outs, especially if you're on the high side of that number, it's not the end of the world if you go to the turn, but you definitely want the pot to be larger when you get there, since check-calling the flop won't net you good implied odds. This opponent will tread cautiously if a heart falls and probably fold to any pot-sized bets.

   In shorthanded NLHE, draws are primarily profitable as semi-bluffing hands. By semi-bluffing, you win the hand by improving or by making your opponents fold.

10. You are both deeply stacked, meaning that against such an opponent, you have plenty of time to sit and wait, which makes folding an acceptable line of play. Calling is okay too, for you have the implied odds of an obliging foe if you hit your hand. You'll need to flop top pair or better to go to war, but with top pair, you'll need to be cautious. Dr. Overbite knows that you are sitting around and waiting, so stacking him with top pair isn't as easy as it may seem. When you hit your hand, your options are to check-call the flop and bet the turn or to check-raise the flop. Betting out on the flop works as well, especially if you're running scripted stop-and-go bluffs as part of your game plan.

    Reraising preflop isn't a great option because you're both so deeply stacked. If you are sure that Dr. Overbite won't get up and leave the game if he wins a big pot, then you can reraise to about $15, prepared to go all-in on the flop with top pair or better. In general, it's better to call and trap against Overbites. Remember: give them time and they'll give you money.

11. Your hand is now an excellent hand with which to go all-in preflop. AT is way ahead of Dr. Overbite's distribution, and because you are short-stacked, you will be called by a large range of inferior hands. Good times!

12. Is he semi-bluffing? Does he have a set? Does he have bottom pair? Who knows? This is what's so tricky about BenBucks. You can call here and see what happens on the turn; however, since you are way ahead of his distribution and since you only have enough to raise $30, you might as well get all the money in the pot when you are ahead—you will be called by pretty much any hand.

Note that if you and BenBucks are both deeply stacked here—say about $200 each—the hand becomes much more problematic. On the flop, you may actually want to check to see what BenBucks does. If he bets, maybe you check-raise him. If you bet and he raises, then you should just call the raise. You don't want to make the pot any bigger with two more rounds of betting action. You are then probably constrained to betting the turn and the river and resigned to folding if BenBucks raises, even though we know he's capable of raising as a bluff, especially if he's aware that you like to employ blocking bets. Maybe you check-call the turn and bet the river. Realistically, you'll need to employ all these lines of play in various hands you play against BenBucks.

Some players in this position will go with the all-in

overbet to avoid being put to further tough decisions by BenBucks throughout the hand. This is about the worst thing you can do, as such large overbets are highly -EV. They will only get called by hands that have you beaten. If you are that scared to go toe-to-toe with this foe, just evacuate the area. Other battles against other, weaker foes abound.

13.

6

♣♠♦♥

SHORTHANDED
TOURNAMENT PLAY

♣♠♦♥

Cash Game Considerations Versus
Tournament Considerations

To this point, we've discussed shorthanded NLHE in the context of cash games, which have several defining characteristics, the key one being that if you bust out you can buy back in. Also, in cash games chips are equivalent to precisely defined monetary payouts; a dollar chip is worth a dollar cash. In other words, your chip EV is equivalent to your monetary EV. Well, for the most part it is; considerations for future hands have to be taken into account because even in a cash game hands aren't independent of each other. We've emphasized that every hand you play leaves impressions in your opponents' minds that you can take advantage of in later hands. In addition, a player nursing a short stack with no intention of rebuying may value his chips, at least psychologically, more than his deeply stacked foes'. Another defining consideration of cash game play is that the blinds never escalate, and even though stack sizes are important for some decisions, players are usually stacked deeply enough so that stack size isn't a primary decision metric in cash games. Finally, in cash games, unlike in tournaments, you can leave any time you want. All of which serve to make tournament NLHE an entirely different beast.

Don't take this to mean that the material we've covered in the cash game section of this book doesn't apply, for it does. But now new variables enter the picture, some of which override typical cash game considerations. The biggest difference between cash game NLHE and tournament NLHE is that chips no longer directly correlate with monetary expectation. In a cash game, a dollar won is a dollar win, but in a tournament, a single chip of the smallest denomination can be the difference between busting out and going on to victory. Since as poker players we're always looking for the main chance—the highest possible profit—when we enter the tournament setting, we need to weigh pure chip EV against other factors that affect overall tournament EV: a money finish and a big payday.

In our discussion of shorthanded NLHE cash games, we noted situations where making marginally -EV moves on a particular hand could result in a higher overall session EV. This idea exists in tournament play, but with a different spin. Usually in cash games, most of the mildly -EV moves you make will be of an aggressive nature, where secondary benefits include image management and table control. In tournaments, more of your -EV moves will involve getting chips into a large pot even though the pot odds may not actually be sufficient for you to be +EV with respect to chips. To carve out an oversimplified example, if you were equally stacked against someone who you knew, 100 percent sure, could outplay you and crush you over time, you'd happily take the short side of a coin-flip situation, your AK versus his pocket fives, say, for the slightly -EV shot at winning the tournament in one stroke, rather than the much larger -EV situation of having to play it out.

Similarly, and taking the skill differential out of the equation, you'll occasionally find yourself in very large pots offering a large percentage of the remaining tournament chips where it may be best to risk your chips even if you know that you're an underdog with respect to pure chip EV. The reverse is also true: from time to time, you may decline situations that are marginally +EV to preserve opportunities for higher +EV down the road. It's tough to imagine ever doing this in a cash game,[1] but doing so is a part of any successful tournament strategy.

Tournaments also depart from cash games in that, apart from tournaments structured as shootouts,[2] most shorthanded tournament situations occur during a tournament's end stage, when players typically have few chips relative to the blinds. This usually means that someone is all-in before the river—probably before the flop. Therefore, the dynamics of shorthanded tournament play differ from the deeply stacked cash game dynamics we've considered up until now. Abusing position, rampant continuation bets, and making bets to get information or to derive value aren't automatic plays in shorthanded tournament settings the way they are in most cash game settings. Opponents' relative stack sizes become an integral part of the decision-making process, especially since the blinds in a tournament continually increase.

In short, if you're a solid cash game player, you have a firm foundation for tournament play, but you'll need to make some key adjustments in order to succeed.

---

1. Though playing against one's wife or girlfriend is an example that comes to mind.

2. A shootout is a tournament that takes place across many rounds. The winner or winners from each table advance to the next round.

Overview of Shorthanded
Tournament Situations

If you are in a shorthanded tournament situation, you are probably in one of a few well-defined situations:

1. You are in a small Multi-Table Tournament (MTT) in which only the final table pays, and only eleven or twelve players remain, meaning that you are playing five- or six-handed at one of two tables until only ten (or in some cases nine) players remain in the tournament.

2. You are in a large MTT that is down to eleven or twelve players. Because it's a large MTT, you are already deep in the money; however, the final table is where the big payouts are. To reach the final table, you must survive five- or six-handed play until only ten (or in some cases nine) players remain.

3. You are at the final table of an MTT, and six or fewer players remain.

4. You are in an MTT satellite event where all spots at the final table pay, and there are only eleven or twelve players left, meaning that you must make it through five- or six-handed play to win your seat.

5. You are in an MTT satellite event where only the top few spots win seats to larger events, and the tournament is down to eleven or twelve players, meaning that you need to get through some shorthanded play to get closer to winning a seat.

6. You are in an MTT satellite event where only the top few spots pay, and you are shorthanded at the final table,

meaning that you only have to outlast one or two more opponents to get your seat.

7. You are in a regular single-table tournament (STT) with a 50/30/20 payout, and you are down to six or fewer players.

8. You are in an STT satellite where the winner or the top two get seats.

9. You are playing in an STT that started with only six players (we'll call this a 6-max STT).

10. You are playing in an MTT that's played exclusively with shorthanded tables.

11. You are in an MTT that's played as a shootout.

12. You are playing in an STT that started as a heads-up freeze out—or you are simply playing heads-up.

While these situations can have wildly varying considerations, they generally all occur at a point in the tournament where the difference between payouts is large. Mistakes made in these shorthanded tournament situations will be much more costly than similar mistakes made in cash games. To be a successful tournament player, you must be good at shorthanded play, good at avoiding key mistakes, and constantly aware of how your specific shorthanded situation differs from general shorthanded cash game play. And the situation can change, literally, from hand to hand!

In this chapter we're going to walk you through all the shorthanded tournament situations just outlined, and give you a strategic overview for playing them correctly. We'll cover all aspects of shorthanded tournament play except for heads-up freeze outs (#12), and heads-up play in the other scenarios...which we'll get to in the next chapter.

Case #1
MTT with Eleven or Twelve Players;
Only the Final Table Gets Money

To get an idea of how you want to play at this stage of the tournament, let's get some concrete numbers in mind. We'll use a sample $100 buy-in tournament with 90 entrants. The typical payout structure for such a tournament will be something like that in Table 6.1.

TABLE 6.1: Payout Scheme for a $100 Tournament with Ninety Entrants

FINISH	PRIZE
1st	$2,500
2nd	$1,700
3rd	$1,150
4th	$900
5th	$750
6th	$600
7th	$500
8th	$400
9th	$300
10th	$200

When you are down to twelve players, your strategy considerations will be dominated by your stack size and your foes' stack sizes relative to the blinds. Given the top-heavy payouts, you generally want to try to play to place in the top three. Some players, of course, rate any money finish as a good day's work, but we here at KPHQ don't ascribe to that notion. "Be in it to win it!" we say,[3] though there will be times when you have four or five opponents with very large stacks compared to yours, and so you might resign yourself simply to sneaking as far up the pay ladder as possible.

Things can get brutal when the last two tables turn short. Sensing a shot at a final table (and the same high money finish you're eying), players snug up and become extremely tight, meaning that if you're relatively short stacked, it's difficult to double up to position yourself for strong final table play. Though many people pay lip service to "be in it to win it," no one really wants to get eleventh place and go home without any money; everyone at this point has a high utility associated with placing in the money. With the possible exception of the chip leaders, no one is playing to win—everyone is simply playing not to die.

If you're deeply stacked, your primary objective is to accumulate even more chips. The worst mistake that you can make as a big stack at this point is to tighten up, play timidly, and go on cruise control into fifth or fourth. This might be a natural reaction—"Let's ride the big stack home"—but the fact of rising blinds means that your big stack won't be big for long, unless you augment it right here and right now. Remember that your foes will trend tentative, so take advantage and raise preflop relentlessly, probably two or three times an orbit.

Test the waters. If your foes fight back, slow down. But if they don't match you pressure for pressure, then the only time you shouldn't raise is if you have a poor holding and there's a short stack of less than 6BB waiting to act behind

---

3. We also say, "Aloneness is the oasis of time," but have yet to figure out why we do.

you. If you raise in that instance and the short stack goes all-in, you're committed to calling the all-in because you'll have proper odds with any two cards; however, even though your opponents already know you're a bigger thief than a Hollywood accountant, there's nothing worse than actually having to show that T3 offsuit you raised with. Talk about squandering your fold equity!

Another time to hit the brakes preflop is if your opponents are willing to call along and play pots with you. In this case, you still want to mix things up, but now you have to play value poker. Since you have a commanding chip lead (and skill lead, image lead, and hack read, having read this book), it's better to play lots of smaller pots than fewer big ones. You don't want to spend your +EV on one or two reckless adventures.

Being a big stack is nice, and it presents the challenge of how to handle prosperity. But what if you're not a big stack? Prohibitive chip leads are rare. What if you're on the short side of medium, jousting around, trying to make things work? First of all, if you have such a stack, don't spook yourself into survival mode. Anytime you're at least within a double up of having an average stack, you're not playing for survival just yet. You still have a chance to go for the kill. To win a tournament, you can't be scared of being knocked out. In it to win it, right?

Trouble is, a short stack is the wrong weapon for trying to steal pots. Or let's say it's a gun with too few bullets. You can't push all-in two or three times an orbit, because you'll only be able to steal so many times before someone wakes up with a real hand and takes a stand. Furthermore, even tight opponents will loosen up their calling requirements if they see you going all-in too rampantly. Selective stealing, then, is your line of play here while you look for a good double up opportunity: one where your chances are better than about 55 percent to win the hand.

Keep your eye peeled for limpers. Some players, usually in the interest of keeping pots small, will choose to limp instead of to raise. If a loose big stack limps, you should be ready to pull the all-in trigger with any ace or any pocket pair. There will be times when the big stack will have limped with a hand like A7, or even AA, and your A2 will be crushed (or, *mirable visu*, you suck out), but usually an all-in here results in the limper and the blinds folding, meaning you're getting 2.5BB instead of just 1.5BB for your risk.

Watch warily for limps from unexpected quarters. A limp from a player who rarely limps or a limp from a player with six or fewer big blinds is usually a trap in a tournament. In fact, against such limpers, you seriously have to consider mucking hands like Big Slick or Slickerella, which are normally huge hands for a short-to-medium stack at a short-handed table.

While limpers are common in this phase, aggressors are equally abundant, and you'll need a plan to deal with them. If there's a highly active big stack at your table, your job is simply to find a hand to push all-in with for value. Against an aggressive big stack, your over-the-top distribution should be something like [AA,22]||[AK,A2]. You may also wish to put KQ in this distribution, and if you know the aggressive player is willing to lay down hands to an over-the-top all-in of 7–8BB, you can also throw in hands like KJ and KT. The key is knowing your foes: is this aggressive raiser someone who will raise with QT and fold to pressure, or is he looking to take his big stack against your smaller stack in what he perceives to be a coin-flip situation? We know that pushing with low pocket pairs is likely to end up putting you in a 56-44 situation (when accounting for overpairs in your opponents' distributions, it's more likely that you are closer to 50-50), but you need to gamble to double up and get chips. Remember that most of the tournament EV lies in the top three spots. Facing a 50 percent chance of elimination is worth it at this point if it drastically improves your chances of placing very high.

Let's now assume that you have around 10BB, a little better than all-in mode. With such a stack, you can sometimes afford to make one raise to 2.5BB or 3BB without sacrificing all your wiggle room if you have to fold. You should probably make this raise either as a complete steal, as the first one into the pot, or with high pocket pairs. With your other highly valuable hands such as AK, you want to push all-in to avoid seeing a flop in a situation where you'll miss two thirds of the time. If you decide to raise without going all-in, keep in mind that when you raise as a 10BB stack, and someone goes over the top, he probably has a legitimate hand because the player going over the top has to assume that you aren't raising as a pure steal. Thus, don't be too quick, as many players are, to call an over-the-top all-in with KQ and bad aces.[4] Players who make this call love to say "I put you on a low or medium pocket pair," but they don't realize—or, more properly, acknowledge—that their opponents are also going over the top with hands like [AA,QQ]||[AK,A8].

If you have 10BB and raise preflop without going all-in, any flat-call will hand you a tough decision on the flop. If you hit the flop or flop a hand with twelve or more outs, you should probably push the rest of your stack to try to take the pot. The only exception might be flopping bottom pair against an opponent—especially a straightforward one—who has already bet into you on the flop. Should you have absolutely nothing on the flop, you'll have to give up if your opponent bets into you. If you're in early position or if your opponent checks to

---

4. In fact, don't be too quick to do anything. At a time when decisions matter most, *think things through.* Even online, where the clock ticks fast, there's always at least a moment or two to collect your thoughts and come to a considered—if not always correct—decision.

you when you're in late position, you may have to push and just hope for the best.

Recognize that some players expect this move—you'd be on the lookout for it yourself. If you can, try to identify these players. They'll call this type of all-in bet on the flop with any pocket pair and sometimes even with ace high. Not only that, they'll check from early position with such hands with the intention of calling your all-in. It's key to have effective countermeasures against this tactic and, simultaneously, to reduce the number of times you actually step into shit.

Let's assume that you're in early position. If your opponent will check behind when he misses the flop but will bet with the hands that he would have called your all-in with, then you're better off checking when you miss the flop, with the intention of folding if he bets, but pushing all-in on the turn if he checks behind. Against opponents who may check behind after having hit the flop, you are better off simply pushing all-in on the flop as not to give them a free card here.

In late position against a player who will check-call instead of betting when he hits the flop, your line of play is most likely a delayed continuation bet. If it goes check-check on the flop and your opponent checks to you again on the turn, then go all-in. It's a rare opponent who will check both the flop and the turn when he's hit the flop. At that point, he wouldn't expect to get paid off anyhow and would probably bet to deny you a free ride to the river. So take two checks at face value and take the pot on the turn.

Okay, that's what to do if you're within a double up of the average tournament stack size. What if you're in much worse shape? What if you need at least two double ups to get back in the hunt? Absent good luck, and then good luck again, you're probably looking at a war of attrition that leaves you, at best, with a low money finish. If you're in this situation, then you switch to "outlast" mode; recognizing, however, that outlast does not mean "fold every hand you're dealt." You can't fold all your hands, even if two or three other players share your plight, for if your other short-stacked opponents go all-in and double up, you'll be all alone in the no-fold equity zone and the other short stacks—now not so short as you are—will lay out and wait to see if you're eliminated on your inevitable all-in. You'll probably have to survive two all-ins before the other short stacks will again have to worry about you as a legitimate contender for a seat at the final table.

To be honest, we hate outlast mode and we hate the no-fold equity zone. We'd much rather make a move while we're still within a double up of average even if it means risking a no-money finish. We gotta go with our man Neil Young on this one: it's better to burn out than to fade away.[5]

If you have something like 5BB, the other short stacks happen to be in the blinds, and they have more than 3BB each, you should consider pushing all-in with any two cards. If the other short stacks are at the other table or if they simply aren't close to your left, you're looking to push any ace or pocket pair anytime you can be the first one into the pot. If your table is still six-handed and you're UTG, you might want to tighten up your distribution to something like [AA,77]||[AK,AT]; otherwise, it's go time!

Your approach to limpers is different when your stack is ultrashort. While you still had some weight to throw around, it was okay to try to throw it against a limper. Now, though, when you're sure to get called, you don't want to mess with limpers unless you have a premium hand like [AA,TT]||[AK,AQ]. Even tossing TT into this distribution is debatable because it opens the door to calls from many more hands against which you'll be only a 56-44 favorite.

To summarize, in most situations when you're down to

5. Why? Because rust never sleeps, that's why.

eleven or twelve players in a small MTT, your approach will be that of calculated aggression. Sometimes you will be highly aggressive, attempting a steal almost every hand; however, you will never let yourself get careless. Remember that every aggressive move and every risk you take should be logically justifiable before you make it. The only time you should lay out completely is when your stack is too short relative to the average chip stack. In that case the probability of you getting a top three finish is so low that you should simply focus on going as deep into the money as possible.

Case #2
MTT with Eleven or Twelve Players; Already In the Money

While this situation is different from case #1, it plays similarly because whether there's a money bubble or not, players typically assign extra psychological value, apart from monetary expectation, to making a final table. This usually puts them into survival mode and causes the same snugging up we discussed in the last scenario. Table 6.2 shows the payout structure for the top twelve from a Sunday Million Dollar Guaranteed Tournament on Party Poker. This tournament was a $200 + $15 MTT with 5,084 players.

Note that as with a smaller tournament where only the top ten places pay, there's no difference in payout between 12th and 11th place. While we'd be the last people on the planet to argue that two additional grand is nothing, as a percentage of the difference between 11th and 1st $\left(\frac{\$2,033.60}{\$154,533.60} = .013\right)$, it's really only 1 percent more than nothing. Thus, the top-heavy payouts still mean that you should be shooting for the top three spots, not just limping to 5th or 6th.

TABLE 6.2: Payouts for the Final Twelve Players in Huge MTT

FINISH	PRIZE
1st	$157,604
2nd	$86,021.28
3rd	$53,382
4th	$43,214
5th	$35,588
6th	$27,962
7th	$20,336
8th	$15,252
9th	$10,168
10th	$5,084
11th	$3050.40
12th	$3050.40

Your edge in this situation is your deep understanding of shorthanded play. Recognize that many of your foes will not know how to play this phase of the tournament correctly, and plan to capitalize on whatever errors they make—even if it means putting your tournament life on the line. At this point it's a good idea to chat up your opponents to discover, if you can, who's in it to win it, who's content just to cash, and who will sacrifice a top prize for the "glory" of a final table appearance. You'd also like to know who has a lot of final table or shorthanded experience of both, and as our mothers used to say, "It never hurts to ask."

If you're deeply stacked, and likely to stay that way for some time, you don't want to take any big risks for a lot of chips. The fact is, though, that the structure of most tournaments means you won't stay deeply stacked for as long as it takes to outplay your lesser foes. Thus, if action is going to become short stacked soon or if it already is short stacked, you need to be willing to push more marginal edges—edges in judgment as well as edges in EV—in turning-point tournament situations such as shorthanded play at the last two tables.

Case #3
Final Table of an MTT

Congratulations, you made the final table! What's more, since this is a book on shorthanded play, we also assume that you've battled through a few spots so that you're only five or fewer places away from the brass ring. Now all you have to do is find a way to grab it! Your decisions and actions here will be heavily stack dependent.

If you are among the shortest stacks at the table, you need to be very aggressive, making lots of preflop all-in moves. Whenever possible, launch your attacks against big blinds who have stack sizes similar to yours. For example, suppose you're the small blind and action folds to you. You have K9, normally a great hand to push with at this point. However, the big blind has a big stack: enough chips so that stealing a big blind from him doesn't mean much. But looking downstream, you see that someone with just 7BB is next to post the big blind. Fold your K9, and preserve your fold equity. Then, if you're able to be the first one in when the 7BB stack posts the big blind, steal no matter what two cards you have. We say this because the short-stacked big blind is more likely to have rags than a real hand and *much* more likely to play it safe and surrender his blind even with a hand like A9, since he knows that after the small blind he'll have a few more free shots at picking up a real hand.

Note that if you have only 4BB or 5BB, you'll need to push

with that K9, for fear of being shut out of steal opportunities when you're on the button or in the cutoff. But if you have around 8BB, then it's probably worth risking being pre-empted, especially since you expect to be dealt a better hand than K9 anyway.

Of course, you could always push all-in with the K9 and then push again on the very next hand, but you're likely to lose some fold equity if you go to the well too often. It's not that your opponents know that you pushed with K9 (they obviously don't); it's that you will have pushed two consecutive hands. Logic tells them that your second push, especially in position, is a naked steal, and either the small blind (remember, he has a big stack) or the big blind may very well decide to look you up. If you're going to make back-to-back pushes, you want the back half of your perfecta to be a premium hand.

Now let's imagine that you're among the chip leaders at this point. If you have a big stack, it's *not* your responsibility to make promiscuous calls to eliminate the short stacks. Instead, your job is to be the aggressor and to deny shorter stacks their vital first-in, all-in opportunities. Raise! Raise! Raise!

But beware of limpers.

You may face some opponents who limp habitually, and against such opponents, you can either limp to play a small pot or raise to keep the hand from going to a flop. But as we've already said, a limp from an opponent who usually enters a pot by raising or a limp from a player with six or less big blinds is a limp that signals big strength. Having a big stack is no reason to throw around chips to satisfy your curiosity or to snap off a bluff that ain't one. If you smell trouble, fold.

Case #4
MTT Satellite with Eleven or Twelve Players; All Final Table Spots Pay

To clarify the situation, we're talking about a satellite into a larger event where everyone who makes the final table gets an identical prize, regardless of order of finish. It may be a buy-in to a bigger event or a travel package including the buy-in, but the key consideration is that there's no premium on finishing first. This is a unique poker situation, and satellites like this veer further from cash games than any other form of tournament poker. Tournament play is always driven by considerations of relative stack size, but end-game play in equal-pay satellites is almost purely a function of this metric. Since all places pay identically in this situation, your only goal is to survive. If you can survive with the chips you have, there's simply no reason to gamble to get more.

What we typically find in this circumstance are a smattering of small stacks scattered across the two remaining shorthanded tables. These stacks face an infinite differential between payouts: nothing versus something. As such, they need to go all-in to try to steal blinds or double up. If there's a chance that others will bust first, they'd rather wait and do nothing, but they can't afford to wait too long. Because players are waiting each other out, they aren't entering pots with a huge range of hands. This is especially true if there's a monstrous stack at the table who can afford to take the worst of it several different times, with the prospect of ending the tournament as his upside and not much of a downside at all. If that prohibitive favorite is you, though, don't feel like you have to call every pesky short stack's all-in. Stick to calling with hands like [AA,77]||[AK,AT]. Of course, you should also be banging away with lots of preflop raising to reduce everyone's stacks or to force an all-in confrontation. If there's more than one big stack at the table, then you and he should implicitly collude to eliminate short stacks. This entails getting out of each other's way in big-versus-small shootouts and/or one big stack overcalling another and then checking it down in an effort to go two against one and blow a short stack into oblivion. It's not nice, but hey, that's poker.[6]

If you are a medium stack or a short stack, you don't want to be calling many all-ins. It's much more in your favor to push all-in when other short stacks are in the blinds. However, if you're in a situation where you're the only short stack at the table and the big stacks are constantly bombarding your blinds, you'll eventually need to fight back with a decent hand like [AA,99]||[AK,AJ]. Before pulling the all-in trigger, make sure you know what's going on at the other table. If you're playing online, have the other table open for your inspection. If you're playing live, stand up and look around. Try to watch some of the action at the other table between hands so that you can figure out how likely it is that a short stack will become involved and go broke over there. Bottom line: unless you're the runt of the litter at both tables, there's a much higher premium on *not* playing hands than on playing them. Save your involvement for the very top of your hand distribution—and even then don't play if you don't have to.

6. We have seen (laughable) situations where big stacks forget this principle and go to war with one another. When that happens, an otherwise imperiled short stack enjoys a pleasant surprise. Situations like these are reminders that your opponents may not always be aware of optimal satellite play, and it's vital that you know who has a clue and who does not.

Case #5
MTT Satellite with Eleven or Twelve Players; Top Few Spots Pay

Say the top three places pay identical prizes. Now you can't afford to wait your way to the final table, because a short stack at the final table is effectively no more useful than a short stack at the last two tables. You need to position yourself to get enough chips to make it to the top three. It's time to shift into accumulation mode.

If your opponents are gambling, sit back and wait for a good spot to take a calculated risk. If your opponents have already tightened up, start being really aggressive. Don't confuse aggression with recklessness, though. No matter how tight your opponents are, you probably shouldn't raise every hand you open. Aim to steal with a frequency slightly higher than two times an orbit. As an alternative, if your foes' postflop play is weak, you can limp more and try to outplay them postflop. Again, remember that you may have a significant skill differential over foes with little shorthanded experience. Bear in mind also that you can't simply sit and wait through another seven or eight places if everyone else is doing the same thing. To give yourself the best shot of getting one of the top prizes on offer, you'll need to open up your play.

Case #6
Final Table of MTT Satellite; Top Few Spots Pay

As in case #4, we're looking at a situation in which an identical prize payout is given to everyone who wins it. To play correctly here, see our previous discussion, but disregard the stuff about spying on the other table since you'd just waste time looking at a table that isn't there.

Case #7
Regular 50/30/20 Cash STT

When a cash STT goes six- or five-handed, some players will have the luxury of having stacks deep enough for some post-flop play, but others will already be in what we call push-and-pray (P&P) mode, where options are reduced to folding or pushing all-in preflop. Apart from monitoring your own stack and being sure of where you are in relationship to P&P, you need to know how—or indeed whether—your opponents take their own stack sizes into account. For the opponents who do change their play relative to their stack size, you need to figure out what moves signal what hand distributions, using stack size as a clue.

Knowing your opponents' mentalities will then shape your strategy, as a further function, of course, of your own stack. If you have 7BB, you're simply looking for an all-in opportunity, and you want to take it before you get down to 4BB. Ideally, you want your all-in to coincide with when another short stack has the big blind; just make sure that the big blind isn't so short stacked (a figure that can range from 2BB to 4BB, depending on the foe) that he'll call with any two cards. The idea behind aiming your fold equity at another shorty at the table is that by taking chips directly from another short stack, you double the differential your all-ins create between you and your short-stacked foes.

If you're able to open from the cutoff or later, you should push all-in with any two cards except when a player is likely to call with any two cards. Even if the big stacks in the tournament are behind you, you shouldn't have to worry about them making loose calls, provided that their stacks are sized such that losing to you will substantially hurt them (and it will if you're pushing to 4–7BB). Warning: don't overuse this tool, or you'll inadvertently loosen up others' calling requirements that, at this point, you'd like to keep tight. So don't push all-in every hand. Limit yourself to an average of somewhere between one and two all-ins per orbit. Even when you moderate your aggression, your foes will become aware that you're pushing with a wide distribution. Thus, you should push all-in with your powerhouse hands like AA when you get them even if you have 8BB. With all the other pushing you've been doing, your opponents won't fall for a limp or a raise to 2.5BB here. In fact, with all the other pushing you've been doing, they'll happily call along with a lesser big pair—and be quite surprised that this time you have the goods. For proper deception:

> *Don't slowplay big hands. Fastplay* other *hands.*

Against bigger stacks that raise a lot and foreclose your first-in opportunities, you want to start going over the top with something like [AA,66]||[AK,A9]. If you don't have enough chips to go over the top, but you still have enough chips to have fold equity when pushing all-in as the first one in the pot, then just don't call if losing in a marginal situation will leave you so short stacked as to have no fold equity. It seems counterintuitive,[7] but pushing all-in later with a random hand is the move that keeps you in the tournament a higher percentage of the time than calling a raise with half a hand. The reason for that is fold equity: if they don't fight, you

---

7. And *scary*—"They have to know I've got nothing!"

win, and often they won't fight. So avoid making calls that can kill your fold equity if you lose. Fold equity is your primary weapon in the STT end game. In other words:

> He who folds and runs away lives to fold equity
> another day.

Now we descend from six- or five-handed to four-handed— the money bubble in an STT. If there was any possibility of postflop play five- or six-handed, it's functionally gone when you get down to four. If you are a short stack when the tournament is at this stage, try to fire your all-ins when the other short stack is the big blind, as just discussed. This will sometimes mean folding hands that might normally be good all-in hands, but it preserves your fold equity—or more accurately, it aims your fold equity at the one player to whom your stack is still a threat. You'll still be pushing all-in against anyone with worthy hands—essentially any ace and any pair—but if a big stack is in the big blind, you may wish to forego otherwise good pushing hands like K9. You would do this to build fold equity for an all-in push with any two cards against a short-stacked big blind—assuming, of course, that you can be the first one into the pot.

If you have a big stack here, you needn't take big gambles. The difference between 4th and 3rd is bigger than the difference between 3rd and 2nd,[8] so usually, with four players left,

---

8. No duh, right? The difference between 4th and 3rd is the difference between nothing and something. We don't look at it that way. Your equity comes not from just making the money but from strategically maneuvering to make the most average money over the long haul. Third place pays 20 units above 4th place, but 2nd place pays only 10 units above 3rd. Considering your overall performance in STTs, the difference between 4th and 3rd is not the difference between no money and some money, but between less money and more money.

you want to get into the money, and only then are you really concerned with playing for first. Just push hands like [AA,66]|| [AK,AT] when you're the big stack, and if a 7BB+ stack is behind you, raise to 3BB instead of pushing all-in. Basically, you want to be aggressive, but you don't want to make lots of wanton calls. Also, remember that if a short stack is in the tournament, an all-in from a medium stack or a big stack means that the player has a big hand. A player usually won't put his tournament life on the line on a complete bluff to steal the blinds when there's at least one cripple left looking to be polished off.

Three-handed, your goal is to be in good position going into the heads-up battle. Many times the stacks at this point will be something like 10K, 5K, and 5K or something like 12K, 5K, and 3K. If you are the big stack in either of these scenarios, play aggressively, but selectively. Most likely, your opponents will have loosened up a tad (because they're in the money—*yay!*) so that you won't have as much fold equity as you had on the bubble. Meanwhile, if you are the 2nd or 3rd place stack in either of these situations, you need to put your foot on the gas. Pretty much anytime you have 8BB or less and you can be first in, your move will be to go all-in. The worst thing that happens is that you get called with only a 35 percent chance of winning the hand, giving you a 35 percent chance of being in good position to win heads-up.[9] A 35 percent chance of being in good position to win heads-up is much better than almost no chance of even getting to heads-up—which would be the case if you let timidity get you blinded away.

---

9. Provided you're better than your opponent at heads-up STT play, which you will be when we get done with you.

Case #8
STT Satellite

STT satellites take many different forms. Some of them are satellites that pay entries into big MTTs. Usually, those types of satellites have payouts so that the winner gets the entry, and either second or second and third get their buy-ins back. For example, Party Poker has $24 + $2 STTs that feed into $200 + $15 MTTs. In these tournaments, first place gets the $215 seat, and second place gets $25. Another type of satellite tournament is a ladder of STT satellites. In this scheme, there are three or four levels of satellites, after which there's a final level with cash payouts. In such a ladder, Level 1 might be a $30 + $3 buy-in tournament. The first few bustouts get nothing, one place might get something like $25, the next few places get an entry into another Level 1 tournament, and either first or first and second get a freeroll into a Level 2 tournament, which has something like $100 + $10 buy-in. After a few more levels with similar payout structures, you eventually get to Level 4 or Level 5, which is a $1000 + $65 or $2000 + $125 buy-in STT, in which the top 4 or 5 players get paid.

In that these satellites are, for all intents and purposes, winner take all, you simply have to play to win once you are shorthanded. There's so much equity in placing first (or in the top two at times) that it typically doesn't matter wherever else you finish. Also, since blinds typically escalate to the point in which there's no postflop play, there's no point in holding out to outplay your opponents. If you have the opportunity to get involved in large pots where you have even a 51 percent edge, go for it. In fact, there are cases where you'd want to contend for a large pot you may only win like 25 percent of the time. Truth? Read on.

Assume that you're four-handed, the relative stacks are 6K, 6K, 4K, and 4K, and you're one of the 4K stacks. Imagine that all three of your opponents have gone all-in before you, and you have a lowly 65 suited. Fourth, third, and second place pay the same, a freeroll to the same level. Only first place wins you a freeroll to the next level. If either of the 6K stacks wins this hand, you'll be a 16K:4K underdog in the heads-up battle, an ugly uphill climb. If the 4K stack wins, the situation will be 12K, 4K, 2K, and 2K. Again, not great news for you. Against the typical distributions for these three players, your 65 suited will be around 20–25 percent to win the hand. In such a situation, you may be forced to call because of the huge hole you'll be in—no matter who wins—if you don't contest this pot.

Or look at it this way: if you don't take this gamble and the 6K stack wins, you'll have to double up and double up again to beat him. If you are fortunate enough to get yourself into two coin-flip situations, you will be about—25 percent to win them both. But that's only if you get the right cards *and* your foe gets the right cards *and* your hand holds up *and* you get to do that again. Yes, you're an underdog, but in this scenario you only have to get lucky once.

When key hands like this develop in STTs or even in any tournament, you need to recognize them, take yourself out of autopilot, and really think things through. What may seem like an obvious fold may, in fact, be a necessary call. So take your time, analyze the situation, consider future situations based on various outcomes, and then act. And don't be afraid of acting. Many a second-place finisher has said to himself, "Well, I got blinded out, but at least I didn't donk off my chips on a reckless adventure with 65 suited." To us, that's someone who didn't give himself a chance to win because he was afraid to look bad in his own or someone else's eyes.

In satellites where the top two or three get the same payout, as usually occurs in STT ladder schemes, your strategy changes a bit. If you're the chip leader, you usually want to avoid big gambles, and if you do get involved, it should be with the intention of slowly grinding down your foes. Because the chip leaders won't do a lot of rampant calling, if you're a small stack, you have no choice but to be aggressive before your stack gets so small that the big stacks become indifferent to losing a pot to you. And if you're a big stack and there's another big stack out there, don't forget to implicitly collude against the small stacks. This is not cheating. It's cooperative action for mutual gain. It's only cheating if you *talk* about it, so keep stumm, but convey through your actions—quick and placid checks behind—how you intend to play.

Things get really interesting in situations where the top two spots get the same payout and you're down to four-handed play. Say the stacks are something like 11K, 3K, 3K, and 3K, and fourth and third place get the same thing, maybe something, maybe nothing, but whatever—the same thing. Assume you are one of the 3K stacks. In this situation, the other two 3K stacks are going to be relatively conservative, meaning that whenever they're in the blinds, you want to go all-in. The best situation is when the 11K stack is to your right because then you can fold if he raises and raise if he folds (i.e., the big stack and you can implicitly collude to put perpetual pressure on the other two short stacks). You may need to fold occasionally since you don't want to hang a big sign on the fact that you're pushing with any two cards.

The worst outcome for you in this case would be for the other 3K stacks to play a pot, eliminating one and leaving the other with 6K. Then you'd be in an 11K, 6K, 3K situation. If the blinds are 200–400 or greater, and they will be, you're pretty much resigned to pushing all-in every time you can be first in, and hoping that luck gets you back in the fray.

Case #9
6-max STT

Of all the tournament situations we've discussed so far, this is the first that enjoys a stretch of deep-stack play. The typical payout has second place getting 40 percent of the prize pool and first place getting 60 percent. Per our earlier discussion, here's another example of when the difference between making the money and not making the money is less about the psychological satisfaction of getting paid and more about the percentage gaps between pay places. Here there's roughly the same equity for finishing either first or second, when measured against third through sixth.

You don't need to take big risks to play for the kill, but you can't just sit back from the start and simply allow your opponents to knock each other out. Since you start out shorthanded, the blinds will hit you faster than they would in the first few rounds of a fullhanded tournament. Let's say you start with 2,000 chips, and that the blinds at the first few levels are 20–40, 30–60, and 50–100. Assuming you pay blinds twice a level, you will pay $2(60) + 2(90) + 2(150) = 600$ in blinds, leaving you with only 1,400 in chips going into the 100–200 level. At that point, you're in P&P mode, and if the tournament is four-handed, your three opponents will have an average of about 3,500 chips. A double up when you have 1,400 chips doesn't even give you an average stack. Sitting on your hands, then, is not the way to go.

From the beginning of a 6-max STT, then, you're looking to grow your garden. You don't want to be reckless, but you do want to be selectively aggressive, and you have to pay close, quick attention to how your foes are going about their business. You should play the beginning of a 6-max STT very much like you would play a cash game, with lots of aggressive small-pot poker and an attitude of *keep pushing till some-*

one pushes back. If you are in a large pot, make sure you have good equity. Try to be at least a 65ish percent favorite when you are deeply stacked and all the chips go in. If you don't feel your odds are that good, look for a different opportunity to score.

Late in a 6-max STT, when you are three-handed, play will most likely resemble that of a satellite where the top two places pay the same. This is because the difference between first and second place is usually half of the difference between third and second place. To proceed from this point forward, then, just refer to our battle plan for case #8 satellites and have at them!

Case #10
6-max MTT

To make money in a 6-max MTT, you have to outlast many foes, and the only way to outlast them is to accumulate chips. Our advice about playing the beginning of a 6-max STT like a cash game applies just as well to the beginning of a 6-max MTT. The only difference between deeply stacked short-handed tournament situations and their cash game counter-parts is that you might not want to risk huge portions of your stack on narrow edges if you have a skill edge over the other players at your table. But while you'd like to avoid risking huge chunks of your stack in uncertain circumstances, you should have no qualms about playing lots of aggressive small-pot poker, just as you would in a cash game.

Controlling the size of the pot is a key consideration here. While we generally counsel aggression across the breadth of poker's landscape, here you want to temper your aggression for the sake of keeping pots small. With your skill edge, you want your stack to be as effectively deep as possible so that your betting can be flexible and creative. If the pot gets too big, that option gets taken away. Retarding the growth of pots keeps your stack deep relative to the size of the pot.

To keep pots small, you may wish to consider limping in position preflop instead of raising. Or you may wish to check behind on the flop or the turn to keep the pot small for tricky river decisions. Always be thinking of your stack size, your opponents' stack sizes, and what you need to keep accumulating chips. Also, don't take this discussion about controlling pot size to mean that you *always* want to play in small pots. Just monitor the circumstance. When you're a prohibitive favorite in a hand, you'd like nothing more than to play a big pot. However, when you're uncertain about where you stand or when you are on a draw, then you may wish to be in a smaller pot where you won't have to commit nearly as much of your stack to make it to the end.

No matter how diligently you accumulate chips, the reality of tournament hold'em is that you will eventually be short stacked with respect to the blinds and eventually be in P&P mode. When P&P time arrives, just follow the advice about late MTT play that we give regarding cases #1–#3.

Case #11
MTT Shootout

Shootouts—where a winner or winners from a given table advance to the next round—are a unique tournament format in two ways: First, you flip-flop between fullhanded and shorthanded play in a way that you do in no other tournament type. To do well consistently in shootouts, you always need to adjust to the changing dynamics of play as a function of the oscillating number of foes you face. The toughest adjustment is probably at the beginning of a new round where you have to slow down from a shorthanded mentality to a fullhanded one. Second, a few different pay schemes exist for shootouts. In some shootouts, like those in most b&m casinos, only the final table pays and only the winner from each table advances to the next round. In other shootouts, especially those online, the last remaining two or three players from each table move on to the next round—taking with them whatever chips they've been able to accumulate.

In shootouts where only the winner advances, you are playing to get all the chips at the table. It's that simple— shootouts of this variety essentially play like a bunch of STT satellites into big tournaments. Shootouts in which two or more players advance, play a lot like the ladder STTs discussed in case #8. There is one key difference, though, which requires a strategic modification: your stack isn't reset. In other words, say everyone at your table starts with 1,000 chips. Suppose that you survive to the next round, finishing at third with 1,000 chips. You take those 1,000 chips to the next round where the average stack size is 3,333. The result of this is that proper play in these types of shootouts is a hybrid between proper satellite play and proper MTT play.

Simply advancing to the next round gives you value (i.e., even though monetary payouts vary from first to third place at each table, each table itself has a relatively flat payout scheme). But there is also value in making sure that you have a big enough stack to play with (i.e., you need to accumulate chips continually to give you a chance at getting to the final table, where the payouts are, of course, the highest). For shootouts in which multiple players advance to the next round, we advocate being in satellite-survival mode if you have an average or above-average chip stack relative to the entire tournament.

It's pretty easy to advance to the next round with such a stack, and having such a stack will make you competitive in the next round, especially since you'll be fullhanded in the beginning where you can play sit-and-wait poker. But we advocate going into accumulation mode if you're a small stack even if you think your chances of merely surviving into the next round are good. If you make it to the next round without a lot of chips, you won't be able to do much damage, and since the payouts increase at each table, you need to take a chance to make yourself competitive at the next table.

Final Tournament Thoughts Before Proceeding to Heads-Up Play

To play successful tournament poker is to strike a working balance between chip preservation and chip accumulation. Because the blinds eat away at you faster in a shorthanded setting, you need to have a plan that will let you accumulate chips to keep pace with the blinds. At the same time, you don't want to be reckless and take unwarranted risks. Though the dynamics of tournament play are much different from the dynamics of cash game play, the bottom line is that controlled, calculated aggression is still your best plan for shorthanded tournament play. Keep a close eye on your opponents' chip stacks and on how they wield those mighty maces, and you should be able to dominate and crush the key shorthanded stages of the tournaments you play.

Exercises

1. When you are in an MTT that's down to twelve or eleven players, how do you expect your opponents to play, and what will your game plan usually be, given the top-heavy payouts of most MTTs?

2. Eleven players remain in a particular MTT in which only the final table pays. Assume that the final-table payouts are similar in structure to those given in table 6.1 (see p. 155). Your table is five-handed. The blinds are 1,000–2,000, and they are increasing to 1,500–3,000 on the next hand. The average stack is 30,000. You have 14,000, and you are on the button. Action is folded to you, and you have T8 suited. The small blind has 5,000 and the big blind has 24,000. What's your play?

3. The STT you're in has a 50/30/20 payout. Action is four-handed. You and another player are the short stacks with 5BB each. The other two remaining players have about 9BB each. You have AT suited in the big blind. The other 5BB stack limps UTG and action is folded to you. What do you do?

4. In Party Poker's Step Higher STT system, Level 1 was a $33 buy-in, Level 2 was a $110 buy-in, Level 3 was a $535 buy-in, and the final level was a $2,150 buy-in tournament with cash payouts. Suppose you are in a Level 3 tournament, where the top two players move on to Level 4, and pretty much everyone else gets knocked down to Level 2.

   With four players left, you are among three players with 3,000–4,000 chips. The fourth player is a dominant chip leader with 10,000 chips. Unfortunately, only about an orbit into four-handed play, your two short-stacked adversaries go all-in against each other. Now three players remain. You have 3,000 chips, the person to your left has 7,000 chips, and the person to your right has 10,000 chips. Blinds are 200–400. You are about eight hands into three-handed play. Every time you have been the small blind, the 10,000 stack has folded his button and you've pushed all-in to pressure the 7,000 stack. You've pushed all-in once from the button as well.

You are now the small blind. The 10,000 stack folds, and you have T3 offsuit. What's your play?

5. Three players remain in a regular STT. The blinds are 400–800. You have 4,000 chips. The other two stacks are 6,000 chips and 8,000 chips. Your opponents have been really aggressive with preflop all-ins. You are in the big blind with A6. The button folds, and the small blind, the 6,000 stack, goes all-in. Do you call or fold?

6. Same situation as in question 6, but now you are the 8,000 stack. Do you call or fold?

Answers

1. You should expect your opponents to be very timid. Most players do not want to place just out of the money or miss out on a final table. As a note, players who are not timid at this point should be considered dangerous opponents going to the final table unless they cross the line from aggressiveness to recklessness.

   Given timid opponents, your game plan will be to accumulate chips aggressively. If you have a large stack, repeatedly pummel your opponents with preflop raises to 3BB (or less if they will fold to smaller raises). If you only have about 6BB or 7BB, you should be willing to risk your tournament life by going all-in to steal blinds unless the average stack is more than double what you have (i.e., play a short stack conservatively only when you have to acquire an overwhelming quantity of chips to put yourself in legitimate fighting position at the final table).

2. If the small blind had more chips, your play here would be to go all-in. However, the small blind's small stack means you don't have much fold equity, for he'll probably make a desperation call. He knows he'll have absolutely no fold equity on the next hand, so he'll most likely choose to gamble with you if you go all-in, correctly assuming that the big blind will usually fold and that he'll be against only one opponent with his tournament life at stake.

Against a random hand, T8 suited wins or ties about 54 percent of the time. If you win, you'll have about 20,000 chips, which still isn't quite average. If you lose, you'll be down to 8,000 chips with the blinds at 1,500–3,000, which is not a party hat you particularly want to wear. Go ahead and fold here, and plan to push all-in on the next hand where your fold equity alone will give you a 60–65 percent chance of having close to 20,000 chips.

It may cross your mind to wonder why one should be afraid of the short stack calling on this hand but not on the next. Here's why: If you fold, the short stack has a shot at putting himself all-in. If he declines to do so, he identifies himself as someone who's holding on for miracle cards and is thus not apt to make a desperation call on the next hand. If the small blind does go all-in here, the outcome of the hand will either see him eliminated or give him enough chips so that a desperation call is (temporarily) no longer a worry.

Considering all possible outcomes, we see that each

leads to favorable pushing conditions on the next hand, and that's why we say that you can (and should) wait and push on the next hand.

3. If this opponent has done a lot of limping as a 5BB stack, then push all-in with what's probably the best hand. However, if this opponent hasn't done a lot of limping, he's trapping here. Usually, players trap with hands like [AA,88]; they'd rather push all-in with unpaired hands like [AK,AJ] to avoid making a decision on a flop they'll likely not hit. Therefore, you shouldn't be worried about being dominated by [AK,AJ] if an ace falls on the board. Against a player whom you suspect of limping with a big hand, your best line of play is to check preflop and to push on the flop if you have a pair of aces or better. (Note that against half his distribution having just a pair of tens on the flop is no good.) If you have less than a pair of aces on the flop, don't invest any more chips on the flop.

4. Push all-in. It's very tough for him to call here, for if he calls and loses, your positions will be reversed. You'll have 6,000 in chips, and you can play a waiting game. He'll have 4,000 in chips and be desperate to double up. In most cases, the big blind will be a nonfactor, side-lined by a very tight calling distribution. Go ahead and grab the very valuable 600 chips out there in the blinds, given that (1) your foe has logical reasons to fold and (2) your opponents will likely implicitly collude to steal your blinds and push you to the felt if you don't stay active.

   As it happens, this question is drawn from a real situation, a Party Poker Step Higher Level 3 tournament that we (and in this instance by "we" here we mean "Tony") recently played. We pushed all-in, confident in the logic of the line of play, confident in the likelihood of getting a fold—and utterly shocked to get called! The big blind had QJ offsuit, and while in a tournament with a substantial difference between first and second place, this call may have been expected and justifiable, given the flat payout scheme of this STT, we figured that QJ would be much worse than the worst hand in our opponent's distribution. Even given all our aggression from the onset of three-handed play, we figured his hand distribution had only dropped from something like [AA,TT]|| [AK,AJ] to something like [AA,66]||[AK,A9]. QJ is *way* outside that distribution, and since this foe had generally been shrewd, we didn't predict so sharp a drop in his calling requirements.

In retrospect, we (and by "we" here we mean "JV") think we ("we" = "Tony"; this could get confusing) forgot to take some realworld considerations into account. As aggressive as "we" had been, it was only a matter of time till this foe decided that, hand distribution be damned, QJ was probably *lots* better than whatever cheese he was facing here. And he may have been right, which doesn't negate the validity of our line of play. In poker, you go with your reads and have the courage of your convictions. Sometimes you're going to be wrong—surprisingly, spectacularly wrong. That's okay:

> *There's no shame in being wrong, only in not learning.*

In further retrospect, we ("we" now being Tony again) recognize the validity of JV's assertion that Tony didn't accurately take a very important realworld consideration into account: you can't assume that opponents will follow what you perceive to be optimal play. That being said, it still seems like the call with QJ in this circumstance is way too risky. Sure, the big blind is correct in knowing that QJ is ahead of his opponent's pushing distribution, but given the size of his stack, he still has plenty of time to wait for a much better calling hand.

"We" retort—oh, never mind. One could argue back and forth about this all day. It puts one in mind of this bit of mythology/philosophy:

> A student asked the master: "What does the world rest upon?"
>
> The master answered: "On the back of a huge turtle."
>
> The student asked: "And what does the turtle rest upon, oh wise one?"
>
> The master answered: "Upon another turtle."
>
> The student, yet again, asked: "And what does that turtle rest on?"
>
> The master, becoming annoyed, answered: "Don't you get it? It's turtles all the way down!"

5. There's a bigger jump in going from second to first place than there is in going from third to second. You need to accumulate chips, and winning this pot catapults you from last to being in legitimate contention to win the tournament. Your A6 stands to be well ahead of your opponent's pushing distribution, and this will probably be your best opportunity since you have only five big blinds. You should call.

6. Your A6 is well ahead of your opponent's pushing distribution, so most wouldn't consider calling to be a bad play. However, with ten big blinds, you'll have more favorable opportunities down the road. Folding here optimizes your monetary EV. Do that, and wait for a better shot.

7

HEADS-UP PLAY

The First Hand Sets the Tone

Heads-up play results from a wide range of circumstances. You might be in a cash game, or you might be in a tournament. Your heads-up match may have started that way, or you may be playing heads-up with the other last man standing, like two punch drunk boxers still going toe to toe long after the referee has rung the bell, the stogie chewing reporters have filed their stories, and all the jaded fans of the sweet science of fight have melted into the night. Regardless of how you ended up here, you're now in a realm of shorthanded play unlike any other. You are in a whole new game. You only have one foe to figure out, so that's your job right now.

This is obviously so if you're starting a heads-up match against an opponent you've never played. But even if you're slugging it out with someone who shared a fuller-handed table with you, you must expect his approach to heads-up play to be different from his full ring strategy and even from his three-handed strategy. At least it should be. If he's not adapting to this ultimate shorthanded circumstance, he's do-

ing something wrong, and while we all like to face foes like
that, we can't count on it. So assume he'll be vectoring his play
in some new direction. You need to figure out where he's
headed—and then head him off. Given that our savvy opponents will be trying to do the same to us, we need to give some
thought to the sort of opening statement we want to make.

In most heads-up settings, the small blind will have the
button, meaning that he's first to act before the flop and last
to act on later rounds. A wacky exception to this is cash game
play on some online sites where if a full game devolves to
heads-up, the big blind will be on the button. As this is a rare
and awkward deviation from the norm, we'll do what prudent
people do when confronted with facts that don't mesh with
their cherished beliefs: we will ignore them. When you start
heads-up play, then, with the button and first action, your options are three: fold, call, and raise. You might think that your
decision is guided by the cards you hold.

Yeah—not so much.

Folding your first hand in a heads-up match communicates
tightness to your foe. Heads-up play is a game of strategic
bluffing—neither player hits most flops. If your opponent believes you're tight, then your bluffing attempts will be more
successful against some opponents. Against others, having a
tight image can make your life extremely difficult. Aggressive
foes will bet into you mercilessly if they think that in your case
tight equals weak. They'll seize the first aggressor advantage
and hold onto it like a puppy with a tug toy. Some of your
more adventurous foes will willfully play back at you. Drawing
no connection between your tightness and your hand distribution, they'll stay in against you regardless of their cards, in-
tending to beat you with bluffs, stop-and-goes and their
whole array of tricky plays. If you essay a tight image in
heads-up action, your best opponents will habitually aggress
in response to your aggression, when it comes, knowing that

you'll only stay in a hand if you have something good (and by now, we know that the probability of that isn't very high).

Calling on the button in the first hand can project several messages to your foe, and his response to your limp may give you immediate information. Your call signals to your opponent that you'll call with okay hands and save your raises for stronger holdings. This opening limp, then, may earn you some fold equity for subsequent preflop raises. Either that or your preflop raises may force your opponent to play with more trepidation postflop. So—fold equity plus information, that's what you're after when you lead with a limp. You won't get a great deal of information from only one hand, of course, but you have to start somewhere, right? How does your foe respond? Does he check his big blind, or does he raise? If he raises, to how much does he raise, and (if you make it to showdown and find out) what does he raise with? Note that if you don't want to call your opponent's raise, you may try to get your opponent to show his cards by chatting as you fold or to show what you're folding and hope the favor gets returned. While we don't favor giving away free information, heads-up or ever, we know that some players have great success with this gambit. If it works for you, we say *mazel tov* and *buona fortuna*.

The last option for your preflop action from the button is raising. You may wish to raise with any two cards simply to see how your foe responds. If he folds without thinking, then you're probably against an opponent who has a preset hand distribution for calling raises. This distribution may change as the match evolves, but in the short term, you should generate as much active aggression as your foe will tolerate. Meanwhile, if your opponent calls almost as a reflex, it means either that he's stumbled on a good hand or that he's not going to establish the precedent of backing down. You'll need to see how your next few buttons go to figure out whether he's playing you or his own hand values, but the pattern will quickly emerge if you're primed to look for it. Finally, if your opponent reraises, that shouldn't necessarily retard your further button aggression. Either he's hit a real hand on the first hand, or else he's just very aggressive out of position. If the former, then you won't see many reraises on future hands; if the latter, strap in for a steep ride, since you're being offered the opportunity to play huge pots in position.

Now let's turn it around; we'll put you in the big blind to start, and think about possible first counters to your foe's opening move.[1] If he folds, you've won some chips, and learned that he's willing to fold his valuable button—unless he's projecting a false image of tightness, which is both possible and very, very common. Here we get into the familiar wheels-within-wheels conundrum of poker thought. You know that your foe's opening move means something. *He* knows this too. Does his opening move reflect his real strategic approach, or is it an intentional feint? If you've been playing against this foe in a fuller-handed setting, now is a good time to think about his prior play. Has he shown himself to be tricky or straightforward? If his true colors have previously emerged, apply them here. If you've never played against him before, treat him as straightforward until proven tricky and gauge his actions accordingly.

If your opponent just calls from the small blind, you may wish to bang in a raise with any two cards, just to see what he does. As we'll discuss later, you generally don't want to keep players from limping when they have the button, for that's a valuable piece of real estate, and they should not be discouraged from squandering its value. Nevertheless, opening

1. And if anyone is thinking "pawn to king four" right now—right on! "Poker equals chess plus luck," it has been said; nowhere does this analogy run more true than in the thrust and counterthrust of a good heads-up NLHE match.

moves do set the tone, and if it's your intention to take an aggressive stance (or masquerade one), then raising a flat-call is the way to go. You might put the fear in him, and give yourself early control of the match.

Finally, if your opponent raises, you can fold, call, or reraise. It's generally not a good idea to reraise the first hand of a heads-up match, for you'll be creating a big pot that you'll have to play out of position against an unmeasured opponent. Fold, then? Well, if you do that, you may embolden your foe to try to run all over you, though you could use the image of tightness to later advantage. Also, it doesn't hurt to avoid investing chips early in a match while you're still sussing out your foe. From where we sit, the best plan is to call raises of 3BB or less. This gives you the option of firing at the flop from first position to see how your foe reacts to a stop-and-go, for if that weapon proves effective, it will be your primary means of neutralizing your positional disadvantage in the big blind. Alternatively, you may simply wish to be straightforward and check-fold if you miss the flop. Whatever your action is, just keep in mind that you'll be projecting some sort of image, and that this image will be the primary building block of the deception trend you'll subsequently create.

Swinging into Action

Your foe's first move in a heads-up match is a sign pointing down a certain road. Over the course of the next few hands, you'll seek to discover, based on his emerging pattern of play, whether this is a true road or a false one. The trick here is to gain a lot of information without risking a lot of chips. After all, you only have one foe to solve, and if he looks to be sticking around for a while, you can afford to be patient. Interestingly, some foes won't stick around. They're uncomfortable in heads-up situations and will run like scared rabbits at the first sign of hyperaggression on your part. (We're speaking of cash game settings, of course, where bailing is an option.) If you get one of these skittish fish on the line, your job is to "tickle the trout," seduce him with soft play and reassuring chat until you can snap him off for a chunk of his stack. At that point, his own tilty stubbornness may keep him in the game. Regardless of whom you face, be he Nervous Norvis or a psycho warrior, there's bound to be some leak in his play that you can exploit. Find it, then hammer it, serene in the knowledge that there are no other foes around to interfere.

Heads-up play is about winning hands without a showdown, since in most cases neither you nor your opponent will be helped by the flop. You need to see how your opponent responds to your preflop raises. Does he usually fold, call, or reraise? Postflop, will he check to you after you have raised? If he checks, does he usually fold if you bet? Does a delayed continuation bet work better than a regular continuation bet? Is your opponent looking to check-raise you? If so, is he generally trapping or bluffing? If your opponent bets into you after you've raised preflop, does he do it infrequently enough that he seems to be betting only his flop hits, or does his frequency indicate that he is using the stop-and-go as a bluff? If he is, will he also use it when he hits, or does he check his made hands on the flop?

So many questions! The same sort of questions we asked ourselves about our various foes in a shorthanded game, only now all our attention is focused on a single enemy. This should make things easier, since we have just the one foe to solve. But not all these betting patterns harmonize with one another. Sometimes the information streams are in conflict; always they're incomplete. This would be a good time to think again about the clear gestalt. Just let all that information wash over you. Your foe's true strategy will emerge—holistically, and in a surprisingly short space of time—if you're open and receptive to the data he transmits and if you keep such negative considerations as greed, ire, ego, and impatience from jamming your reception.

To get a clearer sense of your enemy's true mettle, try varying the size of your preflop raises early in the match, and see how he responds to raises of different amounts. Will he fold to a minimum raise? Call every raise unless it's at least 3.5BB? Once you determine his calling tolerance, then you can dial in a default raise amount. Don't enter a heads-up match with a preconceived notion of the proper preflop raise amount.[2] Let your opponent's reactions determine your optimal preflop raise.

Unless your foe is the weakest Cally Wally in Christendom, you won't be the only one raising, and since you can't surrender all your big blinds without a fight, you'll need to develop effective lines of defense against your foe's preflop aggression. Use this time of early sparring to figure out how to go. First priority: throw in some stop-and-go bets on the flop and see if your foe will fold. Likewise, try some check-raises. Will he aggress with continuation bets but fold when you come back over him? What you're hunting for, generally, are lines of play that lead you to win uncontested pots without risking lots of chips. Against some players, this means betting out; against others, check-raising. Against all foes, your goal is to identify these profitable lines of play and then exploit them as much as possible without making it blatantly obvious that you're doing so. For example, if your opponent is only fighting against your stop-and-goes when he hits a hand, your stop-and-go will be a highly profitable play. However, if you use it *every* time from the big blind, your opponent will eventually adjust, taking that useful weapon away. Therefore, you should use the stop-and-go a high percentage of the time, but disguise it with some checks, check-folds, and check-raises.

2. "3 × BB!" cry the pundits. Everything else is *wrong*!

Just as you won't be the only one raising, you won't be the only one looking for effective lines of play against established betting patterns. So as the match evolves, keep one eye on your foe and the other eye on yourself as your foe sees you. Then be prepared to manipulate his understanding of your betting patterns when key pots emerge. Against some slack-wits, this won't be necessary, since they'll dutifully keep making the mistakes they've been making all along. Against tougher foes (and, sadly, they abound), you need to be ready to provoke a big error in a big situation.

For example, say you're in the big blind, and you've been calling many of your opponent's raises and following up with stop-and-go bluffs. This move has won you many uncontested pots, but now your opponent is playing back at you with increasing frequency. You know that he sees you as a highly aggressive foe, and you know that he now has no respect for your bet on the flop. In response, you dial back on the stop-and-go, using it just enough to convince him that he's got you somewhat, but not completely, tamed in this regard. Now you're in a great position to trap your opponent for a large quantity of chips. Suppose you have AA in the big blind. Your opponent raises. As is "typical" for you, you call along, and then lead at the pot with what looks like the ol' stop-and-go. Your holding is now huge compared to what your foe thinks you have, and his raise of your stop-and-go will put him in a world of hurt. You can either reraise him here or call and bet out on the turn or even check-call all the way down. Thanks to your understanding of his *mis*understanding, you're in position to score a big win with a big hand. In short, for success in key situations:

Establish the meaning of a betting pattern—then change it.

Play Big Pots in Position and
Small Pots Out of Position

Having position for postflop play is a huge advantage in NLHE, so it's in your interest to play smaller pots out of position and larger pots in position. When you raise preflop from the button, you aren't just trying to get your opponent to fold and you aren't just raising based on your cards. You are also making a value bet based on your position. This is why it's good to know how big a raise your foe can stand. Based on this information, you can manipulate him to call out of position or fold in position. Good times!

Not so good times when you're out of position, so let's consider how to play small pots from there. When you're the big blind, most opponents will be raising you a significant percentage of the time. Since nobody likes a bully, it's a typical reflex response to do a lot of reraising. While we generally applaud aggression and acknowledge the reraise as our close personal friend, here's an instance where you have to keep your aggressive tendencies in check because, well, you just don't have position. You should plan on simply calling, rather than reraising, these garden-variety position raises from your foe on the button. Don't get all angry or self-righteous; unfortunately, your foe is playing the game correctly. Fortunately, you'll have your turn—every other hand—when the button devolves to you.

If you adhere to the gospel of keeping pots in the big blind small by refraining from reraising, then on those rare occasions when you do reraise, your strength should be transparently evident to your foe. Not so good. One solution is just *never* to raise preflop, which will certainly do the job of disguising your strength when you have it. But if your foe is an inveterate button raiser, you really don't want to be playing hand after hand after hand out of position, even in minimally raised pots. You need to slow him down somehow, and the reraise is the braking tool to use. Plan to reraise with an appropriate range of hands, something on the order of [AA,88]|| [AK,AJ]. That's a wide enough distribution that he won't be able to put you on aces or kings every time you raise, and he will judge it prudent to dial back on his own button aggression. But the idea here is to have at least a little something going for you on the hand. If you can't have position, you want to have card strength. Be careful, then, not to make your reraising distribution too wide, or else you'll end up conceding both card strength and position to your foe. Remember:

> *bad cards + bad position = bad news*

Controlling Pot Size

Once you've started to shape your actions around the concept of playing large pots in position and small pots out of position, you've entered the realm of controlling the size of the pot. Excellent tournament players are usually familiar with the strategic advantages of this, but it's applicable to cash games as well.

In cash games, the idea behind controlling pot size is to contest large pots when you have an edge and small pots when you're in a marginal situation—and to use your pot-controlling skills to encourage or retard pot growth according to your plan for the hand. Furthermore, as water finds its level, each cash game will achieve an equilibrium around the frequency distribution of how often variously sized pots are contested. For example, perhaps 50 percent of all pots played are less than $100, while just 5 percent of all pots played are above $700. In such a game, you don't want to be on the wrong end of the rare $700 pot, for the dynamics of the game would make it almost impossible to recover your loss. So you control the pot size to make sure this doesn't happen. You avoid reckless adventures against unsolved foes. You seek to build big pots with big hands and big edges. Above all, you strike when you're certain you're ahead.

Even though we've already discussed pot-size control in the context of tournaments, it's worth a review, especially since a large chunk of the heads-up NLHE you'll play is in the form of freeze-out tournaments. (where the event doesn't end until someone wins all) or ultimate clashes at final tables.

Suppose you're heads-up against an opponent whose skills are vastly inferior to yours, and also suppose that you both have 15BB left. If you raise $3 \times$ BB preflop and your opponent calls, the pot will already contain 6BB out of the 30BB in the tournament. In other words, you're forcing the pot to become very large with respect to the total number of chips in play. No matter how well you outplay your opponent, it's very easy for him to get lucky and win such a big pot. Therefore, in a tournament situation in which you have a large playing edge against your opponent, you may actually choose to limp most of the time you're on the button so that you can keep the pots small. Sure, you're sacrificing some positive chip EV per hand because you won't be value betting your position, but if you play much better than your opponent, then you'd prefer to whittle him down over the course of many hands or to get him to call off his chips with second pair (which unskilled opponents routinely do), rather than commit too many chips in a large pot as only a marginal favorite.

Talking of calling with second pair, part of controlling pot size is evaluating how likely your hand is to hold up in a pot of a certain size. Winning hand values go way down in heads-up NLHE; the just-mentioned second pair, or even bottom pair, may very well be a monster. However, players can take this notion of plummeting hand value way too far when they play heads-up. They'll call pot-sized bets on the flop, the turn, and the river thinking that their ace high is good. As a rule, the larger the pot is, the better a hand you'll need to win it. True, players do occasionally bluff large pots into existence, but unless this is their habit, players typically don't create large pots with bottom pair or ace high, meaning that you shouldn't commit lots of chips with such hands either.

Revisiting this notion of whittling down your unskilled foe, then, you can see how starting with a small pot will increase your chances of taking all his chips when you flop top pair. If the pot started out large, he'd be wary of investing too heavily in his second pair. But the small pot—a pot *you* kept small by design—actually lulls him into a false sense of security. He reckons that in an unraised pot, his second pair will be good. And guess what? Most of the time, it'll be good. But in this key hand, a hand that your betting pattern designed and executed, his second pair is no good, and he goes home broke.

At Odds with Odds:
Card Odds, Pot Odds, and Match Odds

In heads-up play, you have three types of odds to consider when making your decisions: card odds, pot odds, and match odds. Card odds are simply the odds of hitting hands. Pot odds refer to the amount of money in the pot relative to how much you're putting in. This includes the notions of implied odds, the amount of money you can expect your opponent to put in the pot on future betting rounds, and reverse implied odds, the amount of money you expect to lose if you hit your hand but still don't win. To these odds we now add a third sort, specific to heads-up play: match odds—your chances of cleaning out your foe completely.

In heads-up play, individual hands serve two goals. Sure, you'd like to use each one to win some chips, but even the ones you don't win may help increase your probability of busting your foe. If you have a skill edge, you don't risk chips in marginal situations, for you know that the longer the match goes on, the more the match odds will tilt in your favor. Leveraging your skill edge works in open-ended cash games, too, provided your foe is sufficiently on the hook that he'll stick around and pay you off. Many players, especially online, treat heads-up cash play as if it were a freeze out. That is, they split after they double up or lose their buy-in. With this in mind, you really want to control pot size, keeping the match roughly in balance until you get a chance to strike a lightning blow.

Some opponents, after winning a large pot from you, may feel confident and will play against you as long as you are willing, but a fair number of players don't like playing with stacks that are too big. In fact, it's somewhat self-selecting—and not to your advantage. A player willing to play with a deep stack is likely to be better than average, and considering that you have to pay the rake, playing a tough player heads-up in an online or realworld cash game is hardly your best bet. To maximize your match odds in this case (or more appropriately minimize your negative odds), simply decline to play. Likewise, if you're in a tournament against a superior foe, with match odds running against you, try to negotiate a favorable deal.[3] You likely won't be able to sucker a tough heads-up player into a tournament deal, but it's always worth a shot. Failing that, look for coin-flip situations and take your chances.

We've already alerted you to the danger of letting ego color

3. If you and your opponent are equally skilled, find your probability of
    winning by taking your stack size and dividing it by the total number
    of chips in play.

your thinking; nowhere is this danger greater than in heads-up play. Heads-up, things can seem *so* personal. Over the long haul, against the long succession of foes you face, your heads-up success will largely be a function of how well you can separate your emotional reactions from the task at hand. Get into an "I'll show him!" mindset and the next nose you cut off will be the one that spites your face. At the same time, be on the lookout for emotional cracks in your foe's armor. If he busts out and buys back in (especially if he buys in *big*), he's evincing signs of tilt you can exploit. Keenly observe how your opponents react to such tipping points in a match and adjust accordingly, using all the weapons at your disposal: hand strength; betting trends; pot control; and some needly chat.

Set Plays and Audibles

In heads-up play, it's not at all unusual for a quick equilibrium to develop, as each competitor develops lines of play that he thinks will be successful. If this equilibrium doesn't favor you, change something, and quick, for it's the textbook definition of insanity to do the same thing over and over again expecting different results. Alternatively, if the equilibrium favors you, then just keep doing what you're doing. At this point, you'll likely fall into a pattern of successfully scripted plays: small blind raise; big blind call and stop-and go; unraised pot DCB; and so on. You're now in a good place, thinking about all the betting rounds in a given hand, with a plan for that hand well mapped out in your mind.

While having and enacting scripts are wonderful things, don't become too complacent in executing your plan for the hand, or you may miss information indicating that you aren't quite in the situation you think you're in. Heads-up play is the most dynamic form of shorthanded poker, where each player's appraisal of his foe is being tweaked and updated on a hand-by-hand basis—sometimes right in the middle of the hand. To play this brand of poker successfully, you need to be able to execute successful scripts, but let's take inspiration from Peyton Manning and call an audible when the situation demands.

Say your foe has fallen into the pattern of raising to $3 \times BB$ from the button and folding to your postflop aggression. Great. But now his opening raise is $4 \times BB$. Is he trying to tell you something? Are you paying attention? Characteristic plays require characteristic counters, but unexpected moves demand insight, creativity, and courage on the fly. His $4 \times BB$ bet might indicate that he generally wants you to pay more to get to the flop, or it may mean that this time he has a hand. You'll need all the power of your reads and hacks to know whether that extra BB is an invitation or a warning sign. Bottom line: stay on your toes. Even against foes who seem to be inferior, be on the lookout for uncharacteristic moves requiring novel responses.

Positional Play on the River

Having navigated a path through the hand—by either script or audible—you'll often arrive at the river with a tricky little problem on your hands. At this point, the pot is at its largest, so the bets going in will be biggest too. This puts a heavy premium on correct decision making. Much is at stake, and not just the pot. There's momentum, psychological advantage, and the tipping point between a healthy stack and an imperiled one; a single right move on a single last bet can often make the difference between winning and losing a tournament match or a cash game joust.

Then there's the practical matter of siphoning chips. Even if you play perfectly on every other round of play, making too many bad calls on the river will most likely make your overall play -EV. Even heads-up, most players are more likely to be betting real hands on the river than making big bluffs. It's just human nature. People tend to bluff when the pots are small and the risks are small. When the pots and bets are larger, they'd rather have a hand. At the same time, not getting in good value bets on the river—large bets because the pot is large—can translate into too many missed opportunities for profit. We need to strike a balance. Let's find out how.

Imagine that you're playing pure value poker on the river and your opponent checks to you. Furthermore, assume that after he checks, he'll only raise if he has a good hand like two pair or better; that is, he won't check-raise bluff. If that's the situation you find yourself in, then you should bet on the river if more than 50 percent of the calls you'll get are from hands that you beat. But it's not enough just to throw a random bet out there and hope he takes the bait. Every value bet is a product placed on the market, and it won't sell if the price ain't right. Think about his calling distribution as a function of your bet size, and find the bet size that maximizes the EV of your river bet. To do this, coordinate two lines of thought: the betting on the hand that's currently in play and your opponent's history of calling in this situation. How much is he good for? That's the question you're trying to answer here.

You may wish to take things further and introduce a bluffing frequency. That is, occasionally bet in position on the river with hands that have no chance of winning when you check behind. You will either derive more profit from the additional pots your bluffs pick up or loosen up your opponent's calling distribution so that you can increase the size of your river bet to a higher "going rate."

Avoid betting in position with hands like bottom pair after

your opponent checks to you. You're really hoping that hands such as these hold up at showdown, but, famously, "Don't bet on the river when the only hand that can call you can beat you." However, if you put your opponent on a range of hands better than yours, and your bet will get your opponent to fold a favorable percentage of hands relative to your bet size, then betting is acceptable because you're no longer betting your hand for value; rather, you're bluffing with the worst hand, and you know it! This type of sophisticated bluff is only good if you're getting correct pot odds, though. Suppose the pot is $30, and you bet $15 as a bluff. This is a profitable play only if your foe will fold at least one third of the time. And here again we see where heads-up play is such a dynamic, ever-changing thing. While your foe may fold at least one third of the time overall, how do you rate the likelihood of his folding *this time?* If you've shown down some big hands lately, he's probably in a folding frame of mind; if you've been caught speeding, he's looking to issue another citation.

Now let's look at what happens when our foe bets into us on the river. To raise here is essentially the same as betting behind a check; the only difference is the hand distributions at play. Raising on a bluff here is something of a double-edged sword. On one hand, it requires a lot of chips to make a meaningful bluff, and so you may end up playing that one overly large pot that makes or breaks a session. On the other hand, such raises carry substantial fold equity against most opponents, and if you can get your foe to lay down a better hand in this situation, you'll enjoy both a monetary and a psychological gain. So have the play in your arsenal, but pick your spots with care.

Should you flat-call his bet on the river? Don't fly by the seat of your pants. Use available information to figure out the correct calling frequency. First look at the pot odds. If they're favorable against your foe's hand distribution, then calling is

+EV, simple as that. If you think the call is +EV, then next examine whether there's higher EV to be gained by raising. And don't forget to think long term. Calling here might keep your foe making loose river bets into you; raising could potentially shut off that flow. Determine the appropriate response you want, and act accordingly.

Of course, if neither calling nor raising is +EV, then you fold. River play in position is very elegant in theory: you have thoughtfully analyzed deception trends, carefully priced value bets, appropriately spaced bluffs, and completely made yourself aware of hand distributions. In practice, it tends to be much more automatic and much less well thought out. Most players act on reflex, without *any thought at all* of their opponents' hand distributions, calling distributions, bluffing frequencies, *anything*. These reflex decisions lead to bad bets, bad raises, bad calls, and bad folds. Don't let that happen to you. When you're on the river in position, you have a marvelous opportunity to put together all your advantages—advantages of skill, awareness, analysis, *and* last action—to gain every last bit of available value. Don't squander this opportunity through quick and careless play. Think things through.

River Play Out of Position

Like river play in position, river play out of position is relatively simple—in theory. The big problem is that you don't have at your disposal the option to end the betting; you don't have last action. This puts more variables into play, and with more variables come a higher potential for bad judgment.

If you understand the concept of betting into calling distributions against which you win more than 50 percent of the time and if you're good enough to accurately read your opponent's hand distributions and calling distributions, you'll squeeze out a fair amount of EV by betting into him on the river. But you can't go blindly firing bets into the pot, even under the honorable flag of value bets. You also need to consider how your opponent will respond if you check to him, for you might get more value from check-calling than you do from betting out. Then again, if you're up against a foe who makes lots of large, tricky bluffs when checked to, then you'd be better off to seize the initiative, using your bets with hands like top pair/bad kicker as blocking bets. Of course, if your foe is *that* tricky, your blocking bets won't slow him down much, and maybe you shouldn't be playing against him at all.

But let's not be coy. Playing big pots out of position on the river is no way to make money in the long run—unless you're against a really bad foe, in which case it really won't much matter what you do. So consider this eventuality from the start of the hand. Given the cards you hold, the foe you face, your relative stack sizes, and the overall match odds, is this a fight you want to fight? Do you want to find yourself out of position on the river on this hand, or would you rather wait until conditions are more favorable to you? And if you *do* find yourself engaged at the river, *engage your mind*. There's too much at stake at this critical juncture for uncritical thinking and rash action.

When the Stacks Are Short

Most of our discussion to this point has presumed that you and your opponent are deeply stacked. This won't be the case if you're the last two players in a STT. In that case, then you and your foe probably have at most 15BB each. That's at most; usually there's closer to 20BB than 30BB total in play when tournament heads-up play begins.

A lot of your strategy at this point is actually a function of what will happen in future hands. By thinking about the future, you can work your way back to the best decision for the hand at hand. Again, here's where a chess player's mentality comes in handy. By creating a mental tree diagram of all possible outcomes, you can take the line of play that travels along the optimal branch. If chess thinking and tree diagrams cause your brain to burn, here's a simple rule of thumb to guide you.

> *In short-stacked play, you never want to have less than one fourth of the available chips.*

Of course even when you're deep stacked, having less than one fourth of the chips is no party, but at least with deep stacks you still have some wiggle room. When you're short stacked and three-to-one outgunned, your back is against the wall; it's better not to reach that point. So think ahead! If you're the small blind and posting the big blind on the next hand puts you in the position of having less than one fourth of the tournament chips, your play is to push all-in no matter what two cards you have.

Sometimes we here at KPHQ get a little self-conscious when we say things like "Push all-in no matter what." We can imagine someone out there looking at their 23 offsuit and thinking, "They said do *that*?" It seems so counterintuitive— so scary—so *wrong*. But here's the thing: Going below one fourth of the tournament chips means that you no longer need just a single double up to become chip leader, or just two big confrontations to win the match. When you're that short stacked, you have to be on the right side of three big pots, one to get off your back, one to take the lead, and one to seal the deal. Let's say you're even on the right side of the coin flip, a generous 55:45 favorite on all three showdowns. Your probablity of winning all three is about .17. Compare this to your odds of winning your all-in push with any two cards against a random hand. Even without taking fold equity into consideration, the very ragged 23 offsuit wins 29 percent of the time and ties an additional 6 percent. Pure math, then, says swallow hard and get your chips in the middle.

When you have between one fourth and one half of the total number of chips in play, you'll still need two all-ins to win, and it would be good if you could reduce that number to one without actually having to put your tournament life on the line. Try to play a little bit with your opponent here. Steal some blinds without going all-in if he'll let you. The best time to try this is when you have about 8BB, because he may believe that he's surrendering no real advantage by letting you "generously" have his blind when it won't put you back in the lead. You can also fire the occasional bluff at a pot on the flop, perhaps after limping from the button—provided that making the bluff and then having to break it off will not push you below that critical one-fourth line after you pay your next blind.

Here's an example of thinking about future hands in the context of the present one, and here's a nifty little script you can run when the time is right. Suppose the blinds are 400–800. Before posting your blinds, you have 7,500 chips, and your opponent has 12,500. You are the big blind. Your opponent completes from the small blind and you check behind with your rags. The pot has 1,600 in chips, and you have 6,700 left. If you miss the flop, your instinct may be to fold, but wait! If you fold you'll probably need to push all-in from the small blind on the next hand (or certainly the one after that), no matter what you're dealt. Instead, why not fight for this pot first? Bet 800 chips and try to take this pot. If you do, you're free from having to push blind on the next hand. If you don't, you're done with the hand (unless you get a free ride to the showdown). On the next hand, you can still push all-in to 5,900, more than one fourth of the chips in play. Your flop bet on this hand, then, has what we might call one-way equity: if the bet does the job, you gain a stronger chip position, but if the play doesn't work, you're no worse off, really, than you were.

Even if you are chip leader in a short-stacked heads-up match, you really don't have too much room to move. While you don't need to panic—you're the chip leader, after all—you can't allow yourself to turn too passive. Just a few surrendered blinds can completely reverse the balance of power. Still, the situation favors you. If you control three fourths of the chips and your foe is canny enough to push all-in blind, look to call with a distribution something like [AK,A2]||[AA,22]||[KQ,KT], for these are the hands that will compete favorably against his random holding. You should be doing some pushing of your own, especially if your enemy will make the mistake of surrendering blinds at this critical juncture. Use a distribution slightly wider than your calling distribution, including hands like QJ, which will play well against desperation calls from your short-stacked foe. Remember that if you're sufficiently deeply stacked—and especially if your opponent will occasionally fold his button—you can afford to fold one or two truly ragged hands in the interest of getting a better opportunity.

It will sometimes happen that a heads-up match is so short on blinds that neither you nor your opponent have much more than 5BB each. If that's the case, you're pushing all-in every hand and calling with hands as marginal as QJ—perhaps even worse. In general:

> *The shorter your stack, the wider your calling distribution should be.*

There's just no point in getting blinded into oblivion. But when you have lots of chips, you don't need to gamble and risk letting your opponent get well at your expense. If you stay aggressive enough, you won't have to worry about folding away your chip lead. But when you don't have lots of chips and you need to win a substantial pot to get back in the game, make sure you push your stack in while you still have some stack to push.

Exercises

1. You hold 77 in the big blind, and your opponent has been raising relentlessly from the button. Postflop, he tends to play his position aggressively on the flop and the turn, though he often shuts down on the river. You both are deeply stacked. What's your plan for this hand?

2. You are heads-up in a STT. The blinds are 200–400. Having started heads-up play with only 5,000 in chips, you now have 11,000 to your foe's 9,000. To this point, when you have had the button, you have limped; your opponent has checked behind; and on the flop when your opponent has checked to you, you have made a minimum bet to which your opponent has folded. When you have been in the big blind, your opponent has usually limped from the button. After your opponent has limped, you have checked behind and bet minimum on the flop no matter what the board is, usually prompting your foe to fold.

    You are the button, and you are dealt 7♠7♣. You limp, as you have on all the other hands, and your opponent checks behind. The flop is 2♥4♥5♣. Your opponent checks, you make a minimum bet, and your opponent raises to 3,000. What do you do?

3. Differentiate between card odds, pot odds, and match odds.

4. You are on the button. The board is 3♦8♥J♣4♥3♦. You have Q♥J♦. Preflop, you raised to 3BB, and your opponent called. On the flop, your opponent checked, you bet 4BB, and your opponent called. On the turn, you bet 10BB, and your opponent called. The pot is now 34BB, and your opponent has just checked to you. Should you check or bet?

5. You are heads-up in a STT. The blinds are 400–800. You have 5,500 chips, and your opponent has 14,500. You are in the small blind, and you are dealt 94 offsuit. What do you do?

6. Your opponent seems to be folding when you have a good hand, and he seems to be betting or raising whenever you don't have a hand. Furthermore, the few times you've had a good hand and you've gone to showdown, your opponent has had you beaten. What should you do?

Answers

1. Reraising preflop is tempting; however, with aggressive play on the flop and the turn to come, you probably want to keep the pot small since you will be out of position. You should usually call preflop; if you don't flop a set, you're probably looking to check-call the flop and the turn. Since your opponent shuts down on the river, you should check on the river if you haven't improved

and fold to a bet, as this will indicate real strength on his part. Check-call the flop if you hit your set, and then either lead on the turn or check-raise to extract maximum value before you get to the river and your opponent shuts down. Alternatively, check-call both the flop and the turn if you think that this line of play will slow down his mid-hand aggression on future hands.

2. You have an overpair, which is typically a good hand heads-up. However, with that board and uncharacteristic aggression from your opponent, how confident are you that your sevens will hold up? If your opponent is semi-bluffing with two overcards and a flush draw, you are a slight underdog to win the hand. His other possible holdings include two pair, a set, a straight, a straight draw, or top board pair, and you're only in great shape against the latter two holdings. The key consideration is that you've been pummeling your opponent, and there's no indication that the pummeling will cease. No need to gamble, then, in a speculative situation. Simply fold here.

3. Card odds refer to you hitting hands. Pot odds refer to money in the pot relative to money required to call: your potential chip return measured against the cost of investment. Match odds refer to your probability of winning the overall heads-up match. If you and your opponent are equally stacked and you go all-in as a 54 percent favorite, your odds of winning the match are 54:46. Alternatively, if you and your foe are deeply stacked and you are better than he is, your match odds may be 65:35 over the long haul. To compete in this pot for all the chips where you are only 54:46 would be to sacrifice your edge in overall match odds.

4. This is a value betting problem. Your opponent has already called two bets of about $\frac{2}{3}$ pot each. The only drawing hand he could have is T9, meaning that, most likely, he hit the flop or he has a pocket pair. Given that he called you on the flop and the turn, he will probably call you on the river with anything from eights and threes to jacks and threes. The only problems are if he called you on the flop and the turn with a pair of threes or if he slowplayed a set or two pair on the flop; however, most opponents will not check the river out of position with these powerhouses unless they have strong reason to believe that you will bet. (So take a moment to see yourself clearly through his eyes.) It seems that you definitely beat over 50 percent of your opponent's calling hands for a bet of up to half the pot, so go ahead and bet that.

Do pause to consider whether your foe is capable of check-raise bluffing; in that case, you may wish simply to check behind for the showdown, given the already large size of this pot. Remember that if a pot is large compared to the average pot size, you would like to take down such a pot as easily as possible. There's no need to try to get another two or three big blinds of EV if it opens the door to a check-raise bluff that will cost you the entire pot.

5. If you take the big blind next hand, you'll be down to under one fourth of the chips in play. Buckle your seat belt and push all-in with your 94 offsuit.

6. Leave the game. Your opponent is better than you are and has you dialed in. If you stay in the game, both your ego and your bankroll will end up bruised, but if you leave, only your ego gets hurt.

8
♣♠♦♥

SHORTHANDED LIMIT HOLD'EM

♣♠♦♡

Same Game—Different Game

If you're like most poker players these days and especially if you've joined the fray within the past few years, you probably only play no-limit Texas hold'em. You may be familiar with other poker variants, having learned Seven-Card Stud as a child, say, or having played a little lowball in a home game somewhere. By and large, though, you find such alternatives risible and strange, for they lack the big-bet rush of NLHE. It's like—uhm—once you're used to jumping out of airplanes, riding an escalator just won't do.

Your authors understand and honor the role that adrenaline plays in poker's appeal, and we've been known to chase a big-bet buzz or two ourselves. Still, we feel that a slavish fealty to NLHE is at least shortsighted and very possibly counterproductive. Suppose you get stuck on a desert island someday with two or three other people who resolutely refuse to play anything other than limit Texas hold'em (LHE)? Where would you be then? Okay, admittedly that's a slim possibility, but still, adding to one's repertoire is never a bad idea. Any good, well-rounded poker player will tell you that it's good to be well-rounded, and in practical terms you may very well one day find yourself in a situation where limit hold'em—and shorthanded limit hold'em at that—is literally the only game in town. Rather than face the grim prospect of *just not playing*, let's take a look at the underlying structure and strategy of shorthanded LHE, with an eye toward adding that game to the lengthening list of ones we play well.[1]

On one level, hold'em is hold'em—the math of the cards remains the same. On another level, LHE and NLHE are much different games. In LHE, you have no choice regarding the size of your bets. Preflop and on the flop, your bets and raises are equal to one unit. On the turn and river, your bets are equal to two units. While some people think that this constraint reduces the game to a cut-and-paste simplicity, it's actually deceptively challenging. It takes a lot of skill to read players accurately when they aren't allowed to change their bet sizes, and given that you sometimes face bets offering better than 10:1 odds, it takes a lot of discipline to fold on the river when you *know* that you're beaten.

The first thing to consider about LHE is that it plays smaller than its no-limit cousin. In the latter game, an average pot size is usually about 20–30BB; in the former, it's more like 15–20BB. That difference isn't huge; the real difference comes when you start to consider what makes a large pot. In NLHE, the rare huge pot is over 100BB, while something north of 30BB would be considered similarly rare and huge in limit. As previously discussed, in shorthanded NLHE, it may be acceptable to make short-term -EV moves if such moves will contribute to increasing the overall EV of your entire session, where such

---

1. One of us (Tony) loves LHE…especially live LHE. Once his serfdom to JV is complete, you'll see him banging away at Commerce Casino's juicy games.

net plus EV comes from forcing your opponents to make bad mistakes in very large pots. When large pots contain many more chips than an average pot, this line of reasoning seems self-evident. In LHE, where large pots contain only slightly more chips than an average pot, one can no longer sacrifice small EV; there's not enough payoff in the big pots. Simply put, you have to find the most profitable line of play on every hand, because the difference between small pots and large ones is not great enough to give up transient EV.

You may still find some ploys that will increase your overall session EV without costing you much money, but such opportunities are rare in LHE. One somewhat successful image play is to bet your draws very strongly in a multiway pot so that all your raises are actually +EV for the pot you are in. Your sophisticated opponents will not question your play, but your less sophisticated opponents, not knowing the math of the game, may think that you are consistently out ahead of your hand, giving you the opportunity to get paid off later with made hands.

Another consequence of the LHE betting structure is that it is often hard to deny your opponents the correct odds to draw. Since shorthanded NLHE is all about fold equity, we need to make a little adjustment to our thinking here and to get used to the idea that fold equity may be modest, or altogether absent, in a shorthanded LHE pot. This means that LHE is primarily a game of value betting.

Don't confuse value betting with not being aggressive. On the contrary, LHE offers you the opportunity to be very aggressive, within the constraints of the structure, as you seek to squeeze all possible value out of every betting round. This can be especially fruitful when you're up against opponents who are unaware or unwilling to admit that they have the worst of it. Here's hyperaggression, LHE style: When you're heads-up and you rate yourself as better than 50 percent to win the pot, you make your opponent pay—and pay—and pay again. Likewise, if you're facing two Cally Wally opponents, throw in your chips at every opportunity in situations where you'll win more than one third of the time. LHE, then, can be simple, but that doesn't mean it's slow or easy.

Shorthanded LHE is a game of repeatedly pushing small edges. Missing a big bet on the river is disastrous,[2] as is missing an opportunity to raise a draw for value.

Value betting, then, is the name of the game because it's tough to punish most foes through merciless bluffing in LHE. But guess what? If you can't deny your foes proper odds, then they can't deny you either. Because of this, you'll be folding fewer hands in shorthanded LHE. This is a tough adjustment for many players accustomed to fullhanded LHE, where sitting and waiting to make big hands is the norm. Even though folding marginal hands when getting proper odds is a mistake, it's a mistake that frequently goes unnoticed in fullhanded LHE games. Especially in lower-limit games, there's usually more than enough dead preflop money in each pot so that you can show a substantial profit even when declining to push slight edges in marginal situations.

In shorthanded LHE, where there's less dead money in each pot preflop, you must religiously assess your outs and your probability of winning a hand—and then you must be bold. If you're getting favorable pot odds to call, call. And don't forget to consider that the relative strength of winning hands goes down as a function of shrinking numbers. In many fullhanded LHE games, you usually need at least top pair with a good kicker to go to war. In shorthanded LHE games, you'll sometimes have to call down with second pair and no kicker. Perhaps, against extremely aggressive oppo-

---

2. Not Hurricane Katrina disastrous, maybe, but certainly Bill Buckner disastrous.

nents, you may need to call down with ace high. Don't get us wrong—aggressive play in LHE is still very important. However, calling down in shorthanded LHE is typically correct a much higher percentage of the time than it is in shorthanded NLHE—especially because the size of the bet you're calling is so severely constrained.

As with shorthanded NLHE, deciphering your foes' betting patterns will be crucial to your shorthanded LHE success, but the information you have is different. In NLHE, the wide range of bet sizes available to your opponents often makes your codebreaking efforts easier, for players give away lots of information with the size of their bets. In LHE, the uniformity of bet size makes it a little trickier to puzzle out their intent when they bet.

Your primary hacking mechanism will be to measure your foes' relative level of aggression against their hand distributions. What percentage of hands does your opponent raise with? What percentage of flops does he bet? What does he hold when he check-raises? Will he check-raise bluff? What does a raise on the turn mean? Does a player need at least two pair to raise on the river? That list goes on—longer than we can record here—but we hope these questions will start you thinking about *when* and *whether* your opponent bets, as opposed to *how much*.

Be on the lookout for textbook players, especially those who are using a fullhanded ring game strategy in shorthanded play. They won't be a huge source of profits, but they are very predictable—and predictably too tight. Make sure you don't give them a lot of action when they have hands, for you'll have trouble recouping your investment from their (nonexistent) loose play. Alternatively, if you're up against a real speed racer in shorthanded limit play, just tighten up your starting requirements and let him bet into you over and over again with inferior hands. In all cases, when you're trying to decode your opponents, you'll find yourself having to build some fairly wide HDMs on the fly, but go ahead and do it and don't be afraid to be wrong. You're much better off making even an undereducated guess about what your short-handed LHE foes have in mind than just blindly blundering through.

Winning Pots Uncontested

In LHE, when you get to heads-up postflop play following a preflop raise, your bet on the flop will lay your foe either 5:1 or 5.5:1 odds to call, depending on the position of the blinds. To call in this instance, your opponent really just needs two overcards, and if he believes that you're apt to continuation bet, then he can confidently call with ace high—not as a draw but as the best hand! Because of this, it seems that a continuation bet on the flop after a preflop raise isn't a great line of play. However, keep in mind that even though you'll be called a lot more than you'd be called in a weak NLHE game, you only need to win one pot for every 5 to 5.5 you lose in order for a continuation bet to be profitable play. Therefore, although your fold equity is greatly reduced, the infrequency with which it needs to be successful means that, in heads-up pots at least, routinely continuation betting is still the way to go.

Note that if you raise a lot with the intention of continuation betting, the line of play isn't offering you a huge overlay. Suppose you're the button and you raise with any two cards. The small blind folds and the big blind calls. The big blind checks the flop to you, and you bet. At this point, you have invested three betting units to win just 3.5 betting units. If you're going to continuation bet routinely, it's vital that you raise preflop with hands that are favored over your opponents' distributions, as part of your "plan B" for your continuation bets. Plan A, of course, is that everyone folds and you win uncontested. But if you bet the flop and get called, you can default to the strategy of checking behind on the turn and getting to the river for the price of one small bet on the flop. That plan will work quite nicely *if* you have the best hand preflop. If you're in there abusing position with rags, then you have to hit the flop to win or else drive off your foes with the force of your bets. We know by now that hitting to win is an untenable strategy shorthanded—as is trying to bet off your foes when you can't swing the big club of a big bet. Yes, you want to win your share of uncontested pots (more than your share, in fact) but temper your aggression. Try to make sure that your distribution has some headroom over your foes'.

Of course, if you raise and continuation bet too much (by their standards), your more observant foes will start check-raising you on the flop (a check-raise that you'll often have to call because of pot odds) and betting into you on the turn—with or without any piece of the flop. To defuse this ticking time bomb, mix up your play by laying off the continuation bet from time to time. By occasionally checking on the flop after raising preflop, you increase your fold equity and reduce the probability of your opponents playing too aggressively against you.

Anyway, it turns out that the turn is a better place to pick up uncontested pots in LHE, for the manifest reason that bet sizes are doubled, and foes holding nothing can easily decide to get away from their hands. Suppose you are playing $20–$40 hold'em. Preflop, you raise from the button, with both blinds calling and then checking the flop to you. If you bet now, you'll be betting $20 into a pot of $120, giving your opponents 6:1 odds with two cards to come. If you let the turn card fall and your opponents check to you, your bet will now be offering only 3:1 odds with just one card to come.

Furthermore, since your opponents have checked to you on the flop and the turn, they likely don't have any piece of the board that they'll call you with, *especially* if an undercard to the flop hits. Use this line of play occasionally even when an overcard hits, but pretty much anytime the turn is a brick: (i.e. it appears to help no one), you should be planning to bet behind.

When you miss the flop out of position, you can use a similar ploy. Check the flop, and if your opponents all check, then bet the turn if it's an undercard to the board. Especially if you've shown that you won't bet every flop you hit, your opponents will have a tough time calling on the turn even if they hit the undercard for a pair. Granted, occasionally an opponent will have slowplayed on the flop, but the math of the game dictates that you have to take such chances.

Now let's look at raising as a weapon to induce opponents to fold. In NHLE, where you can use a big bet as a big club, it's possible to drive foes off their hands with a raise or check-raise on the flop. In LHE, however, these bets are too small to achieve that result and are thus completely ineffective in getting foes to fold. In fact, such aggression often has the opposite of its intended result, for not only do your foes have attractive odds to call on the flop, but by jacking up the pot size, you're often actually pricing them in for a ride to the river, no matter what the action on the turn. While it's true that a check-raise on the flop and subsequent aggression on later betting rounds may unnerve a player with bottom pair or middle pair, many players with such holdings will nevertheless call the turn, drawing to two pair or trips (or validly thinking that their hand is best). And when the river hits, they will usually call again, using the large pot size to justify their call.

Primarily, then, raises and check-raises on the flop should be reserved for value betting and free card plays. Against good players, raises on the turn and the river carry much more clout, and good players may fold hands like TPTK to such raises if your image is tight enough (which given that you're playing shorthanded, it rarely will be). Good players pride themselves on betting for value and not giving up an extra bet when their opponents signal a big holding by raising. As always, observe all hands played at your table, and if you see a player fold to a raise on the turn or the river after betting, then you know whom you can target. Have this play in your arsenal, but use it sparingly, for the fact is that against the majority of opponents, it just won't work.

Passive Play Versus Aggressive Play

In shorthanded NLHE, scalable bet sizes are a key strategic tool and fold equity is the key to success. Without scalable bets, and the big, pot-manipulative club they represent, LHE offers much less fold equity, meaning, of course, that you are going to see more hands through to showdown. With this in mind, you want to be aggressive from the flop forward generally only when you have an edge in cards or when you are against an opponent who will most likely check to you on the turn, giving you a discounted draw.

One particular instance in which you'll be less aggressive is playing out of position on the river. You'll recall our discussion of blocking bet (see p. 106) and of their use even when they're not true value bets. Because they scale the pot on your terms, these bets can potentially save money by averting larger bets on the river in uncertain circumstances. In LHE, there is no longer a need for a blocking bet—there's nothing to block! Your play on the river when out of position in LHE, then, is basically about betting with the best of it and counting on your foe calling "for the size of the pot" with a weaker hand. The only time you should fail to bet the best hand is if you're so certain your foe will fold that the only conceivable way you'll make money is to check and to try to induce a bluff. If you know your foes, you'll know which path to take.

Meanwhile, if you do not see yourself as a favorite against your opponent's calling distribution, then you should check with the intention of calling if the pot odds being offered to you compare favorably to how you stand against your opponent's betting distribution. Remember that at times you will be getting better than 10:1 on your money on the river, meaning that if your opponent bluffs more than one out of eleven hands, you can call on the river with any pair. This argument, while valid, *should not* motivate you to make clearly bad calls. If your opponent knows that you are going to increase your calling frequency, he is much less apt to bluff. Be aware of the symmetry in the logic. Be aware of the pot size when you are contemplating a call on the river, and honestly assess your opponents' betting distributions. Also be aware that calling to catch a bluff, or betting into others as a bluff, has little to no value when there is more than one opponent left in the pot. Someone has something; if you have nothing, you will lose.

Iso Action

The size of bets and raises in fixed-limit poker makes it tough to force players out of pots. However, if the player to your right raises, it is usually possible to isolate him by reraising, and you pretty much always want to try for the iso play whenever you think you have the better hand. The extra dead money in the pot often makes this play extremely worthwhile. For example, suppose you have AK on the button. Play folds to the player on your right, who raises. One option is to call, hoping to hit an ace or a king on the flop; however, you know that at this point in the hand, your AK is a big favorite against your foe's raising distribution. So go ahead and reraise to isolate, and see what happens on the flop. Most of the time, of course, you will miss, but you still want to three-bet (raise a raise, that is, put in the third best) preflop while you yet have a statistical edge, for the increased pot size will make your decisions on subsequent betting rounds easier (i.e., give you odds to call down an aggressive opponent with just ace high). Therefore, three-bet, and make the blinds fold. Assuming the original raiser just calls, you effectively get 4.5:3 on your money preflop.

If your opponent checks to you on the flop after you're three-bet, go ahead and bet. Your fold equity is low, but so is your bet size, so this continuation bet doesn't have to work that often to be worthwhile. You should be aware that you're more susceptible to check-raises after having three-bet, but as long as the proportion of folds is about equal to the proportion of check-raises, you shouldn't have to worry too much. Most of the time, he'll just call.

If you have position and your opponent bets into you then if you have two overcards, you may consider raising, especially if you have ace high on a board with only one high card. The point of this play is to get a free card on the turn when your opponent just calls on the flop and checks the turn. Some, of course, will three-bet you and bet into you on the turn instead. When a foe does this, you need to know whether he's capable of doing it as a complete bluff or whether he's got a big hand and he's trying to get you on the hook for many bets. Nothing is worse than getting into a raising war with a bad hand against an enemy you think is bluffing but is not. Just one such "momentary lapse of reason" can have huge negative consequences on your shorthanded LHE session.

A word of caution: some foes don't know their own strength. They may be three-betting with second pair because they think it's a monster. Others will only attack with two pair or better. Here's where your profiling skills come in handy. You need to know not just whether an enemy is on a big hand but what, exactly, he considers big.

When you're going to be out of position for the duration of the hand, you should keep your three-betting activity to a minimum, especially from the big blind. From the small blind, you can three-bet a little more often, because you'll more frequently get heads-up with dead money from the big blind in the pot, assuming the big blind folds to your iso raise. Mostly you should check-fold or check-call when you miss or barely hit the flop; check-raise bluffs have little fold equity in this instance. When you hit a hand, try to strike a balance between check-raising and betting out. It's important to check-raise and even check-call with very good hands on occasion to force your opponents to put the brakes on when they have position on you. If they have to worry about you having an actual hand when you play passively, then your play of marginal hands will get much easier and life will be good.

In Closing

Value is king in shorthanded LHE. Whenever you force your opponents to give you a favorable return on your investment in a given round of play, you're doing the right thing. Suppose you have a nine-outer with two cards to come. You will hit your hand about 35 percent of the time; the odds against hitting are 65:35 = 13:7, or just under 2:1. If you have at least two foes in the hand and if the pot will continue to give you favorable odds on the turn, you should be in there betting or raising for value. Some of your foes (those who don't understand the math of this) will be baffled and enraged by your "betting on the come." Your subsequent image equity and tilt equity make this play more favorable still.

The bottom line on limit play? You can't sit around and trap players for big pots. You've got to get those gloves off and fight for every small edge you can find!

Exercises

1. Name some fundamental differences between short-handed NLHE and LHE.

2. Why is continuation betting effective in shorthanded LHE, even though your fold equity is much lower?

3. You have Q♦9♣, and the flop is K♦9♦2♣. Preflop, the pot was unraised, and on the flop, all three of your opponents checked after you. The turn is a 4♠. What's your line of play for the rest of the hand?

4. You have K♣Q♣ on the button in a 5-handed game. Preflop, UTG, and UTG+1 limp. You raise, the small blind folds, and everybody else calls. The flop is J♣T♣5♦. Action checks to you. What do you do?

5. In the situation given in question 4, you check the river is the K♦, and everyone checks to you. What do you do?

Answers

1. Given equivalent blinds, the average pot size in NLHE is slightly larger than in LHE, and the size of a big pot in NLHE is much bigger than the size of a big pot in LHE. Structured betting means that you have less fold equity in LHE than in NLHE. In NLHE, you are usually playing to trap opponents in big, key pots; in LHE you push every small edge you can get.

2. The size of your bet compared to the pot is much lower, meaning that your continuation bet doesn't have to work very often for it to be a profitable play.

3. You should be confident that your pair of nines is best here. There's a chance that someone with a king and a bad kicker would've checked the flop, but since it's a shorthanded game and because of the draws on the board, it's not very likely. You should bet the turn for value and the river as well if no scare card comes. If a scare card falls, check. If someone bets, you'll have to base your calling decision on pot size and your assessment of whether your foe will bet with a worse hand or nothing at all.

4. You have fifteen outs that make you a huge hand plus another six that may also win the hand for you. You have two cards to come, so bet for value!

5. Heads-up, or even three-way, this is usually a value bet even if you don't have the draws that you have. Since you have three other opponents, there's a better chance that someone is trying to trap, but given the lack of action on a flop with lots of available draws, it's hard to

imagine that you're beaten here. In the rare circumstance where you are trailing, you still have lots of outs.
Value bet, though if you feel that someone is waiting to
unleash an iso check-raise with a big hand, checking behind wouldn't be the end of the world.

9

STRATEGERIES

Our Back Pages

Back in 2000 (long before the Moneymaker revolution and the Internet poker boom, so, yeah, ancient history), there was a *Saturday Night Live* sketch lampooning then presidential candidates Al Gore and George W. Bush. Gore was tarred with the boring brush, and on Bush they hung the word "strategery," a nod to the man's penchant for such imaginative linguistic somersaults as "Is our children learning?" and "subliminable." The authors of this book take no political sides—at least not here—but we have come, over time, to use the word strategery to mock one another's play or to defend our own, mockingly viz.:

"Why would you call when you can't even beat a bluff?"

"Strategery!"

Now, as it happens, one of the things we did in writing this book was to play a *ton* of heads-up poker, author against author, stack against stack, strategery against strategery, and we glorified this pastime with the grand handle of "research." In our defense, we did take a lot of notes while we played: observations about ourselves and one another; analyses of betting patterns and deception trends; and tactics we could use, or try to use, to bash each other's brains in.[1,2] We also talked our thinking through, and we found the combination of play, thought, notes, and talk to be very effective in clarifying our approach to the game (see the proceeding). Much of what we thought about and talked about found its way, by direct or indirect means, into the text you've read so far. Inevitably, there were some leftovers—observations languishing in our notebooks, stuff worth sharing, but not worth spending whole chapters on. So we've bundled them all together here for you now, and we glorify them with the grand handle of strategeries.

Articulate Dat Shit

If you really want to improve your shorthanded play, or any poker play, do what we did: Sit down across the table from a friend and fellow poker freak, play a few million hands of poker, and talk about everything you do. Pause between hands to show each other what you had, and tell each other what you were thinking. Guess at each other's holdings. Speculate about bet size and bet intention. Discuss lines of attack and lines of defense. True fact: talking about poker while you play will grow your game astoundingly and swiftly.

Understand that when you're in this sort of match, your object isn't to win money but to exchange views, develop strategies, and learn from your mistakes.[3,4] You should play for

1. For the record, I usually won.
2. No, I did.
3. Which mostly he made.
4. No, he did.

at least a *little* money, of course; otherwise your decisions won't matter and you won't play with thoughtfulness and care. But, really, winning your friend's money is secondary. You're there to focus your thinking, and sharing information about your respective approaches is just a great way to do that.

If you think it skews the game to share your cards and secret strategies with one another, well, yeah, it does. But look, shorthanded hold'em is a game of adaptation, and what better way to stimulate adaptation than to have the certain knowledge of your opponent's approach? Yeah, you know he's banging away with stop-and-goes—he told you he is. So you have to find a way to stop him. And he knows you're trying to do that. You're both learning to adapt, and whether those adaptations are based on *known* information or *guessed* information, it's still adaptation, and that's still a skill you need to have.

Articulate dat shit. Everything becomes clearer when you do. Just consider the matter of hand distributions. It's one thing to think, in a vague general sense, about what hands your opponent might hold. It's quite another thing to say the words, "I think your distribution includes all pocket pairs above eights and all aces down to ace-ten." When you do that, you're making a *commitment* to your analysis, and whether the analysis is ultimately right or wrong, the commitment itself is worth something. Talk everything out. Trust us, you'll be glad you did.

Take First Tendencies at Face Value

We're all familiar with the ol' "I know that he knows that I know that he knows" mindfuck. This problem becomes more acute in shorthanded play, where combatants become very familiar with one another's tactics, and adjustments must be made literally from one hand to the next. How do you know whether your foe is weak or just feigning weakness because he knows that's what you expect of him here? Or maybe he's really weak, but playing weak so you'll interpret him as strong when he's not. Or maybe he's strong, playing weak, but masquerading as weak-playing-strong-playing-weak-playing-strong. Or maybe—or maybe—or maybe.

Truly, the head doth explode.

We here at KPHQ think that such thinking is a little too clever by half. How tricky do you think your opponents really are? First of all, they're human, just like you, so they're trying to make the best of imperfect information, just like you. Second, if you think they're that capable of all this third, fifth, and Nth-level thinking, *why are you still in the game with them*? Granted, you could be trapped in a tournament, but still—for the most part, we give our foes more credit than they deserve, especially at the outset of play, when they're unknown to us and therefore a little bit spooky.

Treat opponents as straightforward until proven tricky. Take first tendencies at face value, and use first tendencies as a yardstick against which to measure subsequent moves. If they're really tricky, they'll reveal themselves as such pretty quickly, and you can adjust accordingly (snug up; fight back; go away). In the meantime, don't oversolve the problem. WYSIWYG, right? What you see is (generally) what you get.

The Second Stab

As Doyle Brunson famously observed, it takes a certain amount of fortitude to fire the second barrel—bet again with nothing on the turn after having bet with nothing on the flop. In shorthanded play, the bet with nothing on the flop is common—routine. No doubt you'll make your share of blank bets, and no doubt you'll win your share of uncontested pots on the flop. But you always have to think ahead in the hand. If you bet the flop and get called, will you have the courage to fire that second shot?

There's no law that says you have to blank bet or semi-bluff or engage in any other form of shorthanded stealth. We don't think you can succeed in the game without some larceny in your soul, but that's neither here nor there right now. The issue at hand is one of self-awareness. If you know that you're comfortable taking a stab at the pot, but not too comfortable taking that second stab, then learn to refrain from the first if just throwing in the first isn't enough to make your opponents wilt—either that or learn to follow through. We give much thought to what our foes are capable of; we need to know what we're really capable of as well.

What Is Your Default Value?

In shorthanded NLHE, if your default value is folding, you're thinking about the game wrong. We think this thought process is an artifact of fullhanded play, especially in loose, passive games in which a lot of people see a lot of cheap flops. In such circumstances, the check-fold is a common play. You see a cheap flop; you miss; you fold; next case.

Such a modus operandi has no place in shorthanded NLHE, where fewer people contest more pots, and those who remain uninvolved have a slim prospect for profit. Whenever you enter a pot, your default value should be betting, and your key question should be, "How can I win this hand?" Once more, we see how shorthanded poker turns conventional poker thinking upside down. So many people play poker not to lose—they're obsessed with staying out of trouble. There's nothing terribly wrong in that approach in full ring play, but in the hothouse environment of shorthanded NLHE, *it just won't work*.

Again, what's your tolerance for risk? If you can't hack it— fine, don't hack it. Maybe shorthanded poker isn't your thing. But if you decide that you're going to play the short game, you'd better be in it to win it, because at a shorthanded table, there's just no place to hide.

Intuitive Hand Distribution Modeling

We've talked a lot in this book about HDM, about making a conscious and considered appraisal of the array of hands your opponents might be on. We want to stress that this is *not* about putting your opponent on an exact hand—"I *knew* you had Big Slickina!" Rather, it's about contemplating the range of hands your foe might hold and then using available information—betting patterns, tells, recent history, game state—to narrow that range down to a manageable size. You then think about how your hand compares to various hands in that range. Then you make your move. Winning players work through this process in a logical series of step-by-step calculations and evaluations.

Or—they don't.

In our universe—and no doubt yours—there's something called intuitive hand distribution modeling, wherein you don't think about your foe's holdings in any rigorously ordered way. You just—weigh stuff—until an answer falls into place. Some players are extraordinarily good at this, and we can only applaud their gift of insight. It lets them figure stuff out without actually figuring stuff out. For the rest of us, it's simple: when intuition fails, analysis must suffice.

We're not saying don't rely on your intuitive gifts; just don't use them as a crutch. The fact is that some players rely on an unstructured appraisal of a hand situation (and glorify it by calling it intuitive HDM) because they're yet unfamiliar with—or lazy about or even scared of—the conscious, analytical approach. If you fall into that category, we have two suggestions. First, *try it*. You'll find that the daunting math of the matter becomes a lot less daunting with just a little practice and with, at the end of the day, very little math at all. Second, not to shill for the product line but check out Tony's *Killer Poker by the Numbers*. It will guide you to an understanding of poker's hidden clockworks and help you reach the point where your analytical HDM and intuitive HDM work side by side as allies.

Changing Horses in Midstream

We've talked in this book about having a line of play or a "plan for the hand." Sometimes, these lines of play are well established in your mind before you even receive your cards. If you're on the button against weakly defended blinds and everyone folds to you, your line of play is to raise with any two cards, and your plan for the hand is to have the blinds fold. But the best laid plans of mice and men, they say—or no, you know what, let's quote Bobby Burns exactly:

> But, Mousie, thou art no thy lane
> In proving foresight may be vain:
> The best laid schemes o' mice an' men
> Gang aft a-gley,
> An' lea'e us nought but grief an' pain,
> For promised joy.

When your plan for the hand goes south and when your foes don't do what you expected them to do, the solution is not to switch plans radically, but rather to have a fully devel-

oped line of play, based on all contingencies. To continue
from the example just discussed, your actual and precise plan
is to have the blinds fold *or, if they don't, consider that they have
real hands and play accordingly*. It doesn't mean that you're
done with the hand. It just means that you have considered
the possibility of the hand developing in ways other than the
way you want.

To take another example, say you're out of position against
a very aggressive player, and you hold T9 suited. You call his
raise, with the intention of hitting the flop and trapping him.
If you hit the flop, great. If you don't, don't radically depart
from your *trap* plan into some ill-conceived *bluff* plan. That's
an example of changing horses in midstream, and it's not a
good idea. While flexibility is terrific and "calling an audible"
is sound poker strategy, this is a case of disappointment, not
strategy, driving the bus. You had a nifty plan—hit and trap—
but when that plan didn't pan out, your ire made you switch
plans. Always be aware of where you're at mentally, and always make sure to stay out of your own way, Mousie.

Put Them on a Hand Every Time

You often know you're going to fold. It's automatic. So automatic that you don't even bother thinking about what the
other guy has. Well, you know what? That automatic fold is
actually an opportunity for exercise. Even though you know
you're going to fold, take a moment to see the situation
through the other guy's eyes—around here we call this *ghost-
ing* an opponent—and try to figure out what he has. If other
players are in the pot, you may get a chance to find out how
right or wrong you were. Even if you never get to see his cards,
you *do* gain valuable experience at on-the-fly HDM, and how
can that be a bad thing?

Pots Above the Mean

True fact: you want to be the one winning most of the big pots. While this seems self-evident, it has important strategic impact, especially when big pots are few and far between. When a pot has grown to be well above the mean—much larger than normal—it will have an exaggerated impact on your stack, your foes' stacks, and overall table trends. In other words, whoever wins the rare biggie is going to be in boss command. So you want to win the biggie—even if it means sacrificing some +EV. By sacrificing +EV, we refer to trying to eke out another 3BB with a small value bet when you can just as well take down a 100BB pot immediately with a much larger bet that shuts out all draws.

In a similar vein, don't play big pots in uncharted territory. If you're new to the game or facing a foe who hasn't revealed himself to you yet, there's no harm in declining confrontations. Remember, this is shorthanded play; situations repeat frequently and fast. If you have a skill edge (and by now we assume you do), you'll be much better off waiting for a time when your skill edge is augmented by an information edge as well.

Why Tilt Is Worse Shorthanded

It's not just that you have to make so many more decisions, and thus have more chances to make bad ones. It's that in a shorthanded game, you have nowhere to lurk and recover. Were you playing in a fullhanded game, you could fix your tilt by folding. You could play correctly by not playing at all, hiding behind a tight image till your tilt wanes. That won't work in a shorthanded game, where too tight play is a losing proposition and loose, Cally play (so often the hallmark of tilt) is just a disaster.

Plus, you have to make more decisions.

And you're in no shape to make good ones.

Because you're on tilt.

So ten-handed, you can fold all the bad hands and try not to get hurt too much by the marginal decisions you have to make while you're tilt impaired. At the extreme other end of the spectrum, if you're playing heads-up, you have to make decisions on every single hand. Your foe may very well know you're on tilt, of course, and abuse you mercilessly. Even if he doesn't, though, *you're still on tilt* and still in a position to do damage to yourself on hand after hand after hand.

So let's codify this as the Law of Shorthanded Tilt:

> *The fewer players there are in the game, the worse it is to go off.*

If it's important to get out of a fullhanded game when you're "a cork, bobbing on the sea of poker," it's dead critical that you do so shorthanded. If you don't, you'll be broke before you know what hit you.

But you know that. The problem is never recognizing the danger of tilt. The problem is recognizing the *fact* of tilt. Here's a litmus test: resentment. Anytime you feel resentment, you're on tilt. Whether that resentment is directed at another player or the universe or yourself, it's a warning sign that *you simply must heed*. Tilt in shorthanded play will kill your bankroll. Just kill it.

At What Point Should You Rebuy?

Let's say you're in a cash game and you're running low on chips. Should you try to nurse a short stack back to health, or should you reload now and make your stack a credible weapon? We could give you all sorts of fancy (well, fanciful) mathematical formulas about relative stack sizes, ratio of stack to blinds, phases of the moon, what have you. But it turns out there's a simpler way to address the question, and it has nothing to do with the size of your stack. It has to do with your foes.

You pretty much always want to be deeply stacked if you're better than your opponents. So if the game is good (by which we mean that the players are bad) and if your head is good (absent resentment), then you should reload, top off, or whatever you want to call it at the first opportunity. To play against inferior foes with an inferior stack is to bring yourself down to their level.

Against superior enemies, not only don't rebuy, but don't linger. That's always your best protection against foes you can't beat.

But people often have a sentimental attachment to their buy-in. Having halved their stack, say, they'd rather rebound on their own merit—so that they're only "into the game" for their original buy-in—than rebuy themselves into a deeper hole. Be aware of this. Recognize the times when you're not playing to beat your opponents, but rather just playing to preserve your stack. That's not exactly tilt—but it's not precisely perfect poker either. If you're feeling weak and defensive, either force yourself to reload (against inferior foes), or take a break from the table. Sentimentally nursing a dwindling stack isn't as dangerous as tilt, but it hardly augurs well for positive results.

Heads-Up Play and Ego

One of the hardest things to do, from an ego point of view, is to walk away from a heads-up match. It's such an admission of defeat. It's like putting on a T-shirt that says, "I'm His Bitch." Beneath all these negative feelings is the harsh truth, the bedrock reality that, well, the other guy is just playing better right now. Such a realization is hard to accept. It causes psychic pain. It's doubly hard to walk away from a match when you're losing because, hey, *you're losing*, and nobody likes to book a loss, no matter how practiced you are at taking the long view and calling interim results irrelevant.

We'd like to help you out of this bind. Really, we would, for we've been there, and we know as well as you how hard it is to admit "de-fucking-feat." So how about this? Take pride in leaving when you're beaten; take pride in your discipline and your clear-eyed sense of self; and let that pride be the antidote to psychic pain.

Or if that doesn't work, try this: when you're having trouble pulling out of a nosedive because it feels so bad to go down, just think how much worse you'll feel when you crash. The bottom line is that it takes a tough player to admit defeat. Be that tough player, and be that tough.

Control Freaks

Shorthanded matches, especially heads-up ones, are often about psychological control. When you're calling the shots in a match, you have something that's worth more than cards alone. For this reason, it's often worth surrendering some chips if you can retain overall control.

Let's say you've been abusing someone's big blind and he's been pretty much laying down for you: every time you raise preflop (and you're pretty much raising every time preflop), he folds like a map of Africa. You've not only achieved behavior dominance, but you've got stack dominance as well. Your foe is afraid of you and letting you have your way. Now here comes a hand where, suddenly, he raises you back. You have your usual "whatever" cheese, but you're thinking of getting involved anyhow. Don't do it! Why do you think he raised now? Because he's tired of you pushing him around? No! Well, yes—but also because *he finally has a hand*. Surrendering to this one reraise will not fundamentally change the game state—but playing a big pot and losing could.

Give up the hand and don't give up any more chips. Then go right back and resume your thieving ways. If your foe has truly decided to change gears and come over the top of your aggression, you'll find out soon enough. It's much more likely, though, that he'll revert to his same defensive stance, and you can continue to chip away at his stack.

Momentum is a considerable factor in shorthanded play. If the momentum is running your way, don't willingly yield it.

Another Benefit of Position

We all know that position is great because you get to see what your foes do before you have to act. Beyond this manifest benefit, though, there's what we might call the *bargain of position*, where not only do you get to act last, but you also get to choose not to act at all. From the flop to the turn or the turn to the river, betting in position often means that you get two cards for the price of one.

You flop a flush draw in position. Your foe checks, you bet, he calls. The turn is a brick, but he checks to you again. You may now decide to check behind, picking up a free shot at hitting your flush. In other words, your in-position bet on the flop gets you to the river for free, if you so choose. That's a hell of a bargain, is it not?

Now turn it around. You're out of position with a flush draw. You check-call on the flop. If you check again on the turn, your savvy opponent is going to make you pay again for your draw—and might just bet you off the pot right then and there. Absent a completely flaccid foe, you're just not often going to get to see the turn and river cards for the price of a call on the flop.

We're not saying that you can't play draws out of position, or any hand out of position, for there are, of course, ways to take control of the hand, either by check-raising or by stop-and-go action on the flop or turn. But the fact is that *every* hand plays easier in position, not just for reasons of information, but for reasons of price as well.

When the Other Guy Rebuys

Under the intense microscope of shorthanded play, the true nature of a foe's character is often revealed in the moment when he's felted and forced to rebuy. While it's true that many players can stay on an even keel when the tides of poker turn against them, it's equally true that many players will tilt, and tilt badly, when they have to go back into their wallet or player's account, just to stay in the game. Insofar as tilt is a leak and insofar as shorthanded play magnifies leaks, your foe's post-rebuy phase of play may be an outstanding profit opportunity for you.

First ask yourself if his nose is open. This phrase, if you don't know, is borrowed from boxing. When a fighter's nose is opened (by blows from his opponent), he's likely to bleed out and, ultimately, go down. In poker, a player with his nose open is someone who, due to transient psychic pain, can't presently make quality decisions. So ask yourself if your rebuying foe fits in that category. Next ask how long he's likely to remain in that condition. Is he the sort of player who can quickly right his ship, or is he likely to founder through this rebuy and the next and the one after that?

If he falls into the former category, you'll need to strike quickly. Gear up to a more aggressive stance as soon as your foe rebuys. Put a lot of pressure on, and keep it on, until he demonstrates that he's regained control of himself. Alternatively, if he looks likely to stay on tilt for quite some time, then you take your time. Keep playing your good, adaptive, game. He'll give you everything before he's done.

One common characteristic of the player with a fresh rebuy is *aggressiveness*. Having taken a hit to his stack and his psyche, he'll be looking to get well quickly by building the sort of big pots that will restore his chip count and his confidence. Trap more and call more, for he's likely to be pressing small edges—or even no edges at all. In other words, let him build the big pots—then make his bad situation worse by beating him again!

A Basic Truth About Your Opponents

Fact: most of your foes won't be as sophisticated as you are. It's not just because you've read this book and they haven't. Rather, by reading this book, you have distinguished yourself as someone who is *thinking hard about your game*. Beyond cursory consideration of hand values and a passing nod to pot odds, most poker players just don't bother to do that work. This has three strategic implications:

First, don't count on cleverness from your foes if cleverness is called for to win a hand. It's well known, for instance, that naked bluffs won't work against players who are too stubborn or unaware to fold. They may very well think that their bottom pair is the best hand—and if you're bluffing, they may very well be right. So, whenever you're thinking about essaying a tricky move, ask yourself if your move is "too smart for the house." If yes, save it for a different crowd.

Second, stay away from marginal situations. Say you're holding K9 against an unsophisticated foe and the flop comes AA7. He bets into you. You may very well have the best hand—but go ahead and fold anyhow. Remember that he is a foe you have a skill edge over, and therefore the match odds are strongly in your favor. If he pays you off when you have the best of it, but you don't pay him off when he *may or may not* have the best of it, you can't help but crush him in the long run.

Third, tickle the trout. Make unsophisticated foes feel very good about themselves and about the way they're playing the game. Inflate their self-esteem. Give them the impression that they're in control of the match. In other words, open a gap between their confidence and their capability. Soon, their confidence will give way to recklessness. As a function of not being as smart as they've been led to believe they are, they'll saunter into a big mistake and ship a lot of their chips your way.

Recent History

Because of the rich context density of shorthanded NLHE, current trends count for a lot in the game. Most of your opponents will base their picture of you on what has just happened or what has happened over the last handful of hands. If you're in there banging away with a lot of raises, they'll see you as aggressive. After a while, they'll stop to consider what your raises represent. Should you happen to pick up a big hand in the context of this aggressive recent history, your foes will play into you without even stopping to consider whether this time your bet could be real.

Now contemplate the converse. If you've been playing passively for some reason, your recent history will indicate that you're not a very aggressive player. In this instance, when you pick up a big hand, you're more or less frozen out of betting it strongly, for your foes will read your raise for real strength. This is not the same as analyzing betting patterns and deception trends. Rather, it's a reflex response to recent history. Players who respond in this way aren't very good, and they're very predictable, so always monitor your own recent history and remember to see yourself as your opponents see you. This thoughtfulness will win you many pots and also keep you out of much trouble.

The Good News About Preflop Raises

We come back again and again to the notions of aggressiveness and position. At some point you may begin to wonder whether such a strategy can really be sustained over time. What about all the times that someone plays back at you? Won't your stack really dwindle as a result?

Actually—not so much.

The fact about preflop raises—the really good news about them—is that you can make them all day long in a short-handed game without materially hurting yourself, no matter how many times you have to fold to the pressure of the occasional reraise. Really, the only way your preflop aggression can hurt you is if you trap yourself or allow yourself to be trapped.

This will happen most often when your preflop aggression is going largely unchecked so that you find yourself playing pots with hands like T9 suited, or big cards with bad kickers. Next thing you know, your own confidence and your own recent history get you involved in a big pot where the character-istic weakness of your starting hand puts you in a bind. Say you raise with K8 suited and hit a king on the flop. Sure you're going to continuation bet your top pair—but what happens if you run into strong opposition? That's the time to let that top pair go. Maybe your opponents are wising up to your tricks and are simply taking a stand, but until you have evidence supporting that, assume that your previously uncreative op-ponents will continue to be uncreative.

It's a great game plan to take control of the match by bang-ing away with lots and lots of preflop raises. Just don't deviate from the plan by playing a lot of big pots with marginal hands. Be aware that the very thing that makes your strategy work—preflop aggression with less than prime tickets—puts you at risk for difficult, trappy situations from the flop for-ward.

The Risk of Rhythm

Whenever you're playing shorthanded poker, and especially when you're playing online, beware of falling into a rhythm without considering the consequences of that rhythm. There are two: First, you might be giving away real information about your hand strength and thought process in instances when you deviate from your standard time pattern. Second, your own rhythm can put you on autopilot and make you careless about the choices you make.

Consider taking steps to break up your rhythm artificially and arbitrarily from time to time. For example, make yourself count to five before taking any action. This will yield the twin benefits of forcing you to think things through and of distort-ing your opponents' picture of you. Where once you were act-ing swiftly and with seeming confidence, you'll now appear to be tentative and confused. Believe us, even a five-second stall can really skew things in your foes' minds. The bottom line is that when you change rhythm, you change information, and in terms of moving your enemies out of their comfort zone, that can never be a bad thing.

At the same time, be attentive to the overall rhythm of the table. This will often be a function of recent history. If the table has a "fast" rhythm so that people are making bets and raises without really pondering future play of the hand, you have the opportunity to slip in a larger-than-average bet with a stronger-than-usual holding—ride the rhythm, as it were— and get your foes out ahead of their hands. This is another reason for knowing the going rate for a raise. Within the rhythm of the game, there will be a certain size bet that some opponents will call without much thought and without much of a hand. Know what that bet size is so that you can play accordingly, either staying within the rhythm of that raise in order to get calls, going slightly above it for value, or else blasting well past it to generate folds.

The Friskiness Quotient

On many hands, you will come to a certain crossroads where you'll face the choice of whether to commit to major involvement or not. Facing a bet on the flop for instance, you'll weigh folding to your foe's apparent strength against putting him to the test with an unexpected big check-raise. Obviously, your decision will be colored by everything you know about the situation and about your opponent. But also think of what you know about yourself. Do you get carried away with friskiness? Many players do, especially in shorthanded play, which puts such a premium on friskiness.

Friskiness is good. We like friskiness. Here at KPHQ it's kind of a motto, "When in doubt, be frisky." That said, there's such a thing as too much of a good thing.[5] If your friskiness has been running rampant and especially if you think that your foe is counting on you to engage in battle just because that's what you do, then consider whether this time you might not be better off declining to engage. The battles you don't fight contribute to your bottom line as much as the ones you do.

Sometimes you might want to dial down your friskiness quotient even if you're certain you can still get away with it. Orphan flops are a good example of this. If the flop is 773 and your foe checks into you, there's no reason to believe that you won't win the pot with a bet. But if you've been attacking a lot of orphans lately and if your recent history is trending very aggressive, there's nothing wrong with checking this hand down. You can create the false impression of tight play without sacrificing anything except a small pot—which you may very well end up winning at showdown anyhow.

You might think that such timidity will embolden your foe. If it happened in the context of overall tightness, you might be right. But remember, you're wearing a frisky image right now. Going against the grain of that can only serve to befuddle your foe, which will probably aid your efforts to steal more pots in the immediate hands to come.

When considering your friskiness quotient, then, consider your image, the game state, and the direction you want to take your foe from here. While aggressive play is generally rewarded, there are definitely times—for reasons of strategy, not timidity—to turn down the heat a little.

---

5. This is true, so far as we can tell, of everything except sex.

Don't Not Bet Your Hand

As we've been at pains to point out, it's hard to make a hand in shorthanded NLHE. For this reason, we think your default action should be to bet whenever you think you have the best of it. You may be inclined not to follow this advice when you're sitting on a monster and when you're afraid of not getting paid off. In fullhanded games, this approach often makes sense, since more players in a pot means more players available to do your betting for you. The tendency to slowplay a monster, then, is an artifact of fullhanded play experience. As a strategy, it doesn't do well in shorthanded play and you should abandon it.

Yes, you certainly run the risk of having everyone fold. Yes, you might foreclose on someone's urge to bluff at you. Yes, you might get less than full value from your monster. You know what? That's okay. You're still in command of the match. You're still the one doing the betting. And if you're doing enough betting (*you're* doing enough betting, aren't you?), it may be that your foes won't read you for holding a monster and will pay you off anyhow.

It beats a certain dead horse to say it, but the outcome of your shorthanded session usually turns on the play of a few key hands. The confluence of big hands and big pots is reasonably rare, we grant; however, how is your big hand ever going to win a big pot if you don't get out there and create one? In the movie *Field of Dreams* we learn, "If you build it, they will come." That may or may not be true, but one thing's for sure: if you don't build it, they won't come.

So build it. Build it good. Build it through the image you have of betting cheese in prior hands. Slowplaying is for fullhanded games, and we're not such big fans of it there either.

Betting for Information

When you bet for information, be sure to trust the information you get. If you have raised someone on the flop to gauge the strength of his hand, he reraises, and you still call him down and pay him off, well, you've got no one to blame but yourself.

Consider: You're staring at an orphan flop of 992 rainbow. Your out-of-position foe bets into that flop. You rate him as semi-tricky: capable of betting with a nine, deuce, or pocket pair, but also capable of taking a stab at this pot with a naked ace or even nothing at all. You could always surrender this pot altogether—no harm in that. But let's say you decide to test the waters by throwing out a raise. Now he comes over the top for all his chips. Well, you got the information you were looking for: he has a real hand. Yes, there's a chance that he's bluffing—people do bluff—but if you thought he was bluffing, you wouldn't be raising for information, you'd be raising to resteal the pot. Trust your read. Having sought certain input, trust the input you get.

Of course, this information does take some interpreting. What is his image of you? Does he consider your raise to be a real raise, a bluff raise, or a raise for information? If he doesn't read you correctly *and* if he's capable of a big reraise bluff *and* if you're capable of figuring all that out, then go ahead and snap him off. Otherwise, remember why you made the raise in the first place. Your foe was presenting you with a puzzle. You had several pieces of information in service of solving it and threw in that raise in an endeavor to get the last piece of the puzzle. Having received it, *act accordingly*. Stacks are lost in a heartbeat when thinking suddenly shifts from, "I wonder if he's got it *to* take that, you lying sack of cheese!"

Rising Blinds Squeeze the Streets

We all know that when the blinds rise in a tournament, they put the squeeze on stacks, turning big ones into medium ones and medium ones into small ones. Interestingly, they also put the squeeze on the streets, by which we mean that the higher the blinds get, the less likely there is to be play on later streets.

When everyone is deeply stacked in a tournament, there are ample chips for play across all four betting rounds. You can fire off a bet on the flop and a bigger bet on the turn and still have enough left in your stack to make a sufficiently big bet to control action on the river. As the blinds rise and stacks shrink, you start to lose streets. For a while you can make a big bet preflop and still have some postflop leverage left. Eventually you'll lose that as well so that almost all the action is preflop and almost all the decisions are ones having to do with folding or raising all-in.

This is an overlooked aspect of shorthanded tournament play. Not only do you have more decisions to make in a shorter span of time, but your decisions are all front-loaded. Being a great shorthanded tournament player means knowing how to manage this narrow part of your skill set very well. Work on your preflop play. Get very good at it. If you like, look at it this way: every hand starts with preflop action; as the tournament matures, almost every hand ends there as well.

Where to Sit

If you've been watching a game and paying attention to betting trends, you'll know who the dangerous players are, and you'll know to sit to their left. Of course, you may not always have the luxury of thoughtful, patient, pregame observation—or you may not be thoughtful and patient enough to exploit it. We're not here to condemn you for rushing into a poker game—we've been known to take some precipitous leaps ourselves. But if you're not going to take the time to suss out the table, at least do this: sit behind big money.

We probably don't have to walk you through the logic of this. Mike Caro told everyone long ago that due to the power of position, chips flow clockwise around the poker table, so it only makes sense to sit downstream from the biggest stack. But it also makes sense on a strategic level, for there are generally two strong mechanisms of control in a shorthanded NLHE game: chip stack and position. If you can't have one, at least try to have the other. To yield a chip advantage *and* a positional advantage to one of your foes, especially one who knows how to use these tools, is to put yourself in an untenable bind. Another consideration is that the person with the most money at the table has the highest probability of being the best player at the table. If you have a choice, you'd like to have position on the best player.

ABT: Always Be Thinking

Even when you're certain that you've flopped the nuts and your hand is bulletproof, make it your habit to read your foes and think about what they have. This is no longer a question of *Do they have hands that can beat me?* but rather, *How can I manipulate them to extract maximum value?* The fact is that mostly we only spend energy putting reads on our opponents when we are afraid: afraid of losing the pot and afraid of losing the hand. When we're a lock (or virtual lock) to win, we tend to dial back on our investigative efforts, and why not? A win is a win, right? So there's no urgency.

But yet there is opportunity.

Say you're holding Slickerella and the flop comes A♦Q♦7♠.

Sure, you're likely to win the pot with your two pair, especially if preflop information suggests that your foe doesn't have a set. But what about current information? Does your foe seem interested in the pot? Primed to fold? Can he be tempted into a bluff? Does he have a big, trailing hand like AK or A7 with which he'll let himself get felted? Can you represent a flush draw, or make it look like you're betting phantom outs? These are the questions you want to think about—and then seek answers to by closely analyzing your foes' tendencies and betting trends, their tells, their chip stacks, their hand distributions—the works.

Again, the only reason we don't do this is complacency, the knowledge that no matter how we play the hand, we're likely gonna win it. Don't let winning be enough! Extract the maximum amount of value you can. There *is* an optimal approach out there, you know; there *is* a maximum EV plan for the hand. It's your job to go find it, even when all that's at stake is money or—more money.

Ten Quick Tips

Here are ten quick tips that need no explanation (but get a little anyhow):

1. *Bet all of your made hands and some of your others*. If you're only betting made hands, you're playing too straightforward a shorthanded game.

2. *Value bet on positional advantage*. Given that the cards will all even out in the end, if the pot is x percent bigger when you have position, then you have an x percent edge.

3. *Establish betting patterns*. Because the patterns that you establish can then be meaningfully manipulated according to your goal for the game.

4. *Call sometimes with the intention of bluffing.* This has the benefits of winning you some pots, slowing some enemies down, and prompting others to get carried away with marginal holdings.

5. *A hand doesn't have to be good to be playable.* If you can outplay your opponent, it absolutely doesn't matter what two cards you hold.

6. *Tilt equity goes up shorthanded.* Not all your foes can be put on tilt, but ones who tilt in a shorthanded game will be worth more than ones who tilt in a fullhanded game.

7. *They'll always give you something.* Your foes are always too tight, too loose, too passive, too aggressive, too *something.* It's your job to figure out what, and then use that *too* against them.

8. *Passive play kills.* Shorthanded poker favors aggressive play and first action. A passive player is dead meat, full stop.

9. *Make your opponents make big mistakes.* Manipulate betting patterns and deception trends so that your foes are leaning the wrong way when it matters most.

10. *You can't hide behind your cards.* Hit-to-win will not be a successful strategy in most shorthanded NLHE games.

10

♣♠♦♥

WORDS FROM THE WISE

♧♤♢♡

We here at KPHQ are blessed with friends who are smarter than we are. Being also generous or else wildly susceptible to incessant wheedling, several of them have agreed to share their own views on shorthanded poker, and we are pleased to present those thoughts and observations here. Since not all these opinions mesh with one another (though surprisingly many do), let's bear in mind the old saying that "the ocean is blue, but it's also wet." In other words, there's often more than one right answer, especially in a game such as poker, through which the phrase "it depends" resonates like a mantra. From one person's point of view, the best way to play a certain hand would be to check-raise. Another could conclude that it's best to bet out. Both may be correct. There's just no way to know for sure.

So as you read the following contributions, bear in mind that, viewed through a certain filter, everyone's approach to the game is valid.

Unless they disagree with us, of course. Then they're just wrong.

Daniel Negreanu

Do you like to play shorthanded? Why or why not?

Yes, in fact I much prefer it to ring games. For one, it's less boring since you'll be playing a lot more hands, and two, it's a much more skillful form of poker than playing in a full ring game where tight players can hide.

What strategic adjustments do you make?

The key adjustment is pretty obvious: playing more hands. More important, though, my adjustments will generally depend on my opponents. If my opponents overcompensate for the game being short by playing too aggressively, then I'll look to trap them more. Or if my opponents don't make any adjustments, I will kick it into high gear and get über aggressive on them.

How do you adjust your starting requirements, raising values, and so on?

Basically, anything playable is a hand I would raise with. Having said that, I'd be a little more careful with marginal hands when someone else raised. I'd also be more apt to reraise them with marginal hands.

How important is position?

Essentially, that is the key to shorthanded play. Since the real battle is won in the trenches, when neither player hits the flop, the player with position has an even more significant advantage shorthanded. I'd go so far as to say that a below-average player would destroy me heads-up if I allowed him to be the button every hand. I'd get killed.

What's your approach to defending your blinds?

Very liberal. It's simple math really. Suppose you are playing $100–$200 limit hold'em and a player raises your big blind.

You have 78 offsuit and are getting 3.5:1 odds to call. Considering the $200 raise, the $50 small blind, and the $100 big blind that are already in there, if you fold hands like that playing shorthanded, you'll get creamed.

Defending your blinds liberally is important for other reasons as well. You want your table image to be one where people are afraid of you. In other words, they'd be less likely to steal your blind with K7 than if you were playing tightly from the blinds.

How do you know when you're facing someone you can or cannot beat?

If you are up against an aggressive player who is killing you in the pots where you both flop nothing, you probably won't be able to beat him no matter how lucky you get. If it seems as though every time you hit a hand he folds and every time you miss he outplays you, chances are he is too tough for you.

On the flip side, if you are able to pound your opponent and he is only playing after the flop when he hits a piece of it, you should continue to pound him into submission.

How does your shorthanded approach differ from tournaments to cash games?

In tournaments, the play is always a little bit tighter since you are playing on a limited bankroll. Reraises are generally a much more telling sign of strength than a reraise in a cash game.

What do you love or hate about shorthanded play?

There is nothing to hate about it. What I love most about shorthanded play is that psychology plays an even bigger role, and mixing up your game to fool your opponent is really intriguing to me, for example, check-raising the flop with top pair twice and then next time check-calling the flop and check-raising the turn. There are so many ways to mix up your game, and that is a lot of fun.

DANIEL NEGREANU was the 2004 Poker Player of the Year and (according to Daniel) Sexiest Chest Hair 2005.

Barry Tanenbaum

I love shorthanded play. I remember Mike Caro once saying that whenever he saw a nine-handed game at a casino, he thought, "Wow. You could get three good poker games out of this." I totally agree.

Shorthanded gives the good player two advantages:

1. You use more judgment.

2. You can study your opponent(s).

First, you use more judgment. Because you are playing more hands, including many nontraditional ones, you must use much better judgment to determine if your hand is best. Fewer players also means smaller pots on average, and this effect magnifies errors. Everyone will make errors, of course, but if you make too many bad calls or too many bad folds, you will not be able to catch up.

Second, you can study your opponents. In a nine-handed field, you do not get to see that many showdowns from any specific player. This means it takes much longer to gain a really accurate read on any given player's strategies. In fact, in a typical five-hour session, you can only get very approximate reads on a few players and just good guesses on the others.

But shorthanded, every player at the table is involved in more pots and more showdowns. And there are fewer of them to pay attention to. So your ability to understand how each one plays goes up substantially. And with understanding comes the ability to optimize your play against your opponent's weaknesses while avoiding his strengths.

Online, I play mostly heads-up no-limit tournaments. Having only one opponent means I get to play most hands and only have to study one guy. This magnifies both of the above effects.

BARRY TANENBAUM is a highly successful professional cash game player who offers personalized poker lessons through his website at www.barrytanenbaum.com.

Marcel Luske

As most final table plays of importance are made in the last hands of tournaments, one must know how to play and be ready to play shorthanded. Otherwise, I would be keener to play at a full table, as that gives me more information about the hands I play and more opponent variation.

Your hand selection is dependent on the number of players in the game. With few, weak players left, nearly any two cards are playable. Otherwise, any aggressive player will eat you alive. Position in shorthanded play is very important because this will eliminate a lot of gray areas of possible actions behind you. The more possible actions behind you, the more dangerous it is to play a hand, so be prepared.

The moment someone starts to walk on water is the moment I know to leave that opponent alone. But still your hand selection makes you get involved with them and then makes you a railbird, as you cannot beat LUCK. I hate to outsmart myself and find myself standing on the rail, knowing that I have played well, but that alone is not good enough.

The shorthanded game is beautiful if your opponent plays

weak, not aggressive, and is easy to read. If your opponent is aggressive and fearless, you need cards that make sense to play with, as you know there are going to be a lot of showdowns. Most likely in shorthanded cash games the rake percentage will kill the players, unless the game is very interesting to play (which is to say—very weak opponents with a lot of money). I would rather find a fullhanded game and take my time to spot the weakness without going broke.

MARCEL LUSKE, "the Global Ambassador of Poker," is a fixture at prestigious poker tournaments worldwide.

Lou Krieger

Some poker players love shorthanded play. Others avoid it like the plague. Nevertheless, online poker is the home of short-handed play and on many sites, it's the game of choice. You'll find shorthanded specialists online who never play in full games, and some online poker rooms cater to them by provid-ing marketing and publicizing six- and five-handed games and heads-up games at a variety of betting limits.

You'll find more variance in shorthanded play than you will in nine- or ten-handed games. Players in a full game can afford to sit back and wait for big hands before committing their money. You can't do that in shorthanded play; the blinds come around far more often and will eat you alive un-less you *gamble* enough with less-than-premium hands— hands you'd generally throw away at a full table—to overcome their persistence.

Shorthanded poker requires aggression, and betting and raising with something less than top pair–good kicker is de rigueur. If you're aggressive and clever at reading hands, and playing your opponents, shorthanded play might be right up your alley. It's geared for a loose, aggressive playing style, while tight, passive players—who can at least *survive* in full games—will need to adapt to succeed.

Starting hands change value dramatically as games becomes progressively more shorthanded. Some hands that are playable in full games shouldn't be played at all against five or six opponents, while others—hands that you'd cast away without a moment's hesitation in a full game—are raising hands when the game is short.

Big cards are much more valuable in shorthanded games simply because they can win without improvement. Flush and straight draws, particularly those bereft of high cards, just can't attract the number of opponents in a shorthanded game to make them profitable in the long run. You'll still complete the draws you play with the same regularity, but the payoff at a shorthanded table isn't likely to offset the odds against completing your hand. Some of the hands that offer a positive expected value in full games are big-time losers when the game is short, while some of the hands you'd like to be dealt in a five- or six-handed game are long-term losers in full games.

Blinds come around much more frequently in short games. At a six-handed table, you're in the blind one third of the time, and players are more aggressive as a result. Because midrange suited connectors and similar drawing hands won't attract a sufficient number of callers to make playing them worthwhile, "pump it or dump it" becomes the tactic of choice.

Players no longer require AK or AQ in order to raise. In a shorthanded game, any ace is a potential raising hand. Moreover, if you call a raiser, you won't necessarily know what your opponent is holding. When he comes out betting into a flop that doesn't necessarily figure to have helped him—and in a shorthanded game he most assuredly will come out betting regardless of what the flop looks like—you might have to call all the way to the river even if you're not holding anything stronger than a naked ace.

With aggression the rule rather than the exception and blinds that come around twice as often as they do in full games, position becomes more important because you will probably have to gamble a bit more.

Since big cards increase in value when the game is short-handed, it stands to reason that the value of a pair increases significantly. After all, your middling pair of sixes is probably a favorite against the blinds, particularly if your raise causes at least one of them to fold.

In a shorthanded game, it's tough to determine whether to keep playing if you're called or reraised after you've raised with a midrange pair and the flop contains an overcard or two. Determining whether the flop helped your opponent or he is merely bluffing is seldom easy, and reading your opponent is a crucial skill, because larceny is more prevalent in shorthanded games.

One of the biggest errors I see in shorthanded play occurs when players bet and are raised, or they raise and are reraised, and continue to play hands that just don't figure to be prof-itable. A hand like 98 suited is great in a full game if you can see the flop against a big field for a small bet. When you catch a winner, it makes up for all those other times when the flop misses you completely. But in a six-handed game, you won't get the right price to play these kinds of draws. Much of the time you'll be drawing heads-up, and when the flop misses you, you're trapped in the sunshine with a *nine high*! When you're raised in a shorthanded game, consider folding or reraising. Calling doesn't usually cut it.

If aggressiveness and the higher variance that's a pre-dictable consequence of more risk taking are the bugaboos of shorthanded play, there's plenty of opportunity too. When the game is shorthanded, you'll be able to take advantage of weak players more frequently. By the same token, if you're facing opponents whose skills are superior to yours, the best tactical maneuver at your disposal is to pick up your chips and find a different game.

Shorthanded games are difficult for many players, but these games are neither better nor worse games than full games. They're just different; that's all. But you can learn to beat them. Many players do.

LOU KRIEGER is the author of *Poker for Dummies* and ten other top-selling books on poker. He's also a columnist for *Poker Player Newspaper*, *World Player*, *Inside Edge*, *Woman Poker Player*, and *PokerMagazine.com*, and hosts *Keep Flopping Aces*, a weekly Internet poker show at www.holdemradio.com.

Matt Lessinger

Short(handed) but sweet: regarding shorthanded poker, no matter what type of game you are playing:

- Identify who your most aggressive opponent is.

- Whatever his level of aggressiveness is, stay one level higher.

- Never let someone else be in control of your shorthanded table.

- If you're going to win, you have to be the one to take control.

MATT LESSINGER is a *Card Player* columnist and author of *The Book of Bluffs (How to Bluff and Win at Poker)*.

Vince Burgio

Shorthanded, you must make the obvious adjustment to playing many, many more hands. After that, you adjust to your opponent. Experience is very valuable because you must pay attention to the hands your opponent is showing down and the way he played those hands.

In shorthanded NLHE, you play off your opponent's tendencies. If he's weak-tight you steal more hands. If he's aggressive, you look to trap more hands. You want to maintain a chip lead because heads-up no-limit usually comes down to when both players have big or fairly big hands. So when that hand comes down, which it will sooner or later, you want to be able to bust your opponent and not the other way around. In heads-up limit play, you're more confined by the relative strength of each hand, but still, just as in no limit you're playing another player, so you look to exploit what you see as his weaknesses.

I don't think position is all that important, at least not when there can be three- or four-way pots. Against an aggressive opponent, you may even want to act first, or be out of position, because you know he's going to bet almost every hand so that you can check most of the time, eliciting his bet that is the same as him acting first.

Unless I am playing someone who gives up his blinds consistently or makes overly big bets in no-limit heads-up play, I defend my blinds almost every hand. Of course, I am talking about heads-up play; if there are more players, then naturally I'll defend less. There is a delicate balance, but a key factor is to build up in your opponent's mind the understanding that he can't easily steal from you.

I can usually beat someone who plays too many or not enough hands. If my opponent plays the right amount of hands and he is a good player, it will boil down to the one "big hand" that will surely come up.

VINCE BURGIO is a columnist for *Card Player Magazine*, and a World Series of Poker bracelet holder.

Jeff Madsen

In my short but now illustrious poker career, I have come to realize some key things about the game that are fairly obvious but not understood by all players trying to make a living in the poker world. When it comes to shorthanded play, particularly in no-limit hold-em, there are some general ideas one should understand.

First, because there are fewer players sitting in the game, the value of hands goes up because there is less of a chance that there are other strong or very strong hands in play. For example: In a six-handed game, you are first to act and look down at A8 offsuit. At a full ring, you may raise with this hand but should fold it more often than not because there are still eight or nine players to act behind you, and you are out of position to everyone except the blinds. At a shorter table, you should come in for a raise nearly every time with this hand, because there are now only five or fewer players to act behind you. Although you are UTG, you now have position on a higher percentage of the players remaining to act; if you were playing three-handed, you would actually have position on both of your opponents in the blinds.

Also, the shorter the table, the more you should be aggressive and raise with semi-strong hands that you may not play the same way at a full table, such as ace-rag hands, baby pairs, and suited connectors. In fact, you should realize that because there is a smaller chance of the other players having strong or playable hands, you should be raising to try to steal the blinds as much as the table allows with practically any hand.

Bluffing becomes much more important as the table becomes shorter because the blinds will reach you quicker, and you cannot wait for premium hands to try to accumulate chips; you might end up blinding half your stack down the drain before you pick up a strong pair or AK or AQ. The key to bluffing in these situations is timing. If your table sees you are raising with junk simply to take advantage of the short-handed situation, you may want to wait for semi-strong hands again instead of just raising with anything. If your table has not realized that you are making some moves and stealing blinds, then you should continue being aggressive.

Just as significant as to be aggressive with a wider variety of hands shorthanded is to observe your opponents and try to figure out how well they understand the unique dynamic of a shorthanded table.

Some players may continue to play tight and wait for above-average hands; they will generally not raise with weak hands because they have not been able to adjust to the table. Be sure to make these players miserable by raising before the flop as much as possible. If one of these players reraises you before the flop, you should give them credit for a strong hand and throw your marginal holdings away.

Other players are aggressive, like they should be, for they realize that they must be stealing blinds and opening with weaker hands than normal in order to survive. Against these players you must loosen up your requirements for calling bets and also for reraising before the flop. Marginal hands like the A8 offsuit, for example, shouldn't be calling a bet from a tight or a loose player, but should generally fold to the tight player and reraise the loose player before the flop.

When it comes to bluffing, you must not only be willing to

open with garbage but be able to reraise with garbage before the flop in shorthanded situations when you feel that a tight players will probably fold to a reraise because he knows that he has a tight image and does not feel you would make a play at him or because he has a strong hand but not strong enough to continue. You should also reraise a loose player if he is opening with garbage or if you have established a tight image and he would not expect you to make a play at him.

If you open and a player reraises you, you may decide to fold, call, or raise depending how strong your hand is and how tight or loose your opponents are. Sometimes it is simply about how well you can read your opponents and what their intentions are when they raise: to induce more action or to win the pot right there before the flop.

Bluffing is a huge part of being successful in poker. I have just covered the basics of the dynamic of a shorthanded table and why bluffing should become a big part of your game plan as the table size thins, particularly before the flop. As a hand progresses to the flop and further, keep in mind what your opponent may have, based on his table image, and understand the fact that the value of your own hand becomes greater against fewer opponents. You should generally play your hands aggressively until you feel your opponent is not bluffable or you feel that your opponent actually has a strong hand he will not release. The key is to apply constant pressure despite your holding and know when to release a bluff or even a strong hand when the time is right.

JEFF "THE KID" MADSEN won two bracelets at the 2006 World Series of Poker—at the tender age of twenty-one.

Tom McEvoy

To play or not to play, that is the question. If the shorthanded game is lively with weak players, I am more than happy to dive in. If the game is all tough, aggressive players, the opposite is the case. What if the game is five-handed with two very good players and three weak calling stations? Deal me in, I would say. What if there was only one weak player in it and four tough pros? Well, how bad is that one player, and are any of the pros on tilt? The answers to these questions are not easy. If your idea of a good poker game and an even better time is to win money, then go where the pickings are the easiest. Sometimes people have a different motive than money. They want to test themselves against the best players. Often the better players are the game starters in the casinos. They know that players will join in if they see the game is actually in progress but might not be so quick to help start a brand new game. Therefore, it is the job of the pros to help start games, even if they have to do battle with only each other in the beginning.

If you decide to sit down in a shorthanded game, what strategy do you use? Well, that of course depends on the other players. Against loose calling stations, do not try to bluff. Value bet them with semi-strong hands because they will call with something even weaker. If a relative weak player suddenly starts betting in an aggressive manner, you must decide if he has the goods or is possibly stuck and on tilt. Playing against the solid pros is a different story. They will read you better than the weaker players at the table. You should also be able to read them reasonably well. There will be a reason for their actions. Figure out what it is and play accordingly.

What about starting hand requirements? Well in a shorthanded game, trouble hands like AT or KJ suddenly become raising hands. A hand like AQ might be a hand you reraise with. Remember, always play the players as well as the cards.

Small and medium pairs also go up in value. You can often raise with them when in position, especially if you're the first player in the pot. You often have the best starting hand and good position if you get called.

Speaking of position, exactly how important is it short-handed? Well if it is extremely important in a full ring game, it is even more important shorthanded. You can steal a lot more pots because there are fewer hands out, and it really rewards aggressive play. Playing position strongly is a must if you are going to be successful in shorthanded games.

What about the blinds? Well, it should be obvious that you are going to have to defend them more. Not necessarily with weak hands that are facing big raises, but any reasonable hand is at least worth seeing the flop with. Also, if you are going to call, you should at least think about putting in a reraise to steal the pot. Hands like A5 should generally be played against a button raiser who steals a lot. In fact, at least half of the time I would reraise to slow down the raiser and resteal the pot. Suited connectors go down in value in a shorthanded game, but pairs and any two cards ten or higher are usually worth playing. Ditto for any ace. Just remember that I said *usually*, not always. If a rock raises, be more cautious with these types of hands.

If you think you have the best hand but are not entirely sure, think more in terms of showing it down rather than value betting, or checking and calling your opponent's bet. If you are pretty sure you do, in fact, have the best hand, then your main concern is how to value bet it and get the most profit you can.

In tournaments you eventually have to get down to you and one other player if you are going to win. Practicing your shorthanded play in cash games is a great way to improve your game and maximize your chances of winning tournaments. A major factor in tournaments is the chip counts. Some players may have substantially more chips than you do, or far less. A lot of your strategy must take this into account. Again you must play the player just as much as the cards.

I sometimes love shorthanded play with interesting lively opponents who give a lot of action. If on the other hand I am facing a bunch of pros and tight rocks who have little to say, I want to leave. If that is the case in a tournament situation where I can't leave, then I just tough it out and play my best game at all times. That is all anybody can do.

TOM MCEVOY is the 1983 World Series of Poker champion and the author of many outstanding poker books, including *Championship Tournament Poker* and *Championship No-Limit & Pot-Limit Hold'em*.

Annie Duke

Shorthanded hold'em is simply a subset of fullhanded hold'em. In fullhanded games, situations arise where action is folded to CO-3, and in those pots, action is exactly like a shorthanded game. The two defining characteristics of shorthanded hold'em are that the probability of having the best hand increases (i.e., hand values go down) and that the probability of being able to act last postflop increases. When raising in hold'em, you want to make sure that you are raising either because you have the best hand or because you will have superior position for the duration of the hand. Raising enables you to knock players out behind you to seize the button, to get information about your opponents' hands, and to get the lead on the pot. Shorthanded hold'em is an aggressive game because the positional edge is available a higher percentage of the time.

This mentality is applicable to no limit and limit hold'em.

In NLHE, reraises (especially preflop reraises) may carry significant fold equity. You don't necessarily want to be playing big pots out of position in NLHE; however, if you are in a game where a reraise from the blinds works as a semi-bluff, then you need to be reraising with hands like AK and AQ out of the blinds. If you are only reraising with AA and KK, then your reraise gives away too much information about your own hand.

In limit hold'em, reraises have absolutely no fold equity associated with them. That doesn't mean that you shouldn't be three-betting when you play limit hold'em. In fact, when you have a positional advantage, you should be three-betting a fair amount of the time to isolate the preflop raiser. If you have position and you have a hand that you are not willing to three-bet with, then you should typically fold to a raise. Three-betting to isolate a preflop raiser to play him heads-up is probably the most important play in LHE.

Contrarily, when you raise and someone three-bets you, there is no reason to four-bet. You should just call the third bet, even with AA, because in the long run you will pick up more bets across the later betting rounds.

The only position from which you will be doing a lot of preflop calling is the big blind. When playing limit hold'em and you are in the big blind, the 3.5:1 pot odds you are getting in heads-up pots dictates that you should call raises from the big blind with all but your least playable hands, and your intention should be to check-raise the flop when you hit the flop or flop a big draw. After check-raising, lead out on the turn and the river. Most opponents always continuation bet, so by check-raising the flop, you make them pay the highest price possible. Meanwhile, when you have position and you have hit a flop, call opponents who bet into you on the flop and make them pay by raising on the turn or the river.

Shorthanded hold'em is usually about controlling the

table, but when playing against a maniac in a shorthanded limit game, you should tighten up your starting requirements substantially. Because the average pot size is so big compared to the blinds, you can afford to sit and wait. When you are out of position, raise preflop and make the maniac three-bet you. When you get your AA or KK, do not look to limp reraise, because doing so will result in you being in a crazy multiway pot. By raising and having the maniac three-bet, you are isolating yourself heads-up. When out of position postflop, your most profitable line of play against a maniac when you hit a hand is simply to check-call on the flop and turn, and then stick in a check-raise on the river. If you initiate aggression sooner, you are giving the maniac a chance to fold. Also, do not get in crazy raising wars with marginal hands. This is exactly what the maniac wants. Keep pots small, and let the maniac slowly bleed himself away. When you have position on the maniac, three-bet him preflop to isolate him and, again, just call on the flop and the turn with the intention of either calling the river or making a value raise on the river.

When in a shorthanded tournament situation, either you are at the final table bubble or you are down to the final few. When you are down to the final table bubble, be aggressive. Many players tighten up right before the final table because of the added equity they associate with making a final table. This is the perfect time to accumulate chips. Don't get carried away, but do recognize the steal opportunities that present themselves. Chip position is the biggest factor. If you have a big stack, remember that it is not your responsibility to knock the other players out. As a big stack, the chips that you lose are much more valuable than the chips that you win. But as a big stack, you need to be selectively aggressive. Turn the heat up on the smaller stacks, but don't make lots of loose calls; it only takes a double up or two for a short stack to become a contender.

When playing heads-up, the key consideration is your opponent's willingness to fold. The more willing your opponent is to fold, the more pressure you should put on; the less willing your opponent is willing to fold, the more you should look for value-betting opportunities. Another important consideration when playing heads-up is pot-size control. If you have a significant skill advantage over your opponent, you would much rather play lots of small pots than a few big pots—let skill dominate over variance. Therefore, you may find that it's best for you to do a lot of limping from the button, despite the conventional wisdom that such play is "weak."

Ultimately, poker is a situational game. Every opponent you face is unique, but the guidelines that I suggest should be a good starting point for your shorthanded game.

ANNIE DUKE, the ultimate poker diva, owns two World Series of Poker bracelets and numerous other tournament titles. As one of this era's top poker pros, she enjoys the respect of her peers and the love of fans worldwide.

11

♣♠♦♥

PARTING (SHORT) SHOTS

♣♠♦♥

This is a fact: in most cases, you can be a winning fullhanded no-limit Texas hold'em player without knowing much about the game beyond which hands to play, how to count outs, and a vague sense of your opponents' hand distributions. In short-handed play, though, "that dog don't hunt." To win at short-handed NLHE, you need a much deeper, more complex, and more complete understanding of both the game and your foes. Hit-to-win poker doesn't work. Strictly playing the odds doesn't work. Patented patient TAG poker doesn't work. Why? Because all of those notions turn on the question of what to do when you have a hand, whereas shorthanded play centers on the question of what to do when you *don't* have a hand. In that sense, you could say that fullhanded and shorthanded poker are mirror images of each other, and that's why we say that the most important number in shorthanded hold'em is $\frac{2}{3}$. Two thirds of the time no given player hits the flop. That's the engine that drives shorthanded play. It's really the only one that counts.

To succeed shorthanded, you also need to know that your opponents not only have hand distributions but they also have action distributions. They will call, raise, fold, reraise, check-call, check-raise, check-raise bluff, stop-and-go, continuation bet, *delayed* continuation bet, and even—well, let's see—check-reraise-fold according to detectable, predictable patterns of play. Peering deep into these patterns, reading the chicken entrails of your foes' proclivities, is the art of shorthanded poker. Having read this book, you now have much of the mental framework to be a successful shorthanded NLHE player. Do you have the art? Only you can say.

But we can say this: while much of what happens in fullhanded play is irrelevant or counterproductive to shorthanded success, the opposite isn't necessarily true. Given that even in fullhanded games, make or break moments often come down to *one* decision on *one* hand against *one* foe, we hope and trust that you'll find a lot of these concepts about shorthanded play applicable to full ring games. Caution: *don't* take that two-thirds number with you. In the heavy traffic of a fullhanded game, a flop that misses everyone is the exception, not the rule. To proceed as if no one had a hand would be dangerous, reckless, and just unsound.

You can see, then, why it's so vital to master both forms of poker. In the realm of cash play, fullhanded games will often go short, and when they do, they're a rich opportunity for profit. If all you know is fullhanded poker, you'll be at a loss to exploit that opportunity. It's like not knowing how to swim. You can splash around in the kiddie pool, but you never get to go into the (interesting and profitable) deep water. As for tournaments...wow...to go into a poker tournament without a decent shorthanded skill set is...ah, the simile eludes us. Like preparing a meal but not getting to eat it? Like having money in the bank that you can't withdraw? Like foreplay without— okay, you know what. Let's not go there. Either you get the idea or you don't; we trust that you do.

To those who dove into this tome looking for a cookbook

filled with precise recipes for shorthanded play, we're sorry if we disappoint. Much as we'd love to give answers to questions like, "How do I play A9 suited UTG in a five-handed game?" the more we peel back the layers of the onion that is short-handed hold'em, the more we realize that such questions are meaningless without context. Context is *everything*. We could tell you that a certain river bluff will work 57.3 percent of the time, but only *you* will know whether the guy staring down that bluff will call 100 percent of the time. We can tell you (and have told you over and over again) that positional advantage is huge in shorthanded NLHE, but that won't keep someone in early position from waking up with a hand and that won't keep him from shredding your stack if you're not attentive enough to the patterns of his play to put him on a big hand when it counts.

To be a winner at shorthanded NLHE is to be aggressive, aware, attentive, and many other words beginning with the letter A. To dominate and crush this game is to be brave, bold, brazen, and many other words beginning with the letter B. To win at shorthanded hold'em is to be clever, cunning, creative, and many other words beginning with the letter C.

We could do the whole alphabet but, again, we trust you catch our drift.

The best thing to be in this game is *adaptive*. Where full-handed play often gives you the luxury of a set-and-forget strategy, shorthanded play is so dynamic, so rapidly changing, that the strategy you used successfully—literally—on the last hand can be one that will fry you now. This is especially true online, where foes come and go with lightning speed, and your task is often to figure out how to pick their pockets—*now! quick!*—before they pick yours. And it's especially, *especially* true in end-stage tournaments where the folding of a single blind at the wrong time can put you in a hole too deep to escape.

We don't mean to scare you. Really, we don't. If there's one thing that poker has shown the world in recent years, it's that this is a game that *can* be mastered. Every day new players are entering the game, using the tools available to them, *getting it*, and going to work as confident, competent, successful poker players. There's no reason why they—why you—cannot be successful in the shorthanded realm as well. All it takes is diligence, dedication, doggedness, and many other words beginning with the letter D.

To recap before we close, here's what we rate as the key concepts in this book, the ideas that will keep you headed in the right direction as your shorthanded play unfolds and grows.

No one hits the flop. You knew we'd lead with that, didn't you? Remember, shorthanded hold'em is not about making hands, it's about *not* making hands.

Aggressiveness pays. There's a saying where we come from, "The second liar never has a chance. Be first, be fierce, be forceful. Be the straw that stirs the drink."

Embrace the math. If you're not used to thinking in terms of hand distributions and calling frequencies, now's the time to start. "If you're not slowly getting better, you're slowly getting worse."

Trust your reads. There's no point in putting your foe on a holding if you won't follow through on what you think you know. Don't ever be that guy who says, "I *knew* you had me beat, but I had to call you anyway."

Theft is a must. Stealing the blinds isn't bluffing; it's just taking what's up for grabs in shorthanded NLHE. Get your share of uncontested pots—then get some of their share too.

Position, positioin, position. Everything gets easier when you get to act last. Build big pots when you're in position, and avoid big confrontations when you're not.

Get inside their heads. Shorthanded NLHE is all about predicting and reacting to your foes' betting patterns. If you're thinking what they're thinking *before* they're thinking it, you'll be in command of the match.

Use deception trends. Don't let your opponents get a line on you. Better yet, hook 'em with a false line. Be a hologram: seemingly there, but not there.

Know what hand you hold. Hand values go way up in shorthanded play. Don't measure the quality of your shorthanded holding by fullhanded standards.

Know what game you're in. There's a huge difference between six-handed play, three-handed play, and heads-up play. Shape your strategy to fit the number of foes you face. In a similar vein, if you're beat, retreat.

Save your ego for the cashier's cage. Shorthanded hold'em can be a big dick-measuring contest. The only size that matters is the size of your stack when you're done.

Win the pots that count. Small pots happen all day long. The few large pots are the ones that matter to your session's success, so set your opponents up for a big, key fall.

Adapt. Shorthanded NLHE is a dynamic, fast-moving type of poker. There's no place for rote behavior or autopilot decisions. Use the new information that's *always* heading your way.

Think things through. Every decision counts. Don't make yours in haste.

Fold the crap, raise the rest. Can't think of a better six-word action plan for shorthanded NLHE.

Well, that oughta do 'er. We'd write more, but right now we think we feel a heads-up match coming on. One of us thinks he can kick the other of us's ass. He is, of course, dead wrong.[1]

See you next book, everybody!

—JV & TG

---

1. The authors argued long and hard about who was who in this paragraph. As of this writing, the issue remains unresolved.

Glossary and Guide to Acronyms

BenBucks: Player defined by the willingness and ability to make almost any play at almost any time, one of the toughest types of shorthanded player.

Big Bets Per 100 Hands (BB/100): Metric for determining success in a game. A big bet is equal to twice the amount of the big blind (this terminology originated when most games being played were limit games).

Big Blind (BB): The big blind is a forced bet made before a hand is dealt. It is usually placed by the player two positions to the left of the button, and it is typically twice the small blind. If no one raises, the player who posts the big blind has an option of raising. BB is also used to designate the player who posts the BB in a hand.

Big Slickina: AQ. See also *Slickerella*.

Blocking Bet: An undersized lead bet made out of position designed to discourage a larger one from someone in position.

Button (B): Person acting as the dealer (holding the dealer button), hence, last to act.

Cally Wally: A player who loves to call and who rarely shows aggression. Even though he'll call with a wide range of holdings, his bets and raises signify that he has something powerful.

CB: Continuation bet; a bet made postflop by the preflop raiser.

Cutoff (CO): Person to the right of the button.

DCB: Delayed continuation bet; a bet made on the turn by the pre-flop raiser after all parties have checked the flop.

Deaky: See *Weakydeaky*.

Drag: To slowplay.

Dr. Overbite: Player whose bets and raises are very large with respect to the pot. Some Overbites are loose and wild, but others are a bit more calculating.

Expected Value (EV): Your prospects for profit in a poker game.

Fold Equity: The part of your expected value that comes from having all your opponents fold.

Freeze Out: Heads-up match that's played until one player has all the chips.

Fullhanded: A poker game with seven or more players.

Ghost: To "inhabit" your opponent's point of view and see the hand or hands through his eyes.

Grandstand Overbet: An all-in bet well out of proportion to the size of the pot, either for show or for ego or both.

Hack: A strategy or counterstrategy derived and developed from observing your opponents' betting patterns.

Hand Distribution Model (HDM): Analytic process of putting an opponent on a range of hands and doing the math to see how your holding fares against the entire range.

Hit-to-Win: Paradigm for playing poker in which your primary plan is to sit and wait to hit a hand.

Heads-up Display (HUD): Software package that overlays statistics from poker tracking software in real time at your online table(s).

Iso Play: Reraising the initial raiser to isolate against him and induce heads-up play (used more in limit hold'em than in no-limit hold'em).

Limpede: A preflop phenomenon in which an early position limp encourages everyone else at the table to limp along as well. Also known as a limpfest.

Location Station: A player who plays his position very aggressively. Location Stations like to seize the advantages of position and initial action, and if they can't have them, they'll usually not be involved in a hand unless they have a very good holding.

Loose-Aggressive (LAG): General categorization applied to someone who plays many pots and plays them by doing lots of betting and raising.

Multi-Table Tournament (MTT): Tournament consisting of many tables, where shorthanded play is usually not a factor until at or near the end, unless, of course, you are in a 6-max MTT.

NLHE: Acronym for No-Limit Hold'Em.

Numpty: A hold'em hand of 62.

Out of Position (OOP): You are out of position when you have to act before your opponent(s).

Push and Pray (P&P): Point in a tournament where your only move is to push all-in and hope that you either steal the blinds or win a showdown to double up.

Satellite: Tournament whose prize is an entry into a higher-stakes tournament.

Serial Dater: Player who enters many pots preflop only to end up folding almost everything postflop.

Shootout: Multi-table tournament format played in rounds, where the top player or top few players from each table advance to the next round.

Shorthanded: Game with six or fewer players

Single-Table Tournament (STT): Tournament consisting of one table, either nine- or ten-handed or six-handed or heads-up.

Sit-N-Go (SNG): Originally, SNGs were synonymous with STTs; however, today SNGs can have 2 tables, 3 tables, or even 5 tables. A SNG is therefore a tournament with no scheduled start time: it starts whenever enough people sign up.

6-Max: Game where a maximum of six players can play.

Slickerella: AQ, a.k.a. *Big Slickina*.

Small Blind (SB): Forced bet made by the player to the left of the button. It's usually equal to half the big blind, but it can range from one third of the big blind to two thirds of the big blind.

Sniffer: Poker Tracker or similar software for analysis of online poker play and players.

Stop-and-Go: Betting pattern employed from early position in which you check-call on one round and then bet out on the next round.

Tight-Aggressive (TAG): Playing style defined by not playing many hands (tight) and by betting and raising a lot in hands played (aggressive).

Tighty Tighterson: A predictably weak, cautious, and unimaginative player.

Top/Top (TPTK): Top pair, top kicker, such as AT with a board of T63.

Under the Gun (UTG): Player immediately to the left of the big blind and who, therefore, acts first preflop.

Weakydeaky: Pejorative expression for a timid, untalented, or unimaginative player.

Wheelhouse: Cards ranked from tens to aces; said to be in a player's wheelhouse.

Index

About the Authors

John Vorhaus has been playing poker longer than Tony Guerrera has been alive and writing about it since Tony was in grade school. But Tony, late of the California Institute of Technology, has mad math skills, and his understanding of numbers reduces Vorhaus to a gibbering idiot. Given their complementary skill sets and mutual interest in poker, it was a natural move to hook up as poker co-authors. This is their first joint venture, but such titles as *Killer Poker for Kids, Killer Poker Cookbook*, and *The Killer Poker Dating Guide* are already in the planning stage.

John has served as a poker commentator on television and radio. When not talking about, writing about, or playing poker, he works as an international consultant for television and film script and program development, including such far-flung locales as Nicaragua, where he helped create a television show to "teach young Nicaraguans to think for themselves and practice safe sex." Tony, who routinely terrorizes shorthanded NLHE foes online, is author of *Killer Poker by the Numbers* and the upcoming *Tournament Killer Poker by the Numbers*. When not playing poker or writing about it, he coaches players and makes cash games and tournaments much tougher than they used to be. Both reside in the 626 area code of Southern California.

WEBSITES: John Vorhaus: www.vorza.com
Tony Guerrera: www.killerpokerbythenumbers.com